INVESTING AND SELLING IN LATIN AMERICA

SHIRLEY CHRISTIAN
EDITOR

THE AUTHORS:
Judith Evans
Winston Moore
Bill Hinchberger
Scott Norvell
Holly Johnson
Ruth Sánchez
Steven Gutkin
Carlos Cisternas
Lucy Conger
Esteban Caballero Carrizosa
Peter Hudson
Danilo Arbilla
Jane Knight

Publisher's Cataloging in Publication

Investing and Selling in Latin America / Shirley Christian, editor ;
          the authors: Judith Evans, ... [et al.].
                    p.cm.
                    Includes index.
                    ISBN: 1-887847-00-6.

                    1. United States—Commerce—Latin America. 2. Latin America—Commerce—United States. 3. Business etiquette. 4. Investments, American—Latin America.   I. Christian,   Shirley, ed. II. Evans, Judith.

          HF3065.5.I68 1995   658.8'48'098
                                               QBI95-20454
                                               LCCC95-080153

First edition

Printed in the United States of America

Cover designed by Jim Langford

CONTENTS

—No…that's not exactly what we meant by adapting to local customs….

BEFORE YOU GO

Face it. No matter how serious a person you are, you probably harbor a few stereotypes about how deals are cut and money made in Latin America. You imagine Peter Lorre look-alikes lurking behind palm trees, plumpish men in white suits and spats promising a quick cash profit, maybe a dashing guerrilla type or a smiling colonel looking to make an arms purchase, or an easy-going fellow caught up in tropical politics while just wanting to sell vacuum cleaners á la *Our Man in Havana.*

Jumping onto a PanAm Clipper and landing amidst balmy breezes, you imagine being met by a shoeshine boy who'll give you the latest on who's good and who's bad and guide you into a world where everybody, magically, speaks English with an exotic accent.

Reality is that the PanAm Clipper is no more, and the other things were fiction anyway. Success for the foreigner seeking to do business in Latin America comes after methodically doing your home-work, then legwork, learning languages, and giving some thought to the new culture you're encountering. The businessmen and women whose first-person accounts appear in succeeding chapters make clear that these things are absolutely essential before putting your capital or product on the line. Fortunately, in this post-Cold War era of instant communications and global trade as a way of life, there are plenty of places to turn for information and advice. You'll still get to sip rum or pisco sours under the palm trees, but you'll be ready for doing business without encountering an unpleasant surprise around every turn.

After failing to fulfill its economic promise for decades, Latin America has finally come into its own as a partner in trade and investment. Russia and other countries once part of the Soviet bloc may seem exotic and seductive, but for anyone who looks seriously at the statistics, at market potential, and policy accomplishments, Latin America is the region that is ready for a mature economic relationship with the United States and other developed nations. It offers bigger markets, higher per capita incomes, growing populations, and long familiarity with products from North America and Japan, and to a lesser extent Europe. Although most countries of Latin America still have high poverty levels, they also have large and rapidly growing middle classes that put them well ahead of many parts of the world as export and investment targets.

The 400 million Latin Americans spent $92 billion* on goods from the United States in 1994, almost as much as Western Europe bought. U.S. exports to Latin America have been growing at more than 20 percent a year since 1987 and are expected to reach $232 billion by the year 2010.

The region's infinite variety encompasses two giants, Mexico and Brazil, struggling to modernize their economies and politics at the same time; Bolivia with a small population of mostly Inca descent but one of the world's treasure-troves of untapped natural resources; Peru, which in less than five years changed from a land teetering before a radical insurrection to one with a world-leading economic growth rate; Chile, whose maturing but still growing economy prompts many to compare it to Taiwan or call it the South American Austria, and Argentina, out to reclaim the place it once held among the world's richest nations.

An area once plagued by budget deficits now has most of its public accounts near balance or in surplus; the area that taught the world about hyper-inflation now has very little inflation; the area known for protectionism and import-substitution policies is opening its

---

*The Dollar sign, here and throughout the book is used to denote U.S. currency.

borders at a dizzy pace, often unilaterally. Much of the growth in trade has occurred among the nations of Latin America themselves, and those ever-freer trade channels add to the attractiveness of Latin America for foreign manufacturers or distributors wanting to serve more than one nation.

That growth in intra-Latin American trade, marked by such examples as a six-fold increase in trade between Mexico and Venezuela in just five years, has also helped to bury old grudges between neighbors and will stand the region in good stead even if the United States falls down on its promises to sign additional free-trade agreements around the region.

Politically, Latin America has been going through its longest period of generalized democracy in modern memory. While in the past, democratic governments in Latin America have often been marked by nationalistic or leftist sentiments and economic policies more inclined to redistribute the wealth than create new wealth, today's democratic regimes are marked by a high degree of moderation and practicality. The stability of a few is in question, and there will likely be setbacks, but in most countries there has been a marked improvement in the ability of the political class, military leaders, and other power groups to work things out for the common good.

What is Latin America?

For purposes of this book, Latin America is defined as the land mass beginning at the Rio Grande, which is the border between the United States and Mexico, and extending south and east for several thousand miles to the Strait of Magellan at the southern tips of Argentina and Chile. We've excluded the small Caribbean island nations, even though a few of them have Latin roots, because they tend to function as a trading region separate from the mainland. For the same reason, we've excluded Suriname and Guyana on the South American mainland, which are more oriented toward the Caribbean.

There are other terms to clarify as well. First, consider Central America, which is the string of small countries stretching from the

Mexico

Mexico City ★

Belize

Honduras

Guatemala
El Salvador

Nicaragua

Costa Rica

Caracas

Venezuela ★

Guyana
Suriname

French Guiana

Panama

Bogota ★
Colombia

Ecuador

Peru

Brazil

Lima ★

La Paz ★
Bolivia

Brasilia ★

Paraguay

Chile

Argentina

Santiago ★

Buenos Aires ★

Uruguay

0   500

MILES

Map by Rick Brownlee

southern border of Mexico to the beginning of the continent of South America. In geographer's terms, Central America is, like Mexico, part of North America and consists of six countries: Guatemala, Belize, Honduras, El Salvador, Nicaragua, and Costa Rica. Panama, the next country in that chain, is technically not part of Central America, and not part of either North or South America. It is an isthmus connecting the two continents and, therefore, a world of its own. Panama's dollar-denominated economy and its greater economic wealth still set it apart from Central America, but in today's trade-focused world, it is developing closer ties to its neighbors, so we've included it as the seventh country in Central America.

On the South American mainland, you will hear other regional descriptions, some of which overlap. Among them is the term Northern Rim, a reference to Venezuela, Colombia, and Ecuador. Another is the Andean nations, meaning Ecuador, Peru, Bolivia, Chile, and Colombia. The Southern Cone refers to Chile, Argentina, and Uruguay. These are geographical designations, but increasingly today you will hear of regional trade groupings as well. The most significant so far is that known as Mercosur (in Spanish) or Mercosul (in Portuguese), meaning Common Market of the South, and made up of Brazil, Argentina, Uruguay, and Paraguay.

A Market for Everything

To the exporter or investor, Latin America offers markets for almost every conceivable product and service, investment opportunities for manufacturing, exploration and exploitation of natural resources. It needs housing, roads, and other infrastructure, and particularly has an appetite for better communications at both national and individual levels.

Communications are rapidly improving in most of Latin America, but demand and the ability to pay for better facilities and service are growing faster than supply. It's still almost impossible, for example, to make a call between Quito and Guayaquil, the two largest cities in Ecuador, during business hours. People will beg their relatives and brow-beat employers for money to buy an available telephone line, which Latin Americans recognize as an investment.

Many of the roads being built are to be privately owned or operated. That is, private companies are being awarded contracts to build and operate the roads, then collect tolls on them. Spurred on by the explosion in intra-Latin American trade, most of which goes by land, road usage has soared throughout the region. In Chile, for instance, it has quadrupled in 20 years.

Because of the existence of underground economies in many Latin American countries, even the poorest citizens generally have more disposable income than indicated by GNP figures, and there is a willingness to spend that money on clothing and other items to improve appearances, and on things to build or improve humble homes, which people often build a brick at a time after sinking their life's savings into the land.

Patience Required

That entering the Latin American market is a long-term under-taking for the foreign exporter or investor is obvious in the approach taken by the **Faultless Starch/Bon Ami Company** when it decided to venture into the region. Even though it had been exporting to much of the world for 30 years from its headquarters in Kansas City, the firm chose patience in its approach to Latin America.

First, it hired Kurt Van Keppel, who had learned Spanish as an exchange student in high school and had a fascination with the world beyond the borders of the United States. He had done part of his undergraduate studies in Europe, where he added Italian and French to his language repertory, then he came home to graduate from the University of Kansas with a degree in history. After he had worked two and a half years for **Faultless,** first as a trainee, then as manager of sales to military installations, the firm sent Van Keppel to the American Graduate School of International Management (Thunderbird), in Glendale, Arizona, where he earned a master's degree while also putting together a marketing plan to introduce **Faultless** spray starch in Mexico.

Back on the job and named Latin American sales manager, Van Keppel set out in a methodical way to amass information and analyze the market he was planning to enter. His methods offer a good guide for others planning to get their feet wet in Latin America.

"Fear of the unknown," says Van Keppel, "is the biggest impediment to going into international marketing." And he has developed a system of planning and research that helps cut down on the unknown factors, so much so that he relishes getting on a plane almost monthly to keep up his contacts in Mexico and explore other possible markets in Latin America.

For exporters, he says, there are two ways to enter a new market. One is the "export management" system, which he describes as essentially taking orders by telephone or fax and limiting visits to about once a year. "It's cheap, but may not be lasting," he says. The other method is what he calls "marketing management." It means going to the country, establishing a joint venture or marketing agreement or doing a lot of advertising to introduce your product. "It may be slow and expensive, but we found Mexico quickly profitable."

Van Keppel says he began by studying potential markets for spray starch in Latin America. Wanting to go into a big market, he compared Brazil and Mexico and chose Mexico as his first market because of its higher population density, household income, and educational level, and greater acceptance of foreign products. He has a checkoff list that he recommends exporters use to determine whether to enter a particular market.

The items on the list, which he suggests be weighted according to their importance in the sale of a particular product, are:
- Gross national product
- Geography
- Number of households
- Population density
- Per capita income
- Need for the product
- Competition

● Sales structure
● National politics

As sources of data, Van Keppel uses the public library, the regional office of the U.S. Commerce Department, and the government's **National Trade Data Bank.** In addition, Van Keppel reads *The Economist, The Wall Street Journal,* the Mexico business weekly *El Financiero Internacional,* two newsletters on Mexico, and trade journals for his products.

To set up contacts for an initial visit, he recommends using the various services of the U.S. Commerce Department, state commerce departments, international Chambers of Commerce, and trade associations, all of which will help make appointments with potential retailers, wholesalers, or agents. Van Keppel also used a U.S. Commerce Department service to obtain a market survey on the potential for spray starch in Mexico. Not completely satisfied with the outcome, he went to Mexico and interviewed makers and sellers of washing machines to get his own sense of sales potential.

Even after doing his homework, market surveys, and developing contacts, Van Keppel spent eight months negotiating a sales and distribution partnership with a Mexican manufacturer of household chemicals that didn't have a spray starch. And he now spends a lot of time maintaining that relationship.

A key to succeeding in this long process, he said, is having full management backing. "If the top hasn't made the commitment and communicated it to the rest of the company, you won't get the flexibility and patience you need to penetrate a foreign market," he said. "In general, you can expect the payback period to be twice as long in Latin America as in the United States. So firms should consider very seriously whether they are ready for foreign sales. It may be that there is still more they can do in the United States."

Commerce Department Ready to Help

As Van Keppel's experience demonstrates, the would-be exporter can find a lot of help and information from a single source: the U.S. Department of Commerce through its 73 regional offices spread across the United States and locations in embassies and consulates in 70 countries overseas. The Commerce Department's help is limited to those looking to export, but for individuals and firms considering direct investments, much of the same information can be obtained through other sources. For example, while Commercial Section officers at U.S. Embassies abroad will provide briefing services to exporters, the Embassy's regular political or economic officers will usually provide information for investors. The Commerce Department does not work with firms that lack export experience or have been in business for less than two years. They are referred to the Small Business Administration for assistance.

The Commerce Department provides some of its information free, some for modest fees, and more customized services for higher rates. In addition to the regional offices, which are listed in local telephone books, would-be exporters can make contact with the Commerce Department by calling 1-800-USA-TRADE (872-8723).

Among the non-customized services that Commerce provides are industry sub-sector analyses from many countries, short profiles of specific foreign market conditions or opportunities, an economic bulletin board providing on-line trade leads and other market information, and the **National Trade Data Bank.**

The **Data Bank** is a compilation of the foreign economic and trade data gathered by 17 U.S. Government agencies. Updated monthly, it includes the Foreign Economic Trends reports compiled by U.S. Embassies on virtually every country of the world. The Data Bank can, for example, tell a firm involved in civil construction which countries of the world are receiving international financing for roads and other infrastructure and how to get information to bid on contracts. A manufacturer can find out how many countries in the world are in the market for a given product. The **Data Bank** is available in large libraries or by subscription on CD-ROM for $360 a year.

Among the more tailored services provided by the Commerce Department are these:

- **Customized Sales Survey.** For a fee that varies from $800 to $3,500, depending on country, U.S. Commercial officers abroad will obtain surveys on overall marketability of a particular product, with such additional information as price of comparable products, possible business partners, and distribution channels.
- **World Traders Data Reports.** For $100 per report, a check will be made of the reputation, reliability, and financial status of prospective trading partners.
- **Agent/Distributor Service.** This is an overseas search for qualified agents, distributors, and representatives for U.S. firms. It can be done in 30 days and costs $250 per country.
- **Export Contact List.** For those who want to check out prospective agents and distributors themselves, this database retrieval service provides U.S. exporters with names, addresses, products, and other information on foreign firms interested in importing. The fee is 25 cents per name; $10 minimum.
- **Gold Key Service.** Offered in 47 countries, including most of Latin America, this can be set up with just 13 days' notice before an executive or sales representative wants to travel to a given country. It includes market research, business strategy and orientation briefings, introductions to potential partners, interpreters for meetings, and follow-up planning. It is set up with an intensive schedule that usually begins immediately after someone from the U.S. Embassy meets you at the airport. The fee varies by country.
- **Matchmaker Trade Delegations.** This service, costing $2,200 to $3,500 plus travel and lodging, will "match" U.S. firms with prospective distributors and other business contacts abroad. It is usually set up for a group from a given business or for delegations of people from various firms in a particular state or city.

Some DOs and DON'Ts

People who have spent years in various countries of Latin America have amassed, over time, a number of hard-learned lessons about accommodating oneself to the region and accomplishing goals. What follows is a list of DOs and DON'Ts gathered from the personal experiences of many people, which — if you remember and use them — are almost guaranteed to save you frustration.

First, DON'T make the mistake of believing that if you've had experience in one Latin American country you can automatically transfer all of that to another. Each of the 18 countries in this book has its own traditions, culture, and dynamics, and the people of each believe they are different from their neighbors. There are certain shared characteristics, including the fact that most speak Spanish as the national language, although the sheer size of the only Portuguese-speaking nation — Brazil with its 157 million people — makes that language almost as important as Spanish.

People living in northern Mexico, for example, are much more knowledgeable about the United States than they are about people in the southern reaches of South America, some 5,000-6,000 miles away, and vice versa.

That difference was illustrated in an exchange a few years ago at a dinner party in Buenos Aires, the urbanc capital of Argentina. One couple at the party, both Argentines, had recently returned from their first-ever visit to Mexico and in describing one day of the trip they said they had eaten a plate of tacos for lunch. At that point, another Argentine guest interrupted to ask: "What's a taco?" To most people in the United States the taco is synonymous with Latin America, but the fact is that the taste for the taco pretty much stops at the southern border of Mexico. If tacos make inroads in Central or South America, it'll likely be because **Taco Bell** or some other U.S. fast-food company serves them up.

There was also the case of the Buenos Aires manager of a major U.S. bank who had been transferred to Argentina after serving the bank in Chile. He noted that his superiors in New York assumed the two countries were similar but that, in fact, he thought experience in Italy might have been better preparation for working in Argentina with its strong Italian roots.

That foreigners have not learned the lesson of the great variety and differences within Latin America could not have been more obvious than in the reaction to the Mexican peso devaluation at the end of 1994, when panicky portfolio managers sold off holdings all over Latin America and devastated stock markets in countries thousands of miles from Mexico whose economies and political situations had none of the problems confronted by Mexico.

DO learn languages, and if you're a manager or owner encourage employees to do the same. When you hire, treat language capability in a prospective employee as a strong point. If starting from scratch to learn a language, you can't expect to conduct all your business in Spanish or Portuguese and will have to use interpreters and translators. But being able to say and understand basic getting-around things in Spanish or Portuguese will make you feel much more at home. And once you learn a little of the language, you'll want to learn more. Do not expect the people with whom you want to do business to speak English as a matter of course. There will be many business and service people in the region who will know good English and be willing to use it, but forget the tasteless notion that "They want to practice - I'm doing them a favor."

While in many other parts of the world English is the business *lingua franca,* that is not the case in culturally sensitive Latin America. Europeans visiting the region for the first time have often been more surprised to make this discovery than have people from the United States or Canada, having mistakenly assumed that the area was little more than a U.S. colony. Spanish, the primary language of the region, is spoken in so many countries that Latin Americans don't normally have to use a foreign language in daily life. (This is distinct from Europe or Asia, where many language groups are crowded together). Portuguese is spoken in only one country of Latin America, but that country, Brazil, is the fifth largest nation in the world in size. Like an

American in the middle of the United States, Brazilians may not see the need to be fluent in another language.

The person speaking a second, or foreign, language is always at a disadvantage in a conversation with someone speaking his or her first language, so in a culturally proud area like Latin America many people are reluctant to do so in a situation that would put them at a business disadvantage. The outsider going to an area to look into export or investment opportunities has the responsibility to either speak the language of the country, or arrange to be accompanied by an interpreter — unless the other party offers to speak English and seems completely at ease doing so.

You may find after the first meeting that this is the case and you will no longer need an interpreter. Kurt Van Keppel, the **Faultless Starch** sales executive, says that, in the end, hiring your own interpreter will probably save you money. He says that if you are going to be talking about the drafting of a document it might help to send the document to the interpreter in advance.

If you're going to Brazil and know Spanish but not Portuguese, don't assume that you can speak Spanish and be understood. That may work with taxi drivers and waiters, but for serious discussions make plans for an interpreter unless the other party has already indicated he or she will readily speak English. Many educated Brazilians seem more likely to have learned English as a second language than Spanish.

DO develop a good list of telephone numbers before you leave home. Guard them as if they were money or your passport. No one will intentionally steal them, but if you lose them it could ruin your whole trip. A woman who was mugged on the street during a business trip to a Latin American country a few years ago found that she was less hindered by being punched, shoved down a dark flight of stairs, and having her purse, money, and documents stolen than she was by losing her little black book.

The reason for this becomes obvious when you try to locate people in Latin America. Although telephone service has improved in recent years in most countries of the region, it still has a long way to go to meet global standards. With rare exceptions, such as Chile, you can't rely on the telephone books in Latin America to yield reliable telephone numbers. For one thing, when people move their home or business they almost inevitably have to change telephone numbers because numbers, by tradition, seem to belong to the building, not the person.

Further, if you call someone or a business that has moved you won't get an operator or a recording informing you of the new number. You'll just get the irritated new occupants of the building, who'll likely tell you they haven't the faintest idea where the previous occupants went, then bang down the receiver. Telephone manners are not a strong point of Latin Americans when talking to strangers.

Some businesses deal with this inconvenience by taking out advertisements in newspapers announcing their telephone numbers after they move to new locations. Many telephone books don't get revised and updated for years.

Therefore, any time someone gives you the name of a good contact, be sure to ask for the telephone number. If the person has several numbers, take down all of them. At least one is going to be out of order. In fact, in the process of preparing this book, we found that between the writing time and the editing and checking period many numbers had changed. If you happen to try a number several times and simply don't get an answer, that could be a sign that it is out of order.

DON'T go to Latin America between Dec. 15 and Jan. 6, nor during the week before or the few days after Easter. Latin Americans treat holidays with religious conviction.

If you take the misguided step of going into a country in the days just before one of these holidays be sure you have a confirmed reservation for your return flight and re-confirm it as soon as you arrive because outward flights will be jammed with people on holidays. Among those who stay behind, everyone you'll want to see will have gone to the beach with the family and will probably be unreachable by telephone. Individual national holidays are similarly sacrosanct. Immense cities simply shut down. Except for room service at your hotel, you may find almost nowhere to eat while wandering empty streets alone.

Finally, *DO read books* about the region and the specific country or countries in which you are interested, both fiction and non-fiction. Spending your time on the airplane with a novel about the country you're about to visit may do more to put you in the mood for the visit than studying charts and statistics. You'll also find that an appreciation of literature is common among your business counterparts in Latin America. The region has produced some of the best fiction writing of our time, much of it now translated into English, and there are many highly readable works of non-fiction — politics, history, and economics — in English as well. The editor and writers of this book, with advice from others knowledgeable about the region, have put together a list of recommended books that covers most countries of the region. Except for works by the most famous novelists you may not find many of the books we've recommended in bookstores, but they can usually be ordered directly from the publishers. A few are out of print, but should be available in good libraries. The list appears at the end of the book.

–**Shirley Christian**

For the Computer Literate

Computers, e-mail and the Internet have eliminated in some cases the need for costly international faxes, couriers, lengthy waits for government documents, trips to the library, and other research necessary to doing business abroad.

Now, with the whine of a modem and the click of a mouse, computers can fetch the latest market research reports from U.S. embassies abroad, economic projections from the World Bank and information from the USAID data bases. The so-called Digerati can retrieve stories from international wire services, Latin-America related newsletters and daily newspapers from Buenos Aires to Bogota. With millions of users in nearly every country in the world now, the Internet also offers an unparalleled networking opportunity for international business executives.

Because the face of the Internet is changing daily as new services and software to navigate among them are added, any subject-specific catalog of current offerings on the Internet is necessarily incomplete. What follows, then, is a short guide of on-line items and areas that should serve as a starting point for people interested in using their computer to help them do business in Latin America.

The most fluid area of the Internet is the World Wide Web, often referred to as the WWW or as simply The Web. A collection of literally millions of so-called "home pages" dedicated to particular topics, the Web stands out from earlier generations of Internet technology in that it provides sound, text and pictures in an easy-to-use point-and-click interface.

New users of the Web should head for the Latin American Network Information Center (LANIC) home page at the University of Texas' Center for Latin American Studies (on the Web at <http://lanic.utexas.edu/>, or searchable via the gopher tool at <gopher lanic.utexas.edu>). LANIC is the clearinghouse for most Internet-accessible information on Latin America — including documents produced by the Latin American and Caribbean Center at Florida International University, and fee databases such as the Latin American Database, regional maps, and electronic books about the region.

For hard data on business conditions in Latin America, the best resource is the **National Trade Data Bank,** or NTDB, a massive database (reachable via LANIC, directly at <http://www.stat-usa.gov/ben/html> for a fee, or free via the department's gopher at <gopher stat-usa.gov>) containing reports from U.S. diplomatic missions and commercial officers throughout the region.

NTDB reports run the gamut. Under the heading Country Commercial Guides, for example, are dozens of titles for each country,ranging from analyses of the investment climates and details of trade regulations to lists of the most promising markets and advice for business travelers. The NTDB also lists contacts at American Chambers of Commerce around the world, has guides for small and medium-sized businesses on basic exporting and trade financing, offers the full text of the North American Free Trade Agreement, and houses other reports such as the periodic Foreign Labor Trends on labor activity and regulations and the annual reports on Economic Policy and Trade Practices.

Also available at LANIC is the New Mexico State University Library "Guide to Internet Resources for Latin America." Written and updated regularly by librarian Molly Molloy, the guide is primarily geared toward academic research but also details economic and commercial information available on-line. It is also available directly from the University <gopher lib.nmsu.edu>.

Another Web site at the University of Texas is the Latin American/Spanish WWW & Gopher Services page <http://edb518ea.edb.utexas.edu/html/Latin America.html>. From here, users can easily find their way to most Web connections actually in Latin America and other Spanish-language services throughout the Internet.

Some of the more lively areas of the Internet are the discussion groups, often referred to as Usenet newsgroups. These are essentially unmoderated electronic coffee shops where users post messages seeking answers to questions and offer opinions or help to other users of the group. Most groups deal with one particular subject, usually mentioned in its title, and can be browsed by anyone with the newsreader software (a standard part of all Internet access services now).

Few newsgroups deal specifically with doing business in Latin America. Most instead revolve around individual countries and touch on everything from politics to travel to culture in those countries. People interested in specific countries will find on these newsgroups others — both resident nationals and foreigners with experience in the country — willing to offer tips, advice and recommendations on almost any subject.

Usenet newsgroups dealing with Latin America include:
- soc.culture.latin-america:
- soc.culture.mexican.
- soc.culture.caribbean
- soc.culture.argentina.
- soc.culture.peru
- soc.culture.brazil
- soc.culture.uruguay
- soc.culture.chile
- soc.culture.venezuela.

Mailing lists are similar to Usenet news groups in that they also include postings from people seeking questions or offering answers to others in the computer community. The chief difference is that the messages are electronically mailed out to subscribers instead of being posted for everyone to browse through. Some of the more active mailing lists can clutter a subscriber's mailbox and should be subscribed to sparingly.

Joining these lists is as easy as sending an electronic message to the host computer. Most of the host software (of the listserv, majordomo and listproc variety) will automatically start your subscription; other requests will be read and processed by a human. Subscription queries going to computers MUST be worded exactly as asked or they will not be processed.

Be aware that some lists are more active than others and that, as usual, mailing lists come and go frequently. In addition to the lists mentioned below that should be of interest to those doing business in

Latin America, there are several others dealing with individual countries (Argentina, Chile, Brazil, Mexico, even Bolivia.).

To keep abreast of list developments, subscribe to the NEW-LIST mailing list (write <listserv@vm1.nodak.edu> for a subscription). The NEW-LIST list also provides a database of existing mailing lists searchable by keyword. Molloy's "Guide to Internet Resources for Latin America" also includes a "List of lists."

The following lists deal with Latin American economic or business issues:

LATCO. Maintained by the Latin American Trade Council of Oregon, a forum for trade and economic data about the region and related announcements. To subscribe, send a message with the words "subscribe latco (your first and last names)" in the body of the message to: <lserv@psg.com> Leave the subject line of the message blank.

LATAM-ECON: A list originating in Peru dealing with Latin America's economy overall. To subscribe, send a message with your name, electronic address and institutional affiliation in the message to: <listasrcp@rcp.net.pe>

–**Scott Norvell**

2

ARGENTINA

Wal-Mart Part of New Wave
Of Direct Foreign Investment

By Judith Evans

The mayor helped them to find a building site; the Number Two man at the Economics Ministry put himself at their disposition to untie red tape and designated an adviser to provide them with any information they needed. Could this be Argentina? Indeed it was. When **Wal-Mart,** the famed U.S. discount chain, came knocking on the door in Buenos Aires, it opened so wide that Don Shinkle, the firm's vice president for corporate affairs, was bowled over. "Argentina is a decidedly hospitable country," he says, visibly surprised.

Once a land of "Yanqui go home" sentiments, Argentina has become a Latin American welcome wagon for foreign direct and portfolio investment. So much so that two major multinationals, **General Motors** and **Chrysler,** are returning to Argentina after having pulled out, the first in 1978, the second in 1980. Investors have responded with record capital flows into the Stock Exchange and in direct investment. In 1993, more than $6.2 billion in foreign direct investment poured in, three quarters of which went into the purchase of state-owned companies undergoing privatization. Officials and analysts calculate that Argentina will attract $41 billion in foreign direct investment over the 10-year period starting in 1995.

Wal-Mart's decision, announced in Buenos Aires on Aug. 19, 1994, by Shinkle, was particularly good news for Argentine economic policy makers, who are keen to bring in state-of-the-art distribution experts. One of the factors keeping local prices high, they are convinced, is the lagging development of distribution and commercialization networks. Only 40 percent of supermarket products are sold in stores of more than 350 square meters. The installation of the giant discount store in two locations will, they hope, encourage many imitators.

Only two weeks after VP Shinkle's confirmation that **Wal-Mart** had bought a 10,000-square-meter property on the northern rim of the capital city, he got the green light from headquarters in Arkansas to announce plans for another store. The second **Wal-Mart** was going up on 33,000 square meters of land, already named Alto Avellaneda Shopping, only 10 minutes south by auto from Buenos Aires' central landmark, the Obelisque. Both planned to open in 1995 and to sell the chain's full range of products, including everything from clothes to cosmetics, from auto accessories to toys, from pharmaceutical products to garden equipment. The site of the first of the two **Wal-Marts** was, ironically, the refurbished **Grafa** textile plant, closed down when the economy went into free fall at the end of the 1980s. A warehouse for imports is also planned at that location. In addition, plans were being developed to open **Sam's Clubs,** the **Wal-Mart** wholesale operation.

Shinkle attributes **Wal-Mart**'s Argentine investment plans to the country's enormous growth potential. "There isn't much development of discounting. We can offer the best prices and customers will be able to pay with checks and credit cards," he said. As in all their other outlets, the Argentine stores will count on what Shinkle calls their "work horses" — high quality brands and top notch customer service. But they also bring innovations to the local market such as return guarantees and 24-hour service.

Wal-Mart president David Glass has been obsessed with expanding in Latin America for the past couple of years. Like many companies, **Wal-Mart** got its feet wet in the region when it bet on the success of the North American Free Trade Agreement and moved into Mexico and Canada. The next step — Brazil — was an easy one. The family of Sam Walton, the founder of **Wal-Mart,** had a long and amiable relationship with Brazil's Amaral family, the owners of **Lojas Americanas,** a local department store chain. When the two firms tied the knot in August 1994, Brazilians called it "the marriage of the year."

Wal-Mart will be an innovative employer for Argentina. The chain expects to hire more than 500 people and to provide the same salary and benefit package in Argentina as it does in the United States. In addition to medical insurance, dental care plans, and life insurance, employees can join a stock option plan allowing them to purchase shares with a 15 percent discount from market price. In 1993, the plan paid out 8 percent of total profits.

Wal-Mart Not Alone

Hardly a week goes by now without some foreign firm announcing that it has plans to begin operations in Argentina or to buy or associate with an established local company. Since 1991, with the adoption of the so-called Convertibility Plan for the Argentine currency, dozens of multinationals have set up shop. This new wave of direct foreign investment is the largest since the 1960s, when international companies became involved in starting up the automobile and petroleum industries. According to official figures, direct foreign investment was $4.18 billion in 1992 and a record $6.2 billion in 1993. The acquisition of privatized companies accounts for approximately three-quarters of these amounts. The sale of 45 percent of the former state petroleum company, **YPF,** by public stock offering brought in $3 billion, making it Latin America's largest privatization to date.

With the privatizations, many foreign companies understood that they were being offered a unique opportunity to control regulated monopolies with guaranteed high rates of return. But with 80 percent of the planned privatization now completed, direct foreign investment is veering toward the manufacturing and service sectors.

General Motors has opened a $120 million plant in Córdoba to produce pickup trucks. **Toyota** was looking for a location to do the same. **Chrysler,** in partnership with an Argentine auto parts firm, **Iveco,** planned to produce 4,000 Jeep Cherokees a year in Córdoba, Argentina's equivalent to Detroit. The initial investment for the **Chrysler** plant was estimated at $80 million to $100 million. The U.S. consumer goods giants are also taking positions: **Procter & Gamble, Nabisco** and **Sara Lee** bought local food, health and cleaning products firms. **McDonald's, Burger King** and other fast food chains are already flourishing.

Telecommunications is experiencing a strong take-off following the privatization of **ENTel** and the formation of the two regional monopolies, **Telefónica** and **Telecom.** The two companies have invested $6 billion in the last three years in modernizing the telephone network, which now includes fiber optic cables, state of the art exchanges and satellite services. In 1993, Argentina placed its first communications satellite, Nahuel, in orbit and in October 1994 an underwater fiber optic cable came on line for commercial use. Unisur, as it is called, introduced 64,000 new international circuits, increasing Argentina's foreign communications capacity 20 times.

Mobile phone use is a rage. **GTE** and **AT&T** recently inaugurated a new network to service the interior provinces while in Buenos Aires there are two companies with 200,000 users. Argentina is the largest cable television market in Latin America with 3.5 million subscribers and a $1.3 billion annual business volume.

The privatization of **YPF** and the deregulation of the oil industry have led to a boom in production and exports. Crude oil production was expected to reach 420,000 barrels a day in 1995, and exports reached $1 billion in the first two quarters of the year.

Mining, until now totally unexploited in Argentina, is attracting a number of foreign companies. **Musto** of Canada, along with Australia's **MIM Holdings,** will begin to mine the rich gold and copper fields in Bajo de la Alumbrera in the Andean province of Catamarca sometime in 1995. They estimate a $600 million investment. There are more than 70 international mining companies operating in Argentina and it is estimated that by 1996 investment in the industry will total some $1.5 billion.

Nabisco Buys a Local Competitor

A prime attraction for foreign investors in Argentina is the profit margins, according to Debora Giorgi, a partner in the business consulting firm **Alpha** which has as its clients 40 top manufacturing firms and 30 major national and foreign banks. On the basis of market surveys that **Alpha** has done for several clients, she said return on investment — 20 percent is not uncommon — was "spectacular" compared to other countries. As examples, Giorgi cites the earnings in the expansion of gas lines and distribution, the digitalization of the telephone system and the automobile industry.

She and her partners, economist Pedro Lacoste and banking analyst Hernán del Villar, have completed a number of market surveys that forecast Argentina's future economic development, the future for specific markets and products and the competition. Their results indicate that in the short term the most dynamic sectors will be construction and autos. Both are benefiting from the return of consumer credit, which evaporated over the years of macroeconomic turmoil. Housing construction has been booming, fueled by $800 million in mortgage financing arranged in the last two years. The same is true for auto sales, which have hit records with the introduction of partial payment plans. "In spite of what is happening with international interest rates, here the growth of competition has produced a miracle," Giorgi says, "with rates in decline and lengthening loan terms."

Also revving up construction are the investment clauses in most privatizations obliging new owners to upgrade, expand or improve their acquisitions. In turn, this process is rapidly improving Argentina's neglected infrastructure, which should have a positive impact on competitiveness.

Argentina's new-found economic promise is producing divorces as well as marriages. A wave of mergers and acquisitions and a number of separations are changing the structure of the private sector. In the automotive sector, for example, Argentine growth and the potential of the Mercosur free trade area led the **Autolatina** joint operation between **Ford** and **Volkswagen** to split, and **Fiat** was said to be negotiating a buy back of its part of **Sevel,** the Argentine combination of **Fiat** and **Peugeot.** The return to Argentina of major automakers such as **GM** and **Chrysler** is also at least partly because of the promise of Mercosur's large market. **Chrysler,** for example, plans to export half of its production to Brazil.

The Mercosur trading area now comprises Argentina, Brazil, Uruguay, and Paraguay, and the group wants to negotiate trade openings with other neighbors, particularly those in the Andean-nation bloc.

As Giorgi points out, investors arrive with different agendas and choose diverse ways of entering the market. "**Nabisco,** for example, stayed in the transit lounge for awhile after arriving in Argentina, studying the competition." She said that when **Nabisco** saw that **Kraft General Foods** had benefited by purchasing the local firm **Suchard,** which increased earnings to 15 percent as the chocolate and biscuit market doubled, its own interest piqued in **Terrabusi,** another local biscuit company.

Nabisco is another example of how profoundly the formation of the four-nation Mercosur common market is affecting foreign investment. **Nabisco** plans to spend two years shaping up its Argentine subsidiary, during which time management changes will be gradually introduced and **Nabisco**'s corporate culture and ways of doing things will be adopted. By 1997, the company plans large increases in intracompany trade between **Nabisco Brazil** and **Nabisco Uruguay** based on higher degrees of product specialization in each country.

For some other companies, setting up shop in South America was part of a geographic strategy. The informatics and computer firms began by absorbing or out-competing local distributors as purchasing power grew and the elimination of tariffs and trade restraints made importing much easier.

The LBO Tactic

Leveraged buy-outs are another phenomenon that has taken off in Argentina as micro-adjustment, a mantra throughout Latin America, follows successful macro economic reform. The private sector, after decades of deformed development, has a very small pool of good management talent, but there are many existing companies that, with an injection of new ideas from modern managers, can be serious market contenders. That's where **Exxel** and Juan Navarro come in.

Exxel, the first of only two leveraged buy-out firms in the Mercosur region is, according to its founder Juan Navarro, following in the path of São Paulo-based **Garantia**. The 41-year old Citibank veteran raised $240 million in record time from a number of first class institutional investors, money managers, private pension funds, foundations, and high worth individuals, including **Oppenheimer,** the **Rockefeller Foundation** and **United Airlines. Exxel** opened its doors in December 1992 and has already taken control of 13 companies.

With a group of 11 professionals, **Exxel** tracks very clear criteria in the selection of target firms. "We are only interested in healthy firms," Navarro said. "We look for a disequilibrium in a sector and then for a firm that we think can be shaped to correct it."

One example of **Exxel**'s niche strategy was the purchase of two floundering medium-sized paper companies. Navarro's idea was to produce high quality tissue paper, a product that didn't exist in the local market. **Exxel**'s investment totaled $14 million. The two companies, **Papelera del Plata** and **Papelera Mar del Plata,** were merged, and today the new firm is the market leader with annual sales of $70 million and a profit of $8 million.

Exxel's most recent acquisition has been its most complicated so far. It bought out three medium-sized health maintenance organizations and restructured them into one company, **Galeno Life,** now the third largest HMO in Argentina. The new firm's assets include two hospitals that are undergoing a $15 million expansion. "It's a textbook case of what we like to do: find a sector that will develop along with reforms, in this case the private health care reform, and then, with the management expertise that we bring to the table, make them first rate."

Navarro says he isn't exactly setting **Exxel**'s companies up to be bought out, but he won't be surprised if it happens, either. "Global companies don't have the luxury of not being in this market," Navarro maintains, referring to the entire Southern Cone region of South America. "Sooner or later they will have to be here and the longer they take, the more market share will cost them." Argentina has the edge, in his opinion, over its neighbors because its economy has been so thoroughly deregulated. "The legal conditions are liberal in the extreme," he said, with full liberty to manage funds, to remit profits, pay dividends and transfer money.

Drawbacks: Cronyism and Corruption for Starters

Argentina, according to foreign executives who have been involved with the country for years, was, until the early 1980s, a Third World country with a First World level of corruption — meaning low. However, since the 1980s, they say corruption has been "democratized" and, with that change, has grown exponentially. While there has been no rigorous investigation into corruption, there are several obvious explanations for its growth. For one thing, with the return to elected government, politicians began to look for sources of campaign financing, to use a euphemism. In addition, the huge sell-off of state-owned companies multiplied the opportunities for graft while simultaneously promising to reduce it. Furthermore, the growth of corruption at the end of the military regime, plus the deterioration in confidence among citizens of an operative social contract and in the judicial system gave rise to the conviction that offenders among the rich and powerful act with total impunity.

Within this context, the behavior of government officials often appeared as confirmation of the increasing degree of under-the-table collusion among politicians, business leaders, and the media. This trend began under the Radical Administration of former President Raúl Alfonsín and continued even more flagrantly after President Carlos Saúl Menem was elected in 1989.

Most of the scandals that hit the press are often poorly reported, and there usually are no implications for foreign firms. However, when there have been implications, they've been whoppers. On several occasions, contrary to usual diplomatic comportment, the U.S. ambassador has all but publicly denounced wrong doing.

A recent example involved the promised privatization of the

Post Office, but it has a long history, beginning during the era of military rule, when Ezeiza International Airport in Buenos Aires came under the control of the Argentine Air Force. Subsequent private biddings allotted some important airport services, such as the overnight cargo storage and currency deposit facilities to a firm called **Edcadassa,** which was reported to be 55 percent owned by the Air Force and 45 percent by Alfredo Nallib Yabran, whose name is inevitably followed by the phrase "the mysterious businessman." Yabran was also thought to be the principal owner of **OCA** and **OCASA,** the main firms servicing the postal needs of the Argentine financial world and the first to enter the courier business in Argentina.

Beginning as early as 1990, U.S. officials privately raised the question of harassment of the only U.S.-owned courier service in Argentina, **DHL.** By 1991, the issue had grown to include an apparent stonewalling of **Federal Express** efforts to operate its courier and delivery and deposit services at Ezeiza Airport. This would eventually lead to open hostilities between the U.S. Embassy, then under the stewardship of Ambassador Terence Todman, and former Defense Minister Erman González, and between González and Economics Minister Domingo Cavallo.

In late 1994, when **Encotel,** the state-owned postal service, was scheduled to be privatized, the Argentine Senate took bi-partisan action to exclude any international bidder from acquiring the national postal network, thereby, according to the Economics Ministry, assuring a monopolistic victory to a consortium of firms whose major partner is the same "mysterious" Mr. Yabran. The proposed legislation also prohibited police revision of transport vehicles to be operated by the new owner. Only five senators opposed the bill.

The local press reported that U.S. authorities, beginning with Ambassador James Cheek, who had succeeded Terence Todman, and rising to high State Department officials, made known their objections to the exclusionary clause and their fears that Yabran's operations at the international airport combined with control of the postal service raised serious concerns about increased drugs and arms trade through Argentina.

—*To access our program, type "B-R-I-B-E" and then hit "enter."*

After two weeks of painfully public squabbling during which Cavallo said on one of the nation's most popular television talkshows that Yabran was a frequent guest at the presidential residence, the Senate and the House of Deputies agreed to treat the legislation again when the regular session began in May 1995. President Menem finally came out in support of Cavallo's position and said he would veto any modification that restricted bidding to national firms.

So it did appear that **DHL, Federal Express,** and other foreign firms would be able to contend for the postal service. However, the case demonstrated a continuing battle to force transparency and open competition into a context where back room dealings have become entrenched at high levels of power.

Heat and Light can be Problems as Well

Turning to a completely different kind of problem for investment, it is vital to understand Argentina's critical infrastructure deficit. Decades of scarce to non-existent public funding have resulted in neglect of existing roads, power generation plants, airports, ports, and all other formerly state operated services. To some extent, this situation is being reversed as new private owners improve the facilities in accordance with the privatization contracts. Energy, however, is an exception. As has happened with frequency in recent years, in mid-December of 1994, a week of very warm weather in the capital city of Buenos Aires led to drastic blackouts, leaving whole areas without light, air conditioning and elevators. This has three implications. The most obvious is that energy-intensive or energy-dependent operations have to be prepared to add powerful generators to their investment shopping lists.

The second is that the two consortia that bought the electricity generating plants for Greater Buenos Aires were either not complying or having difficulties in complying with the scheduled improvements. Public debate over the responsibility for the performance of the two consortia, both of which are led by foreign companies, raised the possibility of the contracts being rescinded. In such an eventuality, it is likely that the whole question of privatization and foreign participation will become highly politicized, with consequences that are difficult to predict.

The third factor is somewhat more than an implication. If Argentina sustains its current growth rates, energy generation will continue to be a serious problem well into the medium-term time frame. While the completion of Yacyretá, a dam on the border with Paraguay, was promised for the end of 1995, no other new facilities are on the drawing boards. Summers in Greater Buenos Aires will undoubtedly cause "lights out" with some frequency for years to come.

Argentine Overview

Deregulation a Magnet For Investment, But Labor Costs Pinch

Argentina has one of the most liberal foreign investment codes in Latin America. Soon after President Menem was elected in 1989 his government issued Decree 1125/89, which eliminated all existing requirements for state approval on foreign investment, replacing them with a simple registration scheme. Since then, even the registration requirement has been abolished. There are currently no restrictions of any kind on investment, with one minor exception. The Radio Diffusion Law prohibits majority foreign ownership in the communications field. All other sectors, including those formerly held off-limits as being "strategic," such as the defense and nuclear energy sectors, are open.

These changes in the legal framework have been accompanied by growing public approval of foreign investment. Multinational corporations are viewed as sources of much-needed investment capital and valued "know-how." The public also has the impression that foreign firms treat employees better and provide consumers with higher quality products and services. The vast privatization program implemented by the Menem Administration attracted massive foreign investment with very little political opposition, even from sectors, such as trade unions, that had been hostile in the past. This was most notable in the 1993 privatization of **YPF,** the previously state-owned oil company, which had long been a symbol of national sovereignty and a totem for economic and political nationalists.

The Convertibility Plan, which ties the peso to the dollar, has led to an over-valuation of the local currency that experts estimate to be on the order of 20 percent to 30 percent. This, in turn, has made Argentine labor costs the highest in Latin America. In addition, the employer's social security contributions and other regulatory fees are the equal of more than 50 percent of take-home pay. While labor reform is a declared objective of the Menem government, so far it has been able only to chip away at the costly and inflexible laws governing employment. For example, in 1995 the central government permitted reductions of 30 percent to 80 percent for social security contributions in some provinces. The highest reductions applied to the poorest provinces while the lowest covered the Federal Capital.

According to the Labor Ministry, nominal industrial labor costs, including all contributions, were 1200 pesos a month in 1993, equal to $1,200, up from 907 in 1991 and 776 in 1990. Because of high labor costs, many companies are investing in labor saving technology and equipment with the goal of downsizing the work force. Government support for this reaction led it to place a zero tariff on capital goods imports.

The work week is officially 48 hours and the work day is eight hours. Night shifts cannot be longer than seven hours. Overtime pay is 50 percent more than regular pay during the week and 100 percent for week-ends and holidays. Severance pay is one month's salary for every year of employment and is mandated for any dismissal without just cause (which includes fraud, insubordination, and violent behavior).

If the government is successful in passing the new Labor Law that it submitted to Congress two years ago, many of these practices may change considerably. Under the proposed law, the legal work day would be extended to a 12-hour limit and temporary work contracts would be permitted.

Although Argentina has the lowest rate of illiteracy in the region, the quality of the work force has deteriorated greatly over the last decade. A number of factors explain this decline. The extreme economic volatility led many businesses to close, especially those that employed skilled labor. The historically high rates of unemployment also affected many professionals who then either lost proficiency or fell behind new developments in their fields. Many multinational firm managers complain about the difficulty they have hiring skilled labor or first rate managers. The privatized companies — telecommunications, gas, electricity and water — have resorted to recruiting foreign managers and there are now hundreds of Chileans, Italians, French and U.S. executives employed managing their technical operations.

Stability and Growth Follow Severe Adjustment

Since 1991, the Argentine economy has undergone an unprecedented transformation. Hyperinflation, recession and macroeconomic chaos paved the way for a severe adjustment, which led to a period of price stability and economic growth unrivaled in the hemisphere. Without doubt, the most remarkable achievement was the plummet in inflation rates from the astronomical levels of 1989 — 5000 percent — to an annual rate of 3.5 percent. In itself, this outstanding victory produced enormous changes in how Argentines function economically.

High and persistent inflation over nearly four decades forced businesses to develop perverse strategies in order to survive. Inflation came to be a partner, an ally. With it, debts were canceled with cheapened money, average salaries were forced down when measured in dollars, and profits from financial operations and speculative ventures were possible. Local business executives developed great financial skills and the ability to adapt to abrupt changes in economic policy. In the end, this led to "rich businessmen and poor businesses," a phrase heard often in Argentina.

With stability, many local firms were left "off sides," in a kind of economic penalty zone. The fall in interest rates to levels similar to the inflation rate put an end to financial gains for companies with lots of cash and forced them to compete for clients in the market. Many either wouldn't or couldn't adapt and closed down or sold out. In the last three years a record number of Argentine companies have been bought by multinationals such as **Procter & Gamble, Nabisco, Sara Lee,** and **Unilever.**

Pricing structures and distribution have been revolutionized by stability. There has been a boom in supermarkets and shopping malls, where customers can enjoy comparative shopping, an entirely new pastime in Argentina. International franchised businesses have sprouted all over. **Carrefour,** the largest local chain, had record sales of $1.3 billion in 1993. The return of consumer credit boosted the sales of consumer durables of all kinds, including televisions, refrigerators, and VCRs. In 1994, more than half a million cars were sold in Argentina, 140,000 of them imported.

The construction industry, long in the doldrums, leapt to near capacity with the return of mortgage lending and the pent-up demand for new housing. Today, Argentine banks are able to borrow money in international capital markets for periods of five to 10 years at rates of nine to 10 percent. They re-lend the money in the local market for 16 to 20 percent annually.

Painful Path to Economic and Political Health

More than 10 years since the return to democracy in December 1983, the stability of democratic political institutions in Argentina seems assured. The armed forces, defeated in the Falklands/Malvinas war with Great Britain and having failed in economic management, abandoned their political ambitions and are no longer seen as an important power factor. Obligatory military service was recently abolished, something that would have been unthinkable only a short time ago in a country governed for so many years by military governments.

The international situation, with the end of the Cold War and the collapse of communism, helped the consolidation of democracy in Argentina. The country's 180-degree change in its foreign policy orientation toward support for the United States has not created any controversy, despite Argentina's long history of prickly relations with the United States. Under President Menem, Argentina sent troops to the Gulf War, participated in peacekeeping in the former Yugoslavia and has regularly voted with the United States in the United Nations.

The reinstatement of democracy began with the presidency of Raúl Alfonsín (1983-1989), a leader of the Radical Party. Carlos Saúl Menem was elected in May 1989 and took office in July, six months earlier than expected, as the Alfonsín government lost effective governing ability in the midst of hyperinflation. In 1994, Menem pushed through a constitutional reform that significantly changed the rules of the game. The presidential term was cut from six to four years and re-election permitted; the number of national senators representing each of the provinces went up to three from two, an effort to improve the representation of minority parties; the strong presidentialism of the previous constitution was watered down by the introduction of a chief cabinet minister; the president no longer need be a professed Roman Catholic; mayors of Buenos Aires will now be elected by popular vote rather than being appointed by the president, as was the case in the past.

Menem also initiated the dramatic economic reforms, although some changes in that direction had been attempted under Alfonsín. The reforms have, in addition to macroeconomic stabilization, reduced the economic role of the state and are intended to make way for a dynamic and competitive private sector. The transition is still in process, with several major areas of reform, such as labor law, yet to be implemented and with streamlining what remains of the public sector only barely begun. However, any change in policy direction is almost impossible and a return to past economic turbulence is, therefore, highly unlikely. While there is dissension on social policy and issues such as judicial reform, there is broad consensus on the economic model. Even the Frente Grande, the center-left coalition that was the primary challenger to Menem in the presidential election on May 14, 1995, released a very moderate economic platform that maintained the convertibility of the currency and declared the privatizations to be irreversible. With an impressive 85 percent of the 22 million eligible voters going to the polls, Menem won re-election by a wide margin.

The convertibility of the peso to the U.S. dollar at a fixed parity of one peso to one dollar was the key to the abrupt stabilization of the Argentine economy. Under the plan, introduced by Economics Minister Domingo Cavallo in April 1992, each peso in circulation was backed by international reserves in the Central Bank ($17 billion in June 1994). Typically, when there is a strong peso supply in the market and peso interest rates drop below international rates, the Central Bank buys the excess with dollars from its reserves. Inversely, when peso demand is strong and interest rates go above international levels, the Central Bank sells dollars, injecting more pesos into the market. The key element in the Convertibility Plan's success was that the Central Bank stopped printing unbacked currency because there was no longer a budget deficit.

At the beginning, local inflation remained above U.S. levels, which resulted in the peso's overvaluation. This led to strong pressures for a devaluation, including runs against the peso, but the government successfully fought off these threats. Nonetheless, the peso's record overvaluation does create doubts about the sustainability of convertibility in the medium term.

The government is trying to deal with this problem by means of indirect devaluations such as reductions in the price paid by businesses for labor and energy and lowered taxes. Another policy pursued by the government has been to reward exports by allowing exporters to import high demand products with low duties to be sold very profitably in the local market. Such is the case in the automobile industry, for example.

Despite pressures that mounted in the aftermath of Mexico's currency crisis at the end of 1994, no change in Argentina's one-to-one parity was forecast before the end of 1995. The government planned to continue its efforts to improve the "effective" parity with the dollar with export/import schemes or with some form of subsidies. The upward trend in the valuation of the Chilean peso, which occurred despite the tremors that the Mexican currency crisis sent through much of Latin America, was good news for its neighbor Argentina. Additionally, the possible synchronization of the currencies in the Mercosur free trade zone gave credence to projections of increased intra-regional trade. Argentine exports grew by 17 percent in 1994 with most of the increase being accounted for by sales to Brazil.

The Nation's Roots

After various decades of civil wars following independence in the 19th Century, Argentina began to form as a nation after 1850. The local aristocracy dominated politically until the early 1900s, when massive immigration from Europe brought the Radical Civic Union Party and its candidate Hipólito Yrigoyen into the presidency in 1916. Radicalism would govern until 1930, the year in which a coup initiated a long period of frequent military interventions.

From 1880 to 1930, the Argentine economy experienced extraordinary growth related to its insertion in the agro-export model associated with Great Britain's domination of world trade. Because of Argentina's importance as a source of meat, wool and grains, British businessmen invested in the nation's infrastructure, building railroads, ports and water treatment plants. Up to 1910 Argentina was second only to India in reception of British overseas investments. It was during this *belle époque* that Argentina was known as the world's granary and Buenos Aires was called the "Paris of South America" for the imported architectural tastes of its landowning families.

The Great Depression and the crisis of the 1930s put an end to all that. Argentina turned to a model based on import substitution. This stage, which lasted until 1978, saw U.S. direct foreign investment overtake Britain's.

Peronism, lead by Juan Domingo Perón, won the 1946 election, reflecting the aspirations of the large working class that had been drawn to the large cities by war-induced industrialization. Perón remained in office until he was overthrown by the military in 1955. During his presidency, he continued the import substitution policies initiated in the 1930s and state intervention and regulation of the economy increased steadily. However, under this model, Argentina developed an unusually strong industrial base for a developing agro-exporting country. Among the various industries that grew up during this time were textile, automobile, petroleum, chemical and petrochemical, and steel.

Still there were recurrent boom-and-bust cycles and frequent balance of payments crises. By the early 1970's inflation was on the rise, fueled by political uncertainty. Perón returned after 17 years in exile to lead a troubled country. The famed charisma and political skill were not enough to stall the slide. Argentina was already lurching toward another military coup when Perón died in July 1974. His wife and vice-president, María Estela Martínez de Perón, took over but her inexperience and poor judgment only made matters worse. In March 1976, the military, once again, took command of the state, unleashing a ferocious war against guerrilla violence that quickly escalated into a reign of terror and gave the nation one of the world's worst human rights records.

The military government did attempt to beat back inflation, which continued to erode the financial markets, and to open the economy. However, an overvalued currency and the elimination of high tariffs produced a flood of imports, which led to the closing of many plants, high unemployment, and greatly accelerated capital flight. With the economy in ruin and political protest growing, in 1982 the armed forces invaded the Malvinas Islands, long held by Britain but claimed by Argentina. This provoked the war that would drive the armed forces from power.

The process of economic liberalization begun in 1979 was not reversible and, although the first democratic government stumbled, the policy direction moved ahead and subsequently got a robust push from the Menem administration.

Argentina at a Glance

Population: 33 million (1994 estimated). Labor force: 13.5 million.
Unemployment: 10 percent. Population growth rate: 1.5 percent
Language: Spanish.

Ethnic mix: The Argentine population is very homogeneous, with most people descended from the massive immigration of Italians and Spaniards who began arriving at the end of the 19th Century. Russian and Polish Jews began arriving about the same time but in smaller numbers. Although Argentina had the fifth largest Jewish community in the world in the early 1970s, it is estimated to be much smaller today as many have immigrated to Israel and the United States. There is an influential Arab community that dates back to the first two decades of the century when many fled the collapse of the Ottoman Empire. In recent years, immigration from neighboring countries — Chile, Paraguay, and Uruguay — has increased, especially in border areas. Koreans have also built a sizable community in Buenos Aires and a few of its more suburban areas such as Flores. Finally, people of Northern European ancestry, particularly English, Irish, and German, are a notable presence in business, farming, and the professions, though their actual percentage of the population is small.

Education: The literacy level in Argentina exceeds 90 percent and as recently as the 1970s the country was justifiably praised for its high literacy levels and the quality of its educational system. However, the public school system suffered greatly as economic instability reduced state funding and teacher salaries. Illiteracy has increased in part as a result of the decline in living standards and the growth in immigration from poorer neighboring countries. Nearly two-thirds of all Argentines have completed elementary school or beyond.

Climate and best times to visit: Argentina sprawls southward along the eastern coast of the continent between the Atlantic Ocean and the Andean Mountains. It reaches from a southern latitude of 22 degrees to 55 degrees, giving it a variety of climates that range from tropical to arctic and almost everything in between. Its largest area is in a temperate zone called the *Pampa Húmeda,* where winters are mild and summers very warm and short, lasting from mid-December through February. Heat and humidity make the northeastern provinces subtropical with quite mild winters. The northwest has some pockets of warm, semi-tropical weather in the provinces of Tucumán and Salta but in general it is a dry region in which some areas have high desert qualities. South of the *Pampa Húmeda* lies the Patagonia region which has colder temperatures and greater rainfall.

Although Buenos Aires lies in what is technically a temperate zone, summers can be quite hot, and light clothing is advised. Still, you should pack a summer raincoat for seasonal rain storms and a jacket for cooler evenings and air conditioned spaces. The fact is that the winter months (June-September) are good times to visit Buenos Aires. Most days are sunny, perfect for cafe-sitting, and you'll seldom need more than a light coat or wool jacket. However, the warmer months (December-February) are the best time to go to Patagonia as its winters are very cold with heavy snow and frequently canceled and delayed flights.

Land area: 3.7 million square kilometers.
Economic statistics:
   GDP: $282 billion
   Per Capita GDP: $8,500
   Economic growth rate: 6.5 percent (1993)
   Trade balance: Negative $2.925 billion (1994).
Natural resources, chief agricultural products: With its vast central plain and varieties of climate and terrain, the Argentine economy remains dependent on natural resources to a considerable degree. Agriculture, for example, accounts for approximately 15 percent of GDP, 30 percent of employment and 60 percent of exports. Efforts in recent years have led to a diversification of crops and exports and a major push in the long-neglected mining sector. Oil seeds, especially soybeans, have become the country's most important single crop. Other

significant crops and resources: cereals, forage grains, fruits, vegetables, cattle, sheep, hogs, fish, petroleum, natural gas, zinc, iron, lead, clay, siliceous sand, bentonite, calcite, quartz, salt, gypsum.

Principal exports: Foodstuffs, live animals, fuel, lubricants and related products, vegetable and animal based cooking oils, manufactured products.

Principal imports: Transport equipment, chemical products, manufactured goods. An estimated 44 percent of imports in 1994 were capital goods.

Duties on imports: Argentine duties average less than 8 percent on all imports, but vary widely. Duties on specific imports from all countries not part of the Mercosur trading bloc (Argentina, Brazil, Uruguay, and Paraguay) range from zero to 29 percent. For trade among themselves, the Mercosur countries have a maximum tariff of 20 percent, but each country has a long list of exceptions that change frequently.

Repatriation of profits: No restrictions apply to repatriation of profits by foreign firms, although the 1994 economic crisis in Mexico set off some debate in Argentina on the potential benefits of introducing a minimum time period for foreign direct investment and profit repatriation to reduce volatility and vulnerability in capital flows.

When You Go to Argentina

Visas: Foreign business representatives and tourists do not need a visa to enter Argentina unless they plan to stay more than six months, open a bank account, or enter into a real estate contract. In those cases, a resident visa is required. Visas should be obtained at consular offices and are easier to get abroad than upon arrival or during a stay. They are granted automatically when $30,000 is deposited with cooperating banks, including J.P. Morgan and Citicorp. The money is returned immediately upon receipt of the visa.

Airlines: Aerolineas Argentinas, American, United from the United States; Varig from Brazil; Lan Chile and Ladeco from Chile; Alitalia, Air France, Swissair, British Airways, Lufthansa, KLM, and SAS from Europe, and Air Canada from Canada.

Domestic flights: Flights to the interior of Argentina depart and arrive at the Jorge Newbery Airport, more commonly called Aeroparque, which is a municipal airport located not far from the center of Buenos Aires. However, don't be fooled by the shorter distance. It can be quite chaotic and flights are generally fully booked. Get there more than the required hour ahead of time. The address is Avenida Costanera Norte and the information telephone number is 771-2071. National airlines flying out of Aeroparque include Aerolineas Argentinas, Austral, and LAPA. Flights to neighboring Uruguay also leave from Aeroparque instead of Ezeiza, the international airport.

What to Expect at the Airport:

Passage through immigration has speeded up considerably in the last two years, and, unless weather or other exceptional conditions lead to simultaneous arrivals of several large planes, you can expect to clear both in about 30 minutes. There are two terminals at Ezeiza International Airport, one for Aerolineas Argentinas and Iberia and one for all other international flights. The customs system requires everyone to line up and press a button; green allows you to go through without inspection; red means an inspection, usually perfunctory for foreigners and those with reasonable amounts of luggage.

Once past customs, foreigners are usually amazed to see huge crowds of relatives and friends on hand to meet arriving passengers. This enthusiastic welcome committee can make passing out of the reserved area a bit of a hassle, but the airport is well controlled and there is no gaggle of poor youngsters jostling to grab your luggage and arrange transportation, as is common in many Latin American countries. Even the reliability of luggage carts has improved!

With the U.S. dollar and the Argentine peso on a par, you may as well take advantage of your time in the airport to change some money and not have to worry about it later.

Airport transportation: There are several options for getting into the center of Buenos Aires from the airport, including:

● Car services have proliferated, and if someone locally is arranging your trip, it is the most comfortable way to go. The drivers congregate just beyond the crowd outside customs and will hold up signs with the passenger's name or affiliation. The car-service fares range from $50 to $60, and the ride takes about 30 or 40 minutes.

● There are also special airport taxis, painted black with red trim, that cost somewhat less than the car services.

● There is also a bus service run by a local company called Manuel Tienda Leon, which has a counter near the terminal exit and operates to all of the hotels and has service to some of the outlying suburbs. Fares are substantially less expensive, about $25 to downtown.

● Buses to the domestic airport, where flights leave for other cities in Argentina, are operated by the airlines and are free.

Hotels

NOTE:

   In the last five years there has been a boom in luxury hotel construction in Buenos Aires, and not a bit too soon. The city has always had a surfeit of modest-priced hotels that cater to visitors from the provinces and neighboring countries. But, until recently, the only first-class hotel space was at the Plaza and the Sheraton. The renovation of the Alvear Palace Hotel in the Recoleta section of the city added one, and since 1991 it has been joined by three more top notch hotels: the Park Hyatt, the Caesar Park, and the Inter-Continental. It has to be added that these hotels are very pricey and don't be surprised at unexpected costs, such as very high charges for local phone calls.

   At times, it is difficult to get reservations at the best hotels. In that case, there are a number of smaller hotels that are comfortable, convenient, and prepared for business guests. We recommend the Bisonte, the Claridge, and the Plaza Francia.

   Although many new hotels are being built throughout Argentina, in the interior even the best hotels are generally "no stars," which is why most established industrial operations have their own lodgings for visiting executives.

   A tax of 21 percent is added to all hotel room prices.

Alvear Palace Hotel

Avenida Alvear 1891. Tel: (541) 804-4031. Fax: (541) 804-0034.
Refurbished 1932 Art Deco beauty with business center and a location
sure to please the urbane among us. Health club, pool, and sauna.
Rooms with breakfast begin at $200 plus tax.

Bisonte

Paraguay 1207. Tel: (541) 816-5770. Fax: (541) 816-5775.
Coffee shop, but no restaurant; agreeable staff, good message service,
decent phone and fax services.
Rooms with breakfast begin at $125 plus tax.

Caesar Park

Posadas 1232. Tel: (541) 814-5151. Fax: (541) 814-5148.
Rooms begin at $270 a night and suites go to $2,000.

Claridge

Tucuman 535. Tel: (541) 314-2020. Fax: (541) 314-8022.
Room rates begin at $220.

Inter-Continental

Avenida de Mayo at Moreno 809, Tel: (541) 340-7100. Fax: (541) 340-
7199.
The newest luxury hotel in Buenos Aires, the Inter-Continental is very
close to the financial center and to the main ministries. It has three
floors dedicated to those who need special services, in addition to
those provided by the business center.
Rates begin at $250, with a special business rate of $230.

Park Hyatt

Posadas 1086. Tel: (541) 326-1234. Fax: (541) 326-3736.
Business center, meeting rooms available, good phone and fax service.
Rooms begin at $220, though there are some promotional rates of $150
and $180.

Marriott Plaza

Florida 1005. Tel: (541) 318-3000. Fax: (541) 318-3008.
Sentimental favorite from days when it was just the Plaza; very good
restaurants; the service does not come with a smile; phones are said to
be improved.

Rooms begin at $280, with promotional rates of $179 on weekends according to availability.

Plaza Francia

E. Schiaffino 2189. Tel/Fax: (541) 804-9631.

Overlooks charming park and restaurant row; front rooms are reported to be noisy and back rooms small, so a back suite may be the answer. It's possible to have a computer put in your room.

Rates begin at $135 with continental breakfast.

Sheraton

San Martin 1225. Tel: (541) 311-6331 to 311-6339. Fax: (541) 311-6353 and 312-0346. Business center, travel service, swimming pool; service is much better if you stay in the Tower; construction on an expansion is under way and it may be noisy during the day.

Rooms begin at $200, but promotional rates are available.

Urban Transportation:

Taxis are recommended for getting around Buenos Aires, a big, congested city where the driving style is Basic Italian. The base rate for roaming street taxis is about $1, and a trip of 20 blocks adds about $3, making taxis about the only bargain to be found in Buenos Aires.

Private automobile services: This is a growing industry in Buenos Aires, and the service is usually excellent with good drivers and vehicles that are in good condition. For any travel outside the city or even to the outer suburbs, it's the way to go. Cost arrangements vary and all the hotels on our list will make reservations. A probable charge is $100 for an entire day for auto and driver, plus $1 a kilometer for mileage. Here are two well-known 24-hour services:

● Flash Car, Address: 24 de noviembre. Tel: 304-1946.

● Flota Mayo, Address: Balcarce 381. Tel: 342-6882.

Auto rentals: In recent years automobile rental firms have grown in size and number, leading to a modest reduction in the tariffs. However, by U.S. standards, renting a vehicle in Argentina is still very costly. Occasionally, promotional packages with lower prices are available, but, in general, you can count on $100 a day, plus kilometer charges. If the daily rate is lower there will probably be a higher kilometer charge. Here are three firms:

- Dollar Rent-A-Car, Marcelo T. Alvear 523. Tel: 313-2572.
- AI Rent-A-Car, Marcelo T. Alvear 678. Tel: 313-1515.
- Localiza Rent-A-Car, Paraguay 1122. Tel: 375-1611.

Private air services:

- American Jet, Paraguay 729, 7th Floor, Room 29-30. Tel: 315-3752. Airport Tel: 775-5436 or 775-5487. 24-hour line: 315-3665. Fax: 315-0581. Offers executive jets, national and international passenger and cargo service, helicopters, and turboprop aircraft.
- Angela Rosa S.A., Aeroparque. Tel: 774-7014 and 470-3043. Airport Tel: 772-3022. Offers executive jets, turboprop planes, national and international passenger and cargo service.
- Rent-A-Plane, Tels: 772-6573, 775-1082, 445-4659, 447-2814. Ambulance and international cargo service.

Contacts

FUNDACION INVERTIR (Investment Foundation)
Economy Ministry, 9th floor, Hipolito Yrigoyen and Balcarce Sts.
Tel: (541) 342-7370.
This important organization, set up by Economy Minister Domingo Cavallo, is half public, half private and has developed a good reputation for solving all kinds of problems. Its staff is available to arrange interviews with government officials and to make contacts with business and has, on hand, studies of economic sectors. Not only does the personnel, directed by Jaime Campos and Alicia Caballero, help with paperwork, they also make available translators, telephones, and office space.

Lawyers Experienced in Trade and Investment:

Baker & McKenzie
Avenida Leandro Alem 1110, 13th floor, Tel: (541) 311-5412 and 311-5130.
Contact: Miguel Menegazo Cane

Allende & Brea

Maipú 1300, 10th floor, Tel: (541) 313-9191, 313-9292, and 313-9199.

Contact: José Antonio Allende

Beccar Varela

Cerrito 740, 16th floor, Tel: (541) 372-5100.

Contact: Damian Beccar Varela

Bronsi-Salas

Lavalle 522, Tel: (541) 311-9271 to 9279.

Contact: Horacio Salas

Ernesto Galante & Associados

Cerrito 1136, 3rd floor, Tel: (541) 812-2610 and 812-2786.

3

BOLIVIA

Becoming an Energy Hub
From a Perch High in the Andes

By Winston Moore

It was a former Yale classmate who invited Larry Coben to come take a look at Bolivia, but what convinced him to stay and invest was the country's energy potential, its location at the heart of South America, and the quality of its economic thinkers.

Less than a year after his first visit, in February 1994, Coben's firm, **Liberty Power** Latin America, bought a stake in **Bolivian Power Co. Ltd.,** and Coben became its CEO. **Bolivian Power** is the largest electricity distribution firm and second largest generation company in the country, serving the area around La Paz, the capital. It had revenues of $44 million in 1993. That this commitment to Bolivia occurred almost simultaneously with the currency crisis that sent Mexico reeling and frightened many investors off Latin America entirely didn't seem to faze Coben.

"I am very bullish about the whole continent," he said. "I view the downturns as opportunities to invest, hopefully at a lower cost. I think there is too much pent-up demand, too much potential here for the capitalizations, the privatizations, the investments and the growth not to take place. I have no doubt that sometime during my stay there will be some adverse political development — because there just are."

Other generations of investors encountered a good many of those adverse developments in Bolivia. A poor, landlocked country, it used to be known mainly to the outside world for tendencies to nationalize oil and tin and toss aside governments faster than any of the neighbors. Bolivia has twice nationalized holdings of private oil companies, **Standard Oil** in the 1930s and **Gulf Oil** in the late 1960s. Oil is closely identified with the Bolivian sense of nationhood and a border dispute linked to oil discoveries led to a war with Paraguay in the 1930s. Similar thinking has been applied to the tin mining industry, which was controlled by three so-called tin barons until their holdings were nationalized after the 1952 revolution.

Today, however, Bolivia is a decade into political stability and free-market economics and eight years into currency stability, and Larry Coben is not the only investor excited about its potential.

Fred F. Drew, the U.S.-born vice president and country director of **BHP Petroleum,** says the seriousness of Bolivia's economic reforms had a bearing on the decision of his firm, a unit of Australia's **Broken Hill Proprietary,** to come to Bolivia. In August 1994, **BHP Petroleum** won a bid to build a gas pipeline linking Villamontes in southern Bolivia to Escondida in northern Chile. Its partners include the Bolivian oil company **Yacimientos Petrolíferos Fiscales Bolivianos (YPFB)** and the Chilean counterpart, **ENAP. BHP** and **YPFB** together will provide 90 percent of the cost of the $300 million project and **ENAP** 10 percent. The pipeline will feed thermoelectric plants in northern Chile.

This, and another possible project for a gas pipeline from Santa Cruz in Bolivia to São Paulo, Brazil, highlight the importance that Bolivia places on its more than 150 billion cubic meters of proven gas reserves. As part of its efforts to pull itself up from being the poorest country, per capita, on the South American continent, Bolivia wants to take advantage of its geographical location at the heart of South America to satisfy a significant part of the region's gas requirements.

"The key to **BHP Petroleum** winning the gas pipeline contract to northern Chile," Drew says, "is that we have a lot of common goals with the government, such as to increase self-sufficiency in hydrocarbons and assist in exporting oil and gas, which will increase revenues for the country, and we are looking forward to a long-term presence in Bolivia, rather than just coming in and out."

Both Coben and Drew stress the value of personal involvement and contacts. For Coben, the personal touch mattered even before he had set foot in Bolivia. When he was an undergraduate at Yale, one of his classmates was a Bolivian named Mauricio González. Later, they both did advanced studies at Harvard, Coben in the law school, González in the business school. A decade or so later, Coben's U.S. firm, **Liberty Power,** was developing power plants in other South American countries, and González had become president of the Bolivian oil company, **YPFB.**

"I called him just to kind of see what was happening in Bolivia," Coben said, "and how he was doing personally." González said the Bolivian government was about to embark on its planned program of "capitalization" — a Bolivian-designed form of privatization — of the power industry and suggested that Coben ought to come and take a look.

On that first trip, Coben also met with Carlos Miranda, the national energy secretary, other government officials, and members of the business community. "I was extraordinarily impressed by the extremely intelligent, bright people we met who were working to create a competitive electrical environment," he said.

Coben took a hard look at the Bolivian electricity market, which he admits had not been high up on his "radar screen." He had been more interested in the richer and more populous neighbors: Argentina, Brazil, Chile, and Peru, where his firm was already developing power facilities. During the coming year, he went on to advise the Bolivian government on the drafting of the electricity law, studied the plan to capitalize the **National Electricity Company (ENDE),** and took a hard look at the country and its perspectives.

"I have to say the government did a phenomenal job in being open to investors," he said. "They had these seminars on the new electricity law. Access was very important to us, and I am not sure there is a whole lot that I would do differently."

Soon after Coben's arrival in Bolivia, a dispute surfaced between the government and the **Bolivian Power Co. (COBEE),** a firm listed on the New York Stock Exchange whose largest owner was then New York-based **Leucadia National Corp.** The dispute had to do with plans for construction of a new hydroelectric plant, plus the fear of brownouts in La Paz during the peak-demand winter period, and the separation of **COBEE** into generation and distribution units. **Liberty Power** stepped in, and, with a partner, **Cogentrix Energy Inc.,** bought **Leucadia**'s 18 percent share.

"Our goal was to institute a new strategy to end the fighting with the government and turn this into a vehicle for growth not only in Bolivia, but to export power to neighboring countries as well," Coben said.

Although Bolivian electricity usage is growing at a healthy 7 percent a year, Coben also plans to export electricity to Brazil, Peru, Argentina, and Chile. "The Bolivian market is very fast growing, but in totality it is small," he said. "There is roughly 600mw in Bolivia, and the country needs maybe 900mw, but it doesn't need 60,000mw. In Brazil, just in the border regions, you are looking at 3,000mw to 5,000mw of demand."

The first major expansion in Bolivia's power capabilities under Coben's direction will be the $120 million expansion of **COBEE**'s Zongo Valley installations, to be followed by a number of feasibility studies, including an examination of hydro-power possibilities.

The very nature of the electricity industry requires investors to take a long-term view, but Coben's commitment is unusual because he began to invest long before the arrival of other investors interested in participating in the capitalization of the six leading state-owned companies.

"If I am going to put my money in something I am sure as hell going to be around to be part of that process," he said. "I think being hands-on is critical. I think if you look at the panic over Latin America (after the Mexican crisis) it is partly because of the fact that you had a bunch of people investing who have never been here. I think you have to be part of the business community to be successful in it. No question about that."

Fred Drew and **BHP** showed a similar interest in getting involved with Bolivia on the ground. Drew began visiting Bolivia in May 1993 and set up an office in the eastern lowland city of Santa Cruz in August of that year. **BHP** was attracted to Bolivia because of opportunities to participate in exploration and to help develop gas networks throughout the southern part of South America.

Drew, who grew up in Venezuela and Peru, has traveled the world working for **BHP** since it took over **Hamilton Oil,** his former employer, in 1980. After moving to Bolivia from Malaysia, he focused on letting people in the private sector and government know about **BHP**'s experience and strengths. He emphasized building relationships in Bolivia and, in a reaction similar to that of Coben when he arrived, Drew said he was impressed with the "overall level of professionalism in government" in Bolivia. His first year in Bolivia was an election year, and Drew saw the smooth transition from one president to another that occurred even amid the framework of Bolivia's fractured political spectrum. He called it the "best of both worlds; everyone got to know us and this helped a lot."

Barely a year after **BHP** came to Bolivia, the firm won its first contract, for the gas pipeline to northern Chile, where **BHP** is part owner of the huge Escondida copper mine. He says competitiveness was the main reason **BHP** won the pipeline bidding over **Mobil, Amoco,** and other international firms. "I would say our technical expertise and presentations to the government left no doubt that we were highly qualified to do the job. That, and our strength in northern Chile, I think, were the bottom line."

BHP Petroleum says it will invest $300 million in the pipeline, which is expected to produce $600 million in gas export revenues for Bolivia and an annual rate of return of about 15 percent for **BHP** over 20 years. In addition to the pipeline, **BHP** is engaged in oil explorations at three sites in Bolivia.

Drew said officials and business people in Bolivia are well aware that **BHP** is not solely a petroleum operator, but also has iron ore mining and power generation interests. "Bolivia, obviously, has a mining sector that has been depressed for several years," he said, "and which now needs to receive more investment to help achieve the growth rates projected by the government; therefore, BHP has a lot of opportunities to develop, capitalize and bring new business into the country."

Bolivia Overview

Innovative Ideas Tested
To Reform Economy, Attack Poverty

President Gonzalo Sánchez de Lozada, Bolivia's elected leader since 1993, uses terms such as "silent revolution" and "investment shock" to describe the economic process occurring in Bolivia — an effort to transform the state-centered model of capital accumulation and attain sustainable development through a radical program of capitalization, popular participation, educational and constitutional reform. Doing this, he says, in a country with a history of deep-seated economic nationalism and depressing poverty and ignorance, is a bit like "dragging along a child in a tantrum who doesn't want to go to school."

The cornerstone of Bolivia's economic planning focuses on what Sánchez de Lozada and others on his team call "capitalization" — a term crafted to cover not only the privatization of state companies that is being carried out by many other Latin American countries, but also investment in such firms and in the Bolivian people. The concept was developed partly to get around the deep-rooted distrust of private or foreign ownership of the nation's resources and key industries among some vocal groups in Bolivia, but also to deal with the shortage of investment capital for natural resources and industries, and the needs of the under-educated, poorly fed and housed majority of Bolivians.

It constitutes an innovative effort to move out of underdevelopment without leaving the mostly Indian masses behind, a criticism made of free-market reform programs in many other Latin American nations. Bolivia has vast potential in minerals, hydrocarbons, and agriculture, but lacks just about everything needed to turn that potential into wealth — roads, communications, rural electricity, investment capital, and an educated and trained work force. A 1992 United Nations study found that Bolivia had the worst rural poverty rate in the world.

Unlike privatization programs in other countries, capitalization does not involve outright sale of state-owned assets or payment to the state for a stake in those firms. Foreign investors are supposed to become strategic partners by paying into the coffers of the company in question the equivalent of its market-value in return for half ownership, while at the same time doubling the net worth of the company. Ownership of the remaining 50 percent of each company is to be distributed among all adult Bolivians by means of stock in a newly created pension fund. This is intended to make possible the introduction of a social security and old-age pension system for people who could only dream of it in the past.

The six largest state-owned enterprises are targeted for this treatment, under competitive bidding procedures that began in early 1995. The firms involved are **ENDE,** the electricity generation and transmission company; **YPFB,** the oil and gas company; **ENFE,** the national railways; **ENTEL,** the telecommunications concern; **LAB,** the national airline, and **ENAF,** the smelting company.

ENDE was the first of the six to be sold, with half of it going to three U.S. firms for $139.8 million, well above the $99.1 million set by the government as the minimum price. The buyers of the controlling interest were a unit of **Dominion Resources Inc** of Richmond, Virginia; **Energy Initiative Inc.** of Parsippany, New Jersey, and a unit of the **Baltimore Gas and Electric Co.** Bolivian government officials thought the successful first sale would set a good precedent for future sales under its unorthodox plan.

Even though Bolivia has been averaging 4 percent annual GDP growth, that is not enough to make progress in narrowing the gap with richer nations, so the government hopes that by provoking this kind of "investment shock" it can raise the rate of economic growth to 7 percent and create a half million new or improved jobs.

Intriguing National Leader

Sánchez de Lozada is one of the most intriguing national leaders in Latin America today and would attract much more international attention if Bolivia were richer and more populous. Reared from the age of one in the United States, where his father was alternately the Bolivian ambassador and a political exile, he studied at the University of Chicago, as did many of the Latin Americans now leading the free-market revolutions in their countries. But Sánchez de Lozada majored in philosophy, not business or economics, and his conversation reflects both a worldly intellect and an innovative search for ways to improve the lives of everyone in his backward homeland. He's not a "neo-liberal," he says — the term used around Latin America to describe free-market thinkers. He's just practical.

After finishing his studies at Chicago, Sánchez de Lozada came home and made a fortune in mining before turning to politics as a member of the Nationalist Revolutionary Movement. The party, known as the MNR, led Bolivia's leftist, but non-communist revolution of 1952, but since the mid-1980s has been undoing most of its statist policies and admitting that many of its nationalizations and confiscations were a mistake.

Although elected President only in June 1993, Sánchez de Lozada has put his imprint on the nation's policies for a decade. As Planning Minister in the 1985-89 administration of Victor Paz Estenssoro, the grand old man of the MNR, Sánchez de Lozada drafted the policies that brought order out of the economic chaos inherited from the previous government. Inflation was running at a 24,000-percent annual rate when Paz Estenssoro took office, but in a matter of months it was down to two digits, and has remained low ever since. At the same time, he began laying plans to attract foreign investors, reduce official corruption, and find alternative means of support for farmers growing coca for the international cocaine trade.

At the end of Paz Estenssoro's term, Sánchez de Lozada was

the party's candidate to succeed him and finished first in a field of 10, but without a majority. When the Congress met to pick the next President, the second-place finisher threw his support to the third-place finisher, Jaime Paz Zamora, who ended up as President. Despite his social democratic views, Paz Zamora continued the economic policies of the previous administration. Four years later, Sánchez de Lozada was again his party's standard bearer, this time with an Aymara Indian academician as his vice-presidential candidate, and again finished first. This time, the second-place candidate threw his support to Sánchez de Lozada. On finally becoming President, he put together a broader package of economic reforms intended to increase investment, including the "capitalization" plan.

For 1994, his first full year in office, foreign investment was estimated at $250 million, double the amount for 1993, with two-thirds coming from the United States. The sectors most attractive to foreign investment were hydrocarbons, mining, and agro-industry. Although Bolivia's grinding poverty makes the country of 6.9 million a limited market for imported consumer goods, the government believes small-town and rural markets will expand and see buyers with more cash in their pockets as the result of the capitalization program. The government is also looking for ways to increase the amount of money available for construction of modest homes, perhaps through foreign investment, which would also increase the demand for consumer products.

Bolivia has a low, simple tariff structure, with capital goods coming in with a 5 percent tariff and all other goods facing a 10 percent levy. The customs system is undergoing partial privatization, and consolidated "one-stop window" customs offices for importers have been set up in all major cities. Free trade zones for the temporary storage and repackaging of industrial products are also operating. The increased openness of the Bolivian economy is evidenced by the fact that foreign trade as a percentage of GDP rose from 27 percent in 1983 to 38 percent in 1993.

Bolivia has a relatively simple tax system, which has undergone a number of changes in recent years and is still being examined for possible revisions. A value added tax (VAT) of 13 percent is applicable to all normal economic activity, including sales, rents and leases. A tax of 2 percent is levied on most financial transactions, and there are excise taxes on alcohol, tobacco, and luxury items. Individuals not covered under the VAT system are subject to a 13 percent tax on total income, and property owners pay a sliding scale tax. Businesses pay a 3 percent tax on net capital each year.

Separate rules apply to the mining and petroleum sectors. Mining firms pay what is called an "advance levy on profits" (2.5 percent of net sales), which is a deposit toward the 30 percent tax on net profits. Producers of petroleum products must pay royalties and a national tax equal to 31 percent of gross production. Oil contractors pay a tax amounting to 40 percent of net profits.

The current corporate tax system is unpopular with the business community, which sees it as an indiscriminate and regressive tax on a company's net worth. It does not take into account that most long-term projects carry a four- to five-year negative cash flow. The Sánchez de Lozada administration is considering replacing it with a 25 percent profits tax.

The 1990 Investment Law grants foreign investors rights equal to local investors. There is no restriction on the level of company ownership by foreigners, except in the case of the six state companies in which ownership is to be divided equally between foreign investors and pension funds for Bolivians. There are no restrictions or taxes levied on the movement of capital or the remittance of profits.

To help smooth the administration of justice in business affairs and eliminate corruption, the National Chamber of Commerce has promoted the introduction of a system of arbitration and conciliation under the tutelage of the Inter-American Commission of Commercial Arbitration in Washington, D.C. A center for private commercial arbitration was set up in La Paz to resolve disputes without their having to be heard in court, thus sparing complainants unnecessary expense and aggravation. Some 100 arbiters have been selected and trained, at home and abroad, to work in what is supposed to be a transparent and irreproachable way.

Bolivia has very low labor costs and a trade union movement

weakened by the firings in state companies undertaken in the mid-1980s to slim down the state sector of the economy. The state miners, who were the largest and most combative labor force, have fallen in numbers from 24,000 in the early 1980s to fewer than 2,000 today, largely due to the collapse of tin mining.

The average wage paid to factory workers is about $53 a month, but employers also pay a series of fringe benefits, including bonuses for use in the company store, transportation expenses, and an extra month's salary at Christmas and in August.

But, for employers, the attractiveness of low wages is more than offset by the problems of having a poorly educated and untrained work force. Officially, 21 percent of the adult population is illiterate, but functional illiteracy could be as high as 55 percent. An estimated 70 percent of the illiterate population is rural and 68 percent female.

The government is trying to improve an educational system that is characterized by low staff-student ratios, high rates of course repetition and desertion, and high costs per student, especially for higher education. Language is given as one of the reasons for the high dropout rate. Spanish is Bolivia's official language, but the majority of the population comes from homes where Indian languages, chiefly Aymara and Quechua, are spoken. Many of those Bolivians speak limited, or no Spanish. As the result, instruction in rural elementary schools is expected to shift to Indian languages, a project being pushed by Vice President Victor Hugo Cárdenas, the first Aymara to reach such high office

Bolivia at a Glance

Population: 6.9 million (1993). Labor force: 2.5 million.
Languages: Spanish is the official language, but about half the population speaks one of three main Indian languages: Quechua, Aymara, or Guaraní.

Ethnic mix: 30 percent of the population considers itself mestizo (of mixed European-Indian ancestry), 25 percent Quechua Indian, 17 percent Aymara, 12 percent European, and 16 percent other, including Asian.

Climate and best times to visit: Altitude largely determines climate in Bolivia, a country stretched across the Andes and a series of plateaus, plus tropical lowlands in the east. La Paz, the commercial and governmental capital, sitting at 3,620 meters above sea level (almost 12,000 feet), is crisp and sunny most days. You'll feel warm, sometimes very warm, when you're in the sun, but chilly in the shade or at night because of the virtual absence of humidity. The rainy season runs from January to March, though the rain in La Paz is usually very light, and the coldest months are June to August, but any time of year is suitable for a visit. Santa Cruz, in the eastern tropics is, by contrast, warm and humid year-around. Cochabamba, considered sub-tropical at 2,560 meters above sea level (8,400 feet), is springlike most of the time.

Natural resources, chief agricultural products: Zinc, tin, lead antimony, gold, silver, tungsten, lithium, potassium and other minerals, petroleum and natural gas, cotton, sugar, soya, sorghum, and cattle.

Land area: 1,098,581 square kilometers.

Economic Statistics:

GDP: $6.9 billion (1994)

Per Capita GDP: $1,000

GDP Growth Rate: 4.2 percent (1994)

Main exports: Tin, zinc, lead, antimony, gold, silver, tungsten, hydrocarbons, soya, gold, and wood.

Main imports: Capital goods, vehicles, packaged food items.

Duties on imports: Capital goods 5 percent; most other items 10 percent.

Repatriation of profits: No restrictions.

When You Go to Bolivia

Visas: For most tourists and business visitors a visa is not required.

Airlines: American Airlines and Lloyd Aereo Boliviano from the United States: Lufthansa weekly from Frankfurt; Varig from London via São Paulo; Aerolineas Argentinas from Buenos Aires, Madrid and Paris, Lan Chile from Santiago, AeroPeru from Lima.

What to Expect at the Airport: Customs clearance is usually smooth and quick for those on business or tourist trips. You can bring in portable computers and other business equipment. It is difficult to change money in the international arrival area, so carry a number of small dollar denominations to pay luggage handlers ($1-$2) and for the taxi into town ($6-$10).

THE ALTITUDE

The real shock on landing in La Paz will be the altitude. At 3,970 meters (more than 13,000 feet), the airport is even higher than the city itself. Some people feel the effects immediately, such as a light-headedness or slight dizziness; for others it may take a few hours. But the altitude affects all lowlanders. The standard advice is to take it easy, avoid climbing steps and taking long walks, eat moderately, avoid alcoholic beverages, and sip coca tea (It's the raw material of cocaine, but not the same thing; even U.S. Embassy officials drink it.).

You may notice headaches, insomnia, shortness of breath and heart palpitations. Most visitors avoid a busy schedule on the first day, although, in fact, it'll take longer than that to acclimate yourself. Some people claim to be able to play basketball or jog after a couple of weeks in La Paz; others find they're just beginning to get a full night's sleep by then.

Urban Transportation: Taxis are cheap and widely available on the streets of La Paz, but using them takes some learning. Almost all of them are *colectivos,* which means they pick up other passengers along the route. Some ply a set route, so you have to know the layout of the city to take them. Others will vary their routes according to the needs of the passengers, but you have to speak fairly good Spanish to negotiate these things with the driver. There are also radio taxi services, which can be called from your hotel, and some of the hotels have taxis waiting outside, particularly for longer trips or services by the day or half-day. Such taxis are more expensive, but may be more convenient in a city where you won't want to do a lot of walking.

Hotels

LA PAZ

Radisson Plaza

Avenida Arce. Tel: (591-2) 31-6161. Fax: (591-2) 31-6516.
Recently remodeled and taken over by the Radisson chain, this hotel that first opened in 1977 as a Sheraton has impressive views and large public spaces. It has full business facilities, plus a swimming pool, sauna and massage service, but the voice mail system has been having teething problems. Prices start at $145, including breakfast.

Hotel Plaza

Paseo del Prado 1789. Tel: (591-2) 37-8311. Fax: (591-2) 37-8383.
Location in the center of town on the pleasant Prado makes it the favorite of regular business visitors to La Paz. Full business facilities, excellent roof restaurant, swimming pool, sauna and massage.
Prices start at $145, including breakfast.

Rey Palace

Avenida 20 de Octubre. Tel: (591-2) 39-3016. Fax: (591-2) 36-7759.Excellent family-run hotel favored by businessmen wanting to avoid big hotel treatment. Jacuzzi and mini-bar in all rooms. Reliable message taking.
Executive suites at $95, including breakfast.

COCHABAMBA

Hotel Cochabamba

Plaza de la Recoleta. Tel: (591-42) 8-2551. Fax: (591-42) 8-2558.
Art Deco hotel built in 1930s but fully modernized recently. Has mini-bars, swimming pool, and cable television.
Executive suites at $95, including breakfast.

Hotel Portales

Avenida Pando 1271. Tel: (591-42) 4-8507. Fax: (591-42) 4-2071.

Modern hotel with swimming pool and mini-bar and cable television in all rooms.

Single rooms start at $70.

SANTA CRUZ

Hotel Tajibos

Avenida San Martin 455. Tel: (591-3) 42-1000 through 1004. Fax: (591-3) 42-6994.

Most luxurious hotel in Bolivia. Two large swimming pools, air conditioning, cable television, mini-bars, and good message taking.

Single rooms start at $130, including breakfast.

Contacts

Governmental:

NATIONAL SECRETARIAT FOR INDUSTRY AND COMMERCE

Avenida Camacho 1488, La Paz.

Tel: (591-2) 36-7294. Fax: (591-2) 35-8831.

National Secretary: Carlos Morales

Probably the first stop for foreign business people on arriving in Bolivia.

INVESTMENT PROMOTIONS SECRETARIAT

Foreign Ministry, La Paz.

Tel: (591-2) 37-8877.

Director: Fernando Peredo

Another good starting point for would-be foreign investors.

MINISTRY OF CAPITALIZATION

Edificio Palacio de Comunicaciones, Piso 20, La Paz.

Tel: (591-2) 35-5388 or 35-1859. Fax: (591) 811-2823 (this number correct without city code and with 7 digits).

Assists only companies, banks, and consultants interested in the state firms covered by the capitalization program: oil and gas, telecommunications, electricity, air and rail transport, and smelting. Will go out of business when those state firms have been sold.

BOLINVEST/CARANA

Avenida 16 de Julio 1440, Edificio Hermann, Piso 3, La Paz.

Tel: (591-2) 32-2247. Fax: (591-2) 39-1019.

Program to promote Bolivian exports and investments sponsored by U.S. Agency for International Development.

Executive Director: Donald L. Richardson.

U.S. EMBASSY COMMERCIAL SECTION

Avenida Arce, La Paz.

Tel: (591-2) 43-0251. Fax: (591-2) 43-3900

BRITISH EMBASSY COMMERCIAL SECTION

Avenida Arce 2732, La Paz.

Tel: (591-2) 35-7424. Fax: (591-2) 39-1063.

CANADIAN CONSULATE

Avenida 20 de Octubre 2475, La Paz.

Tel: (591-2) 37-5224. Fax: (591-2) 32-9435.

Business Organizations:

NATIONAL CHAMBER OF COMMERCE

Edificio Cámara Nacional de Comercio

Avenida Mariscal Santa Cruz 1392, La Paz.

Tel: (591-2) 35-0042. Fax: (591-2) 39-1004.

An important resource base, the Chamber serves not only its own members but provides a number of services to visiting foreign business representatives, including the following:

● Members of corresponding organizations worldwide are accorded use of the Chamber premises for office purposes while visiting Bolivia; includes access to telephones, a fax machine, a bi-lingual secretary, and advice on whom to do business with in Bolivia and whom to avoid.

● Foreign sales representatives visiting the country can obtain a list of local importers, organized by product specialty, to help in their search for local distributors.

● The Chamber's library is open for consultation, including a business opportunities bulletin in which goods and services are offered and requested.

● The Chamber's computer system has up-to-date information from the National Statistics Institute and access to the Organization of American States commercial information system, which is used mainly by local importers.

AMERICAN CHAMBER OF COMMERCE (AMCHAM)
Av. Arce 2071, La Paz.
Tel: (591-2) 34-2523. Fax: (591-2) 37-1503.
General Manager: Ana María Galindo.

GERMAN-BOLIVIAN CHAMBER OF COMMERCE
Avenida Mariscal Santa Cruz, Edificio Hansa, Piso 7, La Paz.
Tel: (591-2) 32-7596. Fax: (591-2) 39-1736.

BOLIVIAN PRIVATE BUSINESS CONFEDERATION (CEPB)
Edificio Camara de Comercio, Piso 7, La Paz.
Tel: (591-2) 35-8366. Fax: (591-2) 37-9970.

Useful Publications:

The Membership Directory of the American Chamber of Commerce.

The English-language weekly newspaper *Bolivian Times,* which runs special supplements useful to business people.

Lawyers, who are listed here without recommendation:

Fernando Aguirre
Av. Arce 2071, Piso 1, La Paz.
Tel: (591-2) 32-0237. Fax: (591-2) 39-2055.

Carlos Gerke
Av. Arce, Edificio Illampú, Piso 1, La Paz.
Tel: (591-2) 35-7620. Fax: (591-2) 39-1205.

Eliana Zapata

Av. Mariscal Santa Cruz, Edificio Cámara de Comercio, Piso 13, Of. 1304, La Paz.

Tel: (591-2) 32-8377. Fax: (591-2) 39-1453.

Ramiro Moreno

Av. Mariscal Santa Cruz 1285, Piso 10, La Paz.

Tel: (591-2) 32-9277. Fax: (591-2) 36-5330.

William Scarborough (in Cochabamba)

Tel: (591-2) 042-52448 or (mobile) 014-94133.

Translator:

Eliana del Castillo, La Paz.

Tel: (591-2) 79-4485.

Interpreter:

Niñon Illanes, La Paz.

Tel: (591-2) 79-4325.

Public Relations Consultant:

Susana Sánchez de Lozada G., La Paz.

Tel: (591-2) 32-1168. Fax: (591-2) 43-2087 or 32-3274.

In Case of Illness:

Dr. Ciro Portugal, La Paz. Tel: 34-0978 or 32-0844.

Dr. Mario Tejerina, La Paz. Tel: 35-8871.

Clinica Alemana

Avenida 6 de Agosto 2821, La Paz.

Tel: 32-3023.

Centro Medico Especializado

Avenida 6 de Agosto 2881, La Paz.

Tel: 35-6465.

4

BRAZIL

Staking and Mining a Rich Claim
On the Business Frontier

By Bill Hinchberger

Ask Zeke Wimert what he likes best about doing business in Brazil. He'll tell you it is the frontier-like absence of rules. "What do I dislike most?" counters the man who put the São Paulo-based operations of **Oracle,** the California software firm, on the path to rapid growth. "That there are no rules," he says with a smile.

An unstable land of contradictions? Maybe not the best place to bet the ranch, which is just what Wimert did. He took out a mortgage on his house to cover his end of a partnership he struck with **Oracle** to jump from **Motorola,** where he previously headed the Brazilian subsidiary.

No wonder why Wimert was grinning three years later. He won the wager, paid off the mortgage, and **Oracle** had become one of Brazil's fastest growing enterprises.

It must be tough keeping a straight face when your biggest worry is how to manage expansion. **Oracle**'s gloomy Brazilian operations were registering sales of $2.7 million a year when Wimert persuaded top brass in San Francisco to join him to invest more intensely in Latin America's largest country. After he took over, sales climbed to

$37 million. A 32 person staff multiplied to 160 people, and 250 square meters of office space burgeoned to 8,000 square meters, including a spiffy new building next door to **Arthur Andersen** and down the street from the American Chamber of Commerce.

Oracle sells database software programs. Computer paraphernalia is almost a sure bet in a modernizing economy growing at five percent a year, but Wimert argues that you can sell anything in Brazil with the right approach. "Depending on what you sell, there are between 5 and 90 million people who can buy your product," he says.

He resorts to Brazilian slang to prove his point. "The word *jeito,*" he says. "Any country that has a word for 'Let's made a deal' has to be great for entrepreneurs."

After working with the Brazilian subsidiaries of **National Semiconductor** and **Motorola,** Wimert had developed some definite notions about how to succeed in business Brazilian style. His approach boils down to two fundamentals: keep a no nonsense approach imported from home but reformulate it in a way that fits into Brazil's exuberant interpersonal culture.

Successful foreign executives seem to understand this intuitively. Take Masayoshi Morimoto. He ran **Sony**'s operations in Southern California before taking over in Brazil. "In the U.S., the most important thing is to be fair," he says. "Here, the most important thing is to be friendly."

In his quest for friendliness, Morimoto travels twice a month to meet personally with clients, and in 1994 he took top customers along to Hawaii for **Sony**'s annual worldwide pow-wow. Wimert, for instance, makes sure he's a member of the right country club, to ensure informal contacts along the right lines.

"A lot of business in Brazil is done through friendships," agrees Sérgio Haberfeld, CEO of **Toga,** a Brazilian packaging maker.

Some of Wimert and Morimoto's colleagues lose their balance on the tightrope of doing business in a place where rules and regulations are abundant but selectively applied, and where business is often based on personal relationships. At one extreme, there are those who decline to learn Portuguese and hang out at expatriate-dominated golf courses. At the other extreme, some go native to the extent of even adopting some sloppy business habits. "A lot of people do not maintain the same basic controls that they would in the States. Just because Portuguese is spoken, it doesn't mean that you don't apply basic controls," Wimert notes.

Another mistake is an understandable but fatal tendency to overreact to short-term peaks and valleys. "You have to look at Brazil in the long term," says Wimert. "In any single year, you may make or lose a lot, but over three or four years, you'll make a lot of money."

Wimert, who has since left **Oracle** to run his own consulting firm, plotted a scenario for the software firm's expansion into the end of the 1990s, when he envisions a booming software market. His first year at **Oracle** was devoted to making managerial changes and taking steps to ensure survival. In the second, he focused on publicity and beefing up technological support. During the third year, he worked closely with the sales staff.

One of Wimert's first moves was to replace the president and the finance director. In Brazil's environment of chronic inflation, finance departments can make or break a company: tax planning, investment strategies, cash flow management are all fundamental to protect a firm from the inflationary whirlwind.

With good top executives on board, Wimert used a stint as president of the American Chamber of Commerce to build a high profile in the press. Then he took a page out of Lee Iaccoca's book, starring in his own television commercials. His Gringo accent demanded attention, as did his invitation to potential customers to call during established hours when he would personally answer queries. This touch appealed to Brazilian consumers. But the former Green Beret was bucking conventional wisdom that executives should lie low to keep kidnappers at bay.

On the technical side, the company beefed up communication links with San Francisco headquarters, and began recruiting local talent and putting it through in-house training. Top prospects were sent abroad for instruction. **Oracle** established cooperative agreements with 30 universities for training and recruitment purposes, and offered to work with small firms and individual programmers to develop applications that run on **Oracle** databases. "A company buys the application and also buys **Oracle,**" he explained.

Until the trainees mature, local technicians will be scarce — and expensive. "There is a lack of good people, and the ones out there are commanding salaries that only presidents of multinationals could get two years ago," Wimert noted.

Oracle took "tropicalization" — the adaptation of foreign products to Brazilian conditions — further than most. Rather than superficially translating and adjusting the software, **Oracle**'s Brazilian programmers work inside the software code. Wimert said he wanted to be able to upgrade the product, so **Oracle**'s programmers built along with the international products, and were never more than one stage behind.

After months of breakneck growth, Wimert reckoned it was time to steer the juggernaut in a more precise direction by improving the quality of his salespeople. "I had left sales to the peddlers," he recalled. "We were lucky to have gotten through as well as we did. We sold a lot, but we were losing control of our credit terms." Sales expertise is crucial when some deals require contracts long enough to fill two books, like one with Brazil's federal environmental agency that involved a project in the Amazon with World Bank participation.

Salespeople also got in the habit of routinely offering lots of free training. With 52 products sold in Brazil, **Oracle** has an army of support staff roving the country training people on big ticket software packages that run $150,000 on average. With those kinds of prices, it may seem easy to disregard training expenses, but if there are insufficient controls a company can give away a lot of training.

Such attitudes demonstrate where the no-nonsense business approach takes over from the gregarious nature of Wimert's adopted country. "If I can't make a profit, I don't want to hear about it," he says. "To lose money to gain market share is to sign your own death certificate."

A Factory Site with Shock Capacity

If **Oracle**'s growth wasn't evidence enough of the potential in Brazil's computer market, the decision by **Compaq,** the dynamic United States manufacturer of personal computers, to build a factory in Brazil sent shock waves through the sector. Unlike other firms making electronic gadgetry, **Compaq** declined to locate in the Manaus Free Trade Zone, with its tax and tariff breaks. Instead, **Compaq** opted for proximity to the market, building its plant in São Paulo state.

Compaq's outlook for Brazil is best summed up not in words but in numbers. The $15 million factory will have a capacity of 500,000 computers — more than the 360,000 computers sold in 1993. The Brazilian factory will export to other South American countries, and maybe even Africa. The company determined that Brazil is the perfect launching pad from which to attack the Latin American market, estimated to be worth more than $500 million in 1994, double the figure for 1993. The firm estimated that the Brazilian market for personal computers in 1994 at 600,000 units — half the figure for Canada.

"We reached the conclusion that we had to have a factory near a market this big," explains Jorge Schreurs, president of the Brazilian subsidiary. "In a normal situation, Brazil should represent 50 percent of South America's PC market."

The Brazilian computer market has been far from normal, thanks to notorious protectionist legislation that virtually banned legal imports for 16 years until 1991. A last gasp of import substitution strategy, the restrictive law was aimed at encouraging local production. Instead, it begot a thriving contraband trade and forced local companies to remain in the computer Dark Ages. Abroad, spry young firms like **Apple** and **Compaq,** with flexible and cheap hardware, were challenging the clunky old main frames. Before that revolution, main frame rentals accounted for about 60 percent of the market in both the United States and Brazil. As late as 1992, that number was down to just 4 percent in the United States, but it was still 55 percent in Brazil. **IBM** and **Unisys,** grandfathered around the market restrictions because of their long tenures in the country, continued to rake in comfortable profits from main frame business. Today, Mexico has 4,500 PC's per one million inhabitants; the number for Brazil is just 2,900.

The local plant will allow **Compaq** to take advantage of the tax incentives for computer manufacturing. The web of incentives that replaced the protectionist barriers includes the elimination of a 15 percent industrial tax on computer imports, and partial exemptions on sales and corporate income taxes. Thanks to local manufacturing, **Compaq** will fork over just 15 percent duties on imported components, compared to the 35 percent surcharge on PC imports.

Schreurs estimates an 80-90 percent cost advantage thanks to the local plant. But Brazilians will still pay more than consumers abroad. "Operational costs are higher," explains the executive. "Even with the tax exemptions, the tax load is still high. We're not going to have the same street price as in the U.S."

Compaq established sales operations in January 1993, and decided to build the plant in December of that year. The strategy is to produce personal computers near the biggest market and open underdeveloped distribution channels.

For its plant, **Compaq** settled on a site near Campinas, a growing hub with one of the country's finest universities about 100 kilometers west of São Paulo city. The plant's 400 employees will be Brazilian. Domestic suppliers are scarce, but the company is encouraging Silicon Valley chip manufacturers to consider tagging along in South America. São Paulo state's superior infrastructure — especially its road network, airports and port — tipped the scales on location, says Schreurs.

Proximity to the market was another determining factor. "We didn't want to be outside a 200-kilometer radius of São Paulo city," he explains.

To help tap that market, **Compaq** is encouraging local retailers, ranging from major department stores to specialized outfits,to boost floor space dedicated to computer products. The market is still too small for the retail warehouses common in the United States, but the scarcity of retail outlets is highlighted by the fact that 500,000 visitors crowd themselves into a São Paulo convention center each year for a computer fair called Fenasoft. There they play with the newest mouses, modems and games. Better distribution is considered the best weapon against the accomplished contraband trade, says Schreurs. "Right now, if you want to look at a computer on a Saturday, there's nowhere to go — except to the local contraband dealer who is knocking on your door," he explains.

Shaking Up a Back Alley Business

To make a few copies or print up a personnel manual in Brazil, you generally must traipse down to some back alley printshop.The antiquated equipment conjures up images of Johann Gutenberg behind the counter.

Alphagraphics would rather that Bill Gates came to mind. That means, like other transplanted franchise operations, the modern printshop enterprise must change consumer habits rooted in a bygone era. If **McDonald's** could teach middle class Brazilians to bus their own trays, **Alphagraphics** hopes it can get them accustomed to color copies and self-service machines. **Alphagraphics** wants its shiny high-tech stores to replace the grimy local printer.

In rich northern countries, franchise operations can be taken for granted. Their emphasis on quick service and standard quality fit uniquely with the increasingly rapid-paced lives of many individuals. In megacities such as São Paulo and Rio de Janeiro, the urban verve is no less marked. But many of the convenience services are conspicuous in their absence.

Remarkably, few foreign-based franchise operations detect these opportunities themselves. Instead, well-traveled Brazilians are often the instigators of accords that present them a lucrative market they'd somehow overlooked.

That's how **Alphagraphics** found Brazil in 1991. Or better, was found. A pair of Brazilian entrepreneurs approached company executives in Tucson. They also found a high powered local investor, and armed with the international master license (IML), they began duplicating printshops. Eventually the two were bought out by their cash-rich local partner, and the company moved in professionals to run the show.

Though still nascent, **Alphagraphics**' incursion into Brazil appears successful enough to arouse headquarters' interest elsewhere in South America. The company recently sold an IML to a Chilean company to open shop there and in Argentina, Paraguay and Uruguay.

The first Brazilian store opened in May 1992. In two short years, **Alphagraphics**' Brazilian operation had grown to include a wholly owned store and six franchise shops in São Paulo, Brazil's financial and industrial center, and two franchises in Curitiba, a mid-sized town in southern Brazil.

Curitiba is the consummate test city: medium-sized with a large middle class and literate, but conservative, consumers. "Instead of the Third World, Curitiba is the Second World," says Paulo Cesar de Azevedo Antunes, franchise sales director. The test proved fortuitous for **Alphagraphics** — though for a few others it has backfired. (A world-famous soup company once took it on the chin when its broth appealed to the taste buds of Curitibans, but not to their brethren in other regions, Antunes recalls.)

After Curitiba, São Paulo and its main business districts became obvious initial targets. The company established its own pilot store near bustling Paulista Avenue, partly to serve as a showroom, and it built a training center near its own head offices. The franchise network was established with methodical care.

Employee training became a key to instilling the **Alphagraphics** style in Brazil. In the United States, **Alphagraphics** provides three weeks' training for new franchise owners, who in turn have little trouble finding college students or high school graduates to operate machines and interact reasonably with customers. New Brazilian franchise owners also attend the Tucson course, but when they return and start hiring, the local headquarters offers up to five weeks of instruction for the often undereducated new store staff — introducing new hires to **Xerox** color copiers and other paraphernalia they've likely never seen before, let alone operated. "They are unfamiliar with the equipment," says Jack Burgess, executive director of the Brazilian operations. "But we also had to teach them how to serve the customer, to smile and ask what people need. We had to work on that a lot."

Burgess is an American expatriate, with extensive experience in Brazilian business and married to a Brazilian. He was enlisted to provide a cultural link. "I can turn to the guys in the States and say 'That just won't work here,' and vice versa," he says.

Prudent orientation is crucial for a company striving to adapt a foreign concept and create a new consumer culture. The idea of a quick printshop was so foreign to Brazilians that customers have been known to walk into a store to ask the prices of the fax machines, mistaking the equipment laden outlet for a retail electronics store.

Even those walk-in customers who did understand the concept initially balked at the self-service machines. In a land of low wages, Brazilian consumers are used to armies of attendants: few gas stations maintain self service pumps. But soon a hearty few **Alphagraphics** customers tired of waiting in line for service and gravitated to the empty copiers in the front of the office.

Meanwhile, 80 percent of volume comes from bulk contracts with businesses. Six salespeople scour the city to churn up clients for the newfangled service. "Graphics in Brazil have always been a neighborhood operation," says Burgess. "We had to keep from being seen as a printshop for snobs."

Like most franchise operations, **Alphagraphics** provides infrastructure and back-up support for store owners. In Brazil this extends to assistance with equipment imports, handling negotiations with customs brokers (called *despachantes*) and trying to ameliorate effects of import delays due to things like Chicago snowstorms.

Once approved, prospective owners must shell out about $350,000 for the right to hang out an **Alphagraphics** shingle. The steep entry fee naturally weeds out candidates, most of whom fall into one of two categories, says Burgess: "They're either executives who took early retirement, or younger people with rich parents who want their kid to have his or her own business." Downsizing in Brazilian industry has expanded the pool of prospective franchise operators.

Finding a Local Partner

If **Alphagraphics** had to be approached by Brazilian entrepreneurs, a slew of foreign — often medium-sized — businesses are looking for local distributors or partners to help them extend a few tentative tentacles into the global marketplace.

The Chicago-based **Amco Corp.** makes heavy duty shelves for restaurants and institutional kitchens. President Bob Jaffee looked at the trends, and found his company behind a benchmark of 10-20 percent for international sales. A U.S. business associate told Jaffee about **Emplarel,** a São Paulo-based industrial operation that supplies its own countertops and other equipment to clients in Brazil, such as **McDonald's. Emplarel's** father-and-son operation was earning a reputation distributing products to the growing fast food and restaurant market. "It was serendipity," recalls Jaffee.

Marcos Farah, the junior partner in the family team, explains that **Emplarel** jumped the gun on the import business, distributing hot dog grills for A.J. Antunes in the late 1980s, before tariff reductions began to increase the flow of foreign goods into Brazil. By the time Jaffee expressed interest, **Emplarel** already had a track record. **Amco** was willing to give it a shot.

Today, **Emplarel** represents a handful of foreign companies, primarily in the restaurant and fast food equipment supply sector. Locally sold products often include an **Emplarel** label to facilitate customer contacts for repairs or new purchases. A good portion of their distribution arrangements mean merely walking foreigners through the Byzantine customs bureaucracy.

First, though, Farah and his father Ferdinando like to put potential clients straight on Brazil. "Unfortunately, Americans are lax," says Ferdinando Farah. "They don't come here to see what's really happening here. They see something on the news and are inoculated against the country forever. They think there's no industrial park here."

Ferdinando also criticizes some foreign business people for lumping Latin America in a single basket: "They sometimes will only work through a dealer. And the guy has never set foot in Brazil. He's based in Costa Rica, for goodness sake!"

Although Jaffee credited serendipity, selection of a local partner — for either distribution or direct investment — can be the most important decision a newcomer will make. Some executives, like **Oracle**'s Wimert, argue that it is imperative to have someone on the ground. "You can be from Milwaukee and sell here, but you've got to come and do it," he says. "If you use a local distributor, they can rip you off — like anywhere else."

Bernardo Giacometti, president of **Folio Mkt,** represents the multinationals **Parker** and **Pelikan** in Brazil. For obvious reasons he differs with Wimert, but still warns caution. "Sometimes Americans and Europeans come with 40 pages of contracts, but it is more important to find somebody who is trustworthy." Partners can be found in all the obvious places, and some not so obvious: American, German and other chambers of commerce, trade fairs, international consulting firms, and university alumni associations.

If the goal is direct investment, Giacometti counsels a gradual approach. "Search for a joint venture with an option to buy," he suggests. "A joint venture will allow you access to information, even if you are the minority partner. If you put in money, the money is yours, and if the going gets good, you can buy out your partners."

Brazil Overview

Land of Business Bliss
And Economic Nightmares

Exporters and investors from the United States and elsewhere cannot help dreaming about Brazil. Some have nightmares of 1993's 2,400 percent inflation and social disruption rooted in severe poverty. Others see expanding markets, good industrial and logistical infrastructure, statistics like record trade figures (for exports, imports, *and* the trade balance), and growth rates of 4.5 percent in 1993 and 5.7 percent in 1994.

Regardless of the spirits in their dreams, foreign business people cannot ignore that Brazil has the world's 10th largest economy, the sixth largest population, and the fifth largest geographical area. Foreign governments are driving home the notion: companies that aren't on board yet should buy their tickets now. Former British Chief Secretary of the Treasury Michael Portillo was keen to note that two-way trade between the United Kingdom and Brazil has never been higher, 1.3 billion pounds sterling. "Despite persistently high inflation, the Brazilian private sector is clearly buoyant," he said. Across the Atlantic, U.S. Commerce Secretary Ron Brown included Brazil among the world's 10 Big Emerging Markets — countries where the Clinton Administration set out to concentrate investment and export efforts. During a visit to Brazil, globetrotting Massachusetts Governor William Weld said that only China and Israel matched the dynamism he sensed in São Paulo. Could it be that there will be no further delays of the takeoff of the perennial nation of the future?

Sociologist-cum-politician Fernando Henrique Cardoso was inaugurated president on Jan. 1, 1995. In 1994, as Finance Minister, Cardoso kicked off a policy package called the Real Plan. Wielding an overvalued currency backed by more than $40 billion in hard currency reserves, the Real slashed inflation from nearly 50 percent a month in June 1994 to less than one percent a month in September 1994. By mid-1995, the plan was still holding together. The annual inflation rate for 1995 was projected at 33.5 percent by **Unibanco,** a leading Brazilian bank. That sounds high by international standards, but is low for a country that experienced inflation of 909.7 percent in 1994.

Underlying the Real Plan was an assumption that economic reforms are necessary to transform the monetary slight-of-hand into a full-fledged stabilization program. It can be no small task to quell history's most stubborn chronic inflation: Brazil entered the record books by sustaining annual rates upwards of 50 percent for an unprecedented 15 consecutive years.

"The election of Fernando Henrique is a necessary but not a sufficient condition to lasting stability," noted Roberto Teixeira da

Costa, director-president of **Brasilpar Financial Services.** "The plan," chimed in Gerson Gabrielli, a Salvador-based retailer and president of the National Confederation of Retail Store Owners, "cannot be sustained without structural reforms, principally privatization."

Soon after his election, Cardoso began offering bills to work on revamping the Byzantine tax apparatus, the bankrupt social security system, and the bloated state bureaucracy. Many changes require amendments to the 1988 constitution. Meanwhile, he has to engage in a rear-guard action against price pressures.

Heeding the call to invest or export are firms as diverse as **Raytheon, Blockbuster, Wal-Mart,** sundry makers of distilled whiskey, and virtually all of the world's leading investment banks and computer companies. "Brazil is back on the international radar," declared John Mein, executive director of the American Chamber of Commerce in São Paulo, after the election of Cardoso. Several factors are working in Brazil's favor, said Mein: a tripartite labor-industry-government accord in the automobile sector that spurred record car production; an export boom; good agricultural harvests in 1992 and 1993; and the long-awaited foreign debt accord with creditor banks.

Like a carnival mask, appearances can be misleading. Brazil's reputation as a laggard in regional economic reform (going slow on pension reform, for instance) camouflages fundamental shifts in the economy and business mindset. Brazil has been strengthening democratic institutions, battling corruption, eliminating trade barriers, privatizing industries, and deregulating. Notorious protectionist laws, such as the computer reserve, have been eliminated; import tariffs were slashed from an average of about 80 percent in 1985 to a now competitive 14 percent average; and privatization has liquidated the state's holdings in steel and most of the petrochemical industry. Nobody dares suggest turning back. Federal Deputy Delfim Netto, a former finance minister, commented after one of the last debates of the 1994 campaign that "with small adjustments, ideological differences are disappearing."

Nationalist development policies dating to strongman Getúlio Vargas in the 1930s, reinforced by civilians in the 1950s

and the 1964-85 military regime, awarded Brazilian companies protected markets. The needs of national capital and lucky multinationals outshone those of consumers. For a time, firms expanded
pell mell (more than half of Latin America's 500 largest firms are
based in Brazil). Starting in the late 1980s, growing competition
began to take root amid economic downturn. When President Fernando Collor de Mello engineered an even more severe recession
after his inauguration in 1990, Brazil endured a shrinking economy
for three years.

To top it off, heretofore coddled industry was sent reeling as
Collor bulldozed non-tariff trade barriers and set a gradual schedule of
import levy reductions. Business leaders moaned, but they now admit
that the tariff reductions were indispensable. "That script was the most
important point of the Collor presidency," says Roberto Faldini, a
director of **Metal Leve,** a leading auto parts manufacturer.

To their credit, executives weaned on a protectionist state gradually learned to disregard the government and blaze independent trails.
One symbolic day came in May 1992 when pulp producer **Aracruz**
forged ahead with an international equity issue in New York in the face
of the storm of revelations by then President Collor's brother that
sparked an impeachment process.

If the government has tarried behind Latin American neighbors
on some economic reforms, no matter. Brazilian business embarked on
its own readjustment drive, downsizing and improving productivity by
18 percent in 1993 alone. Does pervasive poverty dampen domestic
demand? Brazilian companies compensated by exporting a record
$43.5 billion in 1994. Industry held its own against a record $33.2 billion in imports, and the economy grew by 5.7 percent.

"With Itamar (Franco) and Collor, business people just turned
their backs on the government," noted consultant Márcio Orlandi of the
São Paulo firm **Fundamental Research.**

Multinational executives like to complain about high taxes,
inflation, government meddling, political instability: if some of them
get going, their grievance lists can seem endless. But as one of their

peers admitted: "If you get them alone and off the record, they'll tell you about all the money they're making."

Foreigners love to tell a tale about Brazil: that two plus two doesn't equal four (sometimes three, sometimes five, the story goes). But for some reason, a lot of foreign companies are willing to put up with this odd accounting. More than 8,500 firms operating in Brazil can boast at least some foreign capital, calculates economist Octavio de Barros. An estimated 2,000 U.S. companies operate in Brazil, says the São Paulo state government, which proudly boasts that 1,300 are based in its state. Of the world's leading 500 companies with international operations, 380 have Brazilian subsidiaries. More than a thousand German companies operate in Brazil, making it first among developing countries as a recipient of German investment. An estimated 42 percent of Brazil's exports are made by foreign companies.

Many firms, including multinationals, are doing quite well. The Japanese electronics maker **Sony** was estimating Brazilian sales of $200 million in 1994, up from $150 million for the previous 12 months. Brazil is one of **Sony**'s three fastest growing markets: the others being the United States and China. "We make profits here, and Tokyo allows us to reinvest them here," says Masayoshi Morimoto, director-president of **Sony**'s Brazilian subsidiary.

Gross direct foreign investment is on the upswing after a few rocky years early in the decade, says economist Barros. In 1990, foreigners put $1.26 billion into Brazil, followed by annual figures of $1.17 billion (1991), $1.67 billion (1992), $1.31 billion (1993), and an estimated $2.9 billion in 1994. Foreign investors in Brazilian capital markets increased their outlays from $154 million in 1990 to $5.4 *billion* in 1993.

That's a pretty good base for a country still lacking macroeconomic stability and prosperity for the poor majority among the 150 million population.

Some business leaders are optimistic that these problems are starting to be addressed. In little over a decade, successive governments adopted no fewer than 10 schemes aimed at whipping inflation into line. Many Brazilians are jaded, but business leaders hope that the most recent Real Plan, implemented in mid-1994, can hold if the initial currency changeover is followed up by structural reforms like further privatization, tax reform, social security reform, and reduction of state spending.

The initial currency stabilization effort was based on a considerably overvalued Real in relation to the dollar. For years, Brazilian governments directly controlled the official commercial dollar rate to ensure a competitive position for exporters. A formally illegal but tolerated black market generally reflected lack of confidence in the local currency, pushing the dollar rate extraordinarily high. When direct exchange controls were eliminated, the Central Bank regulated the exchange rates via open market operations. In late 1992, **Barings Securities** reported that the currency was fairly valued but warned that "There is risk of strong export growth being checked if the (currency) becomes overvalued." Although the exchange rate was experiencing some fluctuation, by mid-1995 one U.S. dollar was worth roughly 90 cents on the Real.

Even if the Real Plan were to fail, most business leaders believed in late 1994 that Brazilian society was ready to make the sacrifices necessary to exorcise the inflationary devil. "One thing is clear," stressed Ângelo Calmon de Sá, president of **Banco Economico.** "Stability is going to come."

A boom could be on the horizon, predicted Harry Simonsen Jr., president of the São Paulo consultancy **Simonsen Associados.** He based his prognostication on a study by his firm that showed an increase in investments announced publicly by companies — up by about 30 percent from 1991 to 1993. The figures were not exhaustive, he acknowledged, but he saw them as good indicators. "GDP was down in 1992, but based on this same study, we were able to predict growth in 1993," he notes.

Independent of the destiny of the Real Plan, **Lloyds Bank** was working with a single scenario after President Cardoso took office at the beginning of 1995. Luiz Roberto Martins, director vice-president, said **Lloyds** anticipated a debate about the role of the state, with constitutional reform, expanding privatization, and tax reform.

Consultant Márcio Orlandi, head of **Fundamental Research**, believes that healthy growth in 1993 and 1994 set the stage for explosion. "In 1995, companies will take investment projects out of desk drawers, and we'll also see lots of mergers and acquisitions," he predicted. "In 1996, there will be massive investment. 1996 could be the best year in history."

Growth itself could create infrastructure bottlenecks if moves are not made quickly to improve port facilities, telecommunications, energy, transportation and irrigation services, said the consultant.

Concerns about infrastructure in even well-developed outlying areas helped convince at least one firm to locate a new plant in an industrial suburb of São Paulo city, even though some analysts believe the region to be nearly saturated. "If we start to grow by 6-7 percent, which we need to address poverty, everything could collapse," warned Sérgio Haberfeld, CEO of the Brazilian packaging firm **Toga**. "I'll try to at least put my plant where the disaster will be smaller."

Lower Barriers and Welcome Mats

Despite recurring bouts of xenophobia, partly reflected by restrictive clauses in the 1988 constitution, Brazilians and their economy are generally receptive to foreigners and their businesses. "Brazilians need foreign partners and they need capital," says Bernardo Giacometti, whose **Folio Mtk** represents the multinationals **Parker** and **Pelikan** in Brazil.

Icatu, founded in 1989 as an asset management company, broke into investment banking as the government's lead adviser in the 1992 sell-off of steel company **Acesita. Icatu** director José Luiz Osorio is hardly fazed that foreign institutions like **Morgan Stanley, Merrill Lynch** and **Bear Stearns** are hiring big name Brazilians and opening local representations. "We believe that there will be a restructuring of the sector," said Osorio. "Inflation will fall, and all the big houses are here. We are going to have to associate — always. We know we'll have something to offer."

"Brazilians like Americans," says consultant Orlandi. "There's no 'Yankee Go Home!' sentiment here. It is easy to form partnerships with Brazilians."

Democratization has begun to allow this sentiment to manifest itself in the legal code, said attorney Durval de Noronha Goyos Jr. Under military rule, some foreign companies profited handsomely thanks to safeguarded markets or participation in state-led initiatives, but opportunities for foreigners were limited. Sometimes the military's preoccupation with national security and geopolitics worked against foreign firms. Sometimes secret decrees would squelch them, said Noronha. With post-1985 redemocratization, "Everything that had to be done in the ex-Communist countries had to be done here, too," the attorney noted. Noronha predicted that Brazil's adherence to the most recent General Agreement on Tariffs and Trade (GATT) will force fundamental changes in the country's treatment of foreigners. These shifts will come on top of reforms like rule changes for profit remittances and royalty payments to headquarters implemented over the last few years.

Despite their general receptivity to foreigners, Brazilians — not unlike people anywhere else — don't appreciate folks coming down and telling them how to do things. "You've got to meet with them and try to speak Portuguese, even if you don't speak that well," advised Zeke Wimert, former president of **Oracle**'s Brazilian operations. "Brazilians don't want to hear that we do everything better — even if they agree."

Foreigners may need to deal with companies whose owners are diehard nationalists. These might be family-owned firms awaiting generational turnover, where older patriarchs are more likely to resist foreign initiatives. Be modest and friendly, suggests Haberfeld, whose packaging firm **Toga** is experienced in both international trade and joint ventures involving foreigners. "Why not tell them that they're great?" he asks.

If general sentiment favors foreign investment, special interests have successfully lobbied for legislation to protect specific sectors. Some restrictions are engraved in the 1988 constitution. That document limits foreign investment in petroleum, telecommunications, mining, power generation, nuclear activities, fishing, internal transport, health care services, financial institutions, and print and electronic media. State monopolies are guaranteed in petroleum and telecommunications. In other sectors, foreign investment is limited to less than half of voting capital. Another clause gives national firms priority in government bidding. Though not a constitutional issue, the lack of adequate industrial property protection is a major impediment for many foreigners.

Labor Union Evolution

The confrontational trade unionism that bucked both employers and the military government starting in the late 1970s has gradually evolved into a more pragmatic approach — less strident if no less militant. More skilled sectors, such as bank workers, tend to be organized.

Vicente Paulo "Vicentinho" da Silva, head of the Unified Workers Central (CUT), the country's most dynamic union federation, represents a new, pragmatic strain in labor leadership, one who puts a high priority on industrial competitiveness. In his previous post as president of the metalworkers union in the industrial suburbs of São Paulo city, Vicentinho was instrumental in negotiating the 1992 and 1993 agreements in the automobile sector that helped spark record production of 1.55 million units in 1994. Vicentinho agreed to check wage increases at 6.3 percent a year, despite the low $2.79 an hour paid to shop floor workers. In exchange, he got a no-layoff promise. As part of the deal, the government lowered taxes and manufacturers agreed to trim profit margins.

Labor belligerency in Brazil is diminishing overall, partly due to economic uncertainty and layoffs, particularly in the São Paulo metropolitan region. In 1989, 183 strikes generated a loss of 107,982,218 work hours in Brazil in all sectors; in 1992, there were just 52 strikes and 11,727,196 lost work hours, according to the Inter-Union Department of Socio-Economic Statistics (DIEESE), a labor funded think tank. With 21 percent of the work force unemployed or underemployed, the "specter of potential job losses" helps to avert strikes, says consultant Orlandi.

"Recently, strike problems have been more concentrated in the public sector than in the private sector," noted Humberg.

—*It'll be kind of expensive to set up your company in Brazil: there's my brother-in-law in the Ministry, Silva in Customs, João in the notary office.*

Labor Quality

Brazil faces a sticky incongruity: an oversupply of unskilled labor and a shortage of skilled personnel. In fact, the labor quality balance somewhat resembles that of income distribution, where the poorest 10 percent of Brazilians receive just 0.8 percent of income and the richest 10 percent get 48.7 percent. More tellingly, only 39 percent of young people ages 12-17 are enrolled in school. Regional differences are also profound: the southeast (including São Paulo and Rio de Janerio) has 14.7 percent illiteracy; in the northeast (including Salvador and Recife), the figure jumps to 42.6 percent.

Direct wage costs are among the lowest in Latin America. The minimum wage of $111 a month is about a third less than that in poorer neighbor Paraguay. "Nobody wants cheap labor that produces cheaply and inefficiently. The type of work force Brazil has to offer isn't interesting anymore," says Orlandi.

Taxes, social security contributions and other government surcharges virtually double the average company's wage bill, says a study by the São Paulo Industrial Federation (FIESP). Haberfeld, whose company also operates in the United States, says the firm's American employees earn considerably more than their Brazilian counterparts, but that the extra government levies make the wage costs almost comparable.

Companies spend precious time and money on education and training, sometimes leaving foreign partners flabbergasted. "That's not your core business," Sérgio Haberfeld recalls hearing when he showed visitors the in-plant high school classrooms. Haberfeld estimates that his firm spends an average of $120 a month per employee in extras, from basic education to hospital bills. One example of extra costs: "We pay taxes that are supposed to help provide public transportation, but we also have 10 buses to get workers to the job site."

Companies that can afford the extra outlays find they pay off. Auto parts company **FNV** was able to meet ISO 9000 European production standards — thus expanding its potential market — only after providing some employees with basic remedial education.

Thanks partly to such measures, select Brazilian-based multinationals are achieving productivity results impressive enough to ring bells back home. Morimoto, president of **Sony**'s Brazilian subsidiary, says that after two or three weeks of training, assembly line personnel in Manaus can perform at least as well as those he oversaw in San Diego. "Of the 20 television factories worldwide, we consistently rank in the top five on quality," Morimoto boasts. A handful of assembly workers are now planning to attend university, he said with pride.

"Our people from all over the world have been coming here to see what **General Motors do Brasil** is doing in 'lean' processes," noted **GM** CEO Jack Smith during a visit to São Paulo. Production managers at **GM**'s automobile operations are loathe to divulge their manufacturing secrets. But the lean trend is evident at its **Delco** subsidiary's battery plant in Piracicaba, São Paulo state. The **Delco Remy** operation, a Brazilian adaptation of Japanese techniques, manages the complicated task of changing a heavy mold in 15 minutes, one-fourth the world average.

"Other Latins can be undisciplined, individualist, and think they know it all," says Alberto R. von Ellenrieder, director of the accounting and consultant firm **Bouchinhas & Campos.** "But Brazilians have two virtues: they are disciplined and they like to work on the shop floor. They embrace total quality and teamwork with enthusiasm."

As the **Oracle** experience demonstrates, top technical people are in short supply and come tagged with puffy salary requirements. In the post-downsizing era, however, managers are widely available. Financial officers, thanks to years of chronic inflation, are probably among the world's most sophisticated. Yet inflation and protectionism have created some bad habits. Many managers tend to opt for price increases rather than search for ways to cut costs or improve productivity, says a report by the London-based Economist Intelligence Unit.

The flip side of the labor quality issue is structural unemployment — and simmering, interrelated social problems. Ney Araujo, president of the agribusiness firm **Agroceres,** recalls a conversation he had with a labor leader: "What we need are 13 million jobs at $100 a month each, I told him."

Brazil's growth, despite inflation, has produced a scant number of these slots. "Growth has been good for increasing the income of some people, but not for adding jobs," says José de Freitas Mascarenhas of the Bahia State Industrial Federation (FIEB). "Efficiency for its own sake makes little sense if it doesn't generate jobs."

Salvador-based economist Armando Avena notes that industry accounts for 35 percent of Bahia state's output, but employs just 7 percent of the economically active population. Agriculture employs 40 percent. "Industry is the dynamic sector, but it doesn't employ," he says. "And when agriculture modernizes, it reduces employment."

Mascarenhas suggests that new positions "have to come from small businesses, which are good at creating employment." But small business loans are complicated by the fact that most new small businesses are in the informal sector, making it impossible for banks to analyze them and to make loans. "Small and medium businesses are good at generating jobs," agrees economist Carlos Eduardo de Carvalho, "But a good part of these companies are on the border of legality. How do you make a loan to them?"

Education is an obvious response, but the effects of that are at least a generation away. "The problem of structural unemployment is a worldwide one," says Mario Ernesto Humberg, director of the São Paulo consultancy **CLA**. "You no longer resolve employment with growth. I think Brazil has an additional problem, education. It is difficult to incorporate uneducated people. But this problem will only be resolved in 20 years — if we take measures now (to improve educational levels)."

In the meantime Humberg believes that unskilled labor can only be absorbed through growth in public services like trash collection and (unless it comes via privatization) the installation of telephone lines.

Imports, Investments and Infrastructure

Some sectors are more primed than others to profit from a new growth cycle. The attractions of the computer sector are evident. A

Barings Securities report offered other likely beneficiaries: infrastructure (telecommunications, electricity and roads), agribusiness, steel, aluminum, metalworking industries, paper and pulp, consumer goods, "and especially the retail trade." The U.S. Commerce Department expects Brazilian needs to partly match those of nine other countries it classifies as Big Emerging Markets (from China and India to Argentina and Mexico): telecommunications, environmental technology, health care, transportation and power generation. "We picked these sectors on the basis of what the Big Emerging Markets are going to need to grow, and what we think we can supply," says Jeffrey Garten, undersecretary of Commerce for International Trade. Automotive parts, tractors and other farm equipment, fast food, and foodstuffs are other sectors cited by business experts.

The tourism industry is experiencing a boom in the sun-drenched, folklore-rich northeast. Road building, good old boosterism, and natural competitive advantages helped Bahia state attract $220 million in private hotel investment in just two years. In mid-1994, construction firm **Odebrecht** announced a mega-project envisioning total investment of $2 billion over 15 years to build a tourism complex in Bahia's capital, Salvador.

Direct investment, often via mergers and acquisitions, could outdistance growing interest in the São Paulo Stock Market. "Many banks," says **Arthur Andersen** partner Francisco Papellás Filho, "are organizing themselves to serve as a conduit for foreign direct investment in companies — as happened in Spain. Today you can buy risk investment for a low price. Some (banks) will want to do due diligence for foreigners, others will want to buy in directly."

Brazil's **Banco Itamarati** signed an operating agreement with the U.S. bank **JP Morgan** to explore opportunities in the electric energy sector — including privatization, construction and renovating existing plants, said Antonio Hermann Dias Menezes de Azevedo, executive vice president. **Itamarati** signed another accord with the U.S. investment firm **Donaldson, Lufkin and Jenrette** to keep an eye out for opportunities in the telecommunications realm.

Infrastructure projects are expected to offer enormous potential. Strapped public budgets mean that outlays have been cut for partially completed hydroelectric and nuclear plants. Road maintenance has been lax, and ports are in dire need of modernization.

To get around tight public budgets, the São Paulo state government is helping spearhead an effort to leverage public spending into greater private sector infrastructure investments. The key project is a $20 billion mega-project in the Tiête-Paraná river basin of South America's Southern Cone. Opportunities appear likely in such areas as railway expansion, port development, road concessions and telecommunications. Project oversight is done by a private-public Tiête-Paraná Development Agency (ATDP).

Several projects in a more traditional vein are underway or on the drawing board: a natural gas pipeline from Bolivia into Brazil's south-central industrial heartland attracted several bids; the Inter-American Development Bank (IDB) is reportedly ready to help pay for the duplication of the main roadway linking southern Brazil with Argentina and Uruguay; and the IDB awarded its largest loan in history ($1.2 billion) to the São Paulo state government to help finance the clean up of the polluted Tiête River; the bays of Baía de Todos os Santos (Salvador) and Baía de Guanabara (Rio de Janeiro) are slated for extensive environmental clean-up initiatives.

Franchising in Brazil is a $32 billion a year business, growing by an average of 25 percent annually. A report by the London-based Economist Intelligence Unit ranks Brazil third, behind only the United States and Japan, in such activity. Legal changes in 1992 facilitated the licensing arrangements and royalty payments of franchises. The boom is led by the fast food sector.

Exporting into Brazil has never been more enticing. Economic growth, the likelihood of a strong Real (as part of the anti-inflation drive), and lower tariffs will create opportunities almost across the board. In 1995, as part of the Southern Cone Common Market (Mercosul) accord, maximum tariffs for all but one-tenth of imports will fall from 35 percent to 20 percent. That will further reduce average duties, already down to 14 percent in 1994, compared to 80 percent in 1985.

Opportunity should not overshadow caution in some sectors —
particularly where the informal economy boasts clear competitive
advantages thanks to systematic tax evasion. "The first rule is: if your
business is in a sector where the informal economy is strong, forget it.
Your tax burden will keep you from competing," warns businessman
and former government minister Shigeaki Ueki. "In textiles, for example, you can bring in the most modern equipment, but it won't matter."
By some estimates, the informal sector accounts for as much as half of
the country's GDP.

Regions

Brazil is divided into 26 states and the federal district of
Brasília. Most developed are the south-central and southern regions,
including the states of São Paulo, Rio Grande do Sul, Minas Gerais,
Paraná, Rio de Janeiro and Santa Catarina.

Of the 30 Brazilian cities with the best business environments,
18 — including the top three — are located in the state of São Paulo,
according to a study by the consultancy **Simonsen Associados,** which
applied objective factors of infrastructure and other amenities. "The
interior of São Paulo state is the best Brazil of Brazil," notes **Simonsen.** Companies like **Dow Chemical** and **DuPont** maintain their Latin
American headquarters in or near São Paulo city. Sixty-two percent of
the country's banks are based in the state, which accounts for about a
third of Brazil's GDP.

The central role of São Paulo in the Brazilian economy may
come as a surprise to foreigners, many of whom still think first of Rio de
Janeiro, the capital until 1960. Since losing its status as political center,
Rio de Janeiro has gradually seen finance and industry seep to São Paulo
or other environs. The declining economy has been accompanied by
growing security concerns: "With the kidnappings in Rio, many multinationals decided to move to São Paulo," notes Ellenrieder. When
Noronha Advogados, a leading law firm, resolved to close its office in
Rio de Janeiro, senior partner Durval de Noronha Goyos Jr. commented
matter-of-factly: "It is close enough to São Paulo to handle from here."

"Why would anybody establish their offices in Rio?" asks Brazilian business leader Bernardo Giacometti, incredulously recalling foreign business people who put down roots in Rio de Janeiro before thinking about anything else. Many of these individuals tend to become regulars on the Rio-São Paulo air shuttle.

Using a purchasing power index, market potential was measured by advertising association Grupo de Mídia. It found that São Paulo state accounts for 31 percent of the country's purchasing power, followed by Rio de Janeiro state (13 percent), Minas Gerais (10 percent), Rio Grande do Sul (7 percent), and Paraná (6 percent). Then come the northeastern states of Bahia (6 percent) and Pernambuco (4 percent).

These facts of life generally convince executives to locate within a certain radius of São Paulo city. Companies interested in exploring regional opportunities in the Mercosul tariffs union with neighbors Argentina, Paraguay and Uruguay are often attracted to the south. "Argentinean investors like Curitiba. It is more European," says Ellenrieder. "In the south, there is less poverty and educational levels are better."

Of special note is the Manaus Free Trade Zone. A remote city in the Amazon, Manaus began receiving favorable treatment in 1967 by a military government keen on integrating jungle regions into the rest of the Brazilian economy for geo-political reasons. Tax breaks helped attract more than 600 manufacturing plants, some with names such as **Sony, Honda, Philips, Bosch,** and **Gillette.** The zone has become one of the world's largest, with the electronics industry leading the way.

Even those who defend the zone admit that industry would not locate in Manaus without myriad tax breaks. Operationally, many Manaus-based companies are considered inefficient. Geographical isolation from both markets and suppliers results in high transportation costs.

Some analysts report good business climates in the states of Bahia and Tocantins.

Corruption: the Gray Areas

Some foreigners adapt quickly to Brazil, but many never fully adjust to the absence of clear standards of conduct, either legally or informally. "The gray zone for Americans is smaller than for South Americans, or even for Europeans," remarks businessman Haberfeld.

Companies that refuse to pay bribes or at least dip into the gray area of small gifts can find that their goods clear customs more slowly or their documents take longer to process. One business person told the story of a Brazilian friend who quit a sales job with a multinational because the firm prohibited bribes and allowed Christmas gifts only worth less than $50. "He decided that it would be impossible to do business," says the executive.

In Brazil, laws are often on the books but ignored or selectively enforced. Some believe this a bureaucratic tactic to make things difficult so that a regulator can "sell" an easier way around.

Attorney Noronha believes that selective enforcement generates mistrust among the less privileged populace. "In a country where the arbitrary is the norm, rules are largely set to endorse the law of the fittest. That creates lack of confidence in rules. And anomie," he believes.

Arbitrary and seemingly capricious delays can occur at customs — sometimes because an official wants a payoff, sometimes because he or she may use the letter of the law to pursue an individual nationalist agenda. Customs agents (called *despachantes*) are indispensable for importers, although one Brazilian business person admits: "It is hard to tell the honest and dishonest ones apart."

Some of the biggest mistakes are made by multinational executives who think they understand how things work. "They think that they can live outside the law like a northeastern Brazilian," says Orlandi. Haberfeld warns that if the government decides to crack down on hanky-panky, foreigners are the likely first targets.

Most executives and consultants believe that finding a good and reputable local partner is the best answer to the dilemma of cultural uncertainty.

Brazil at a Glance

Population: 157 million
Labor force size: 57 million (1992)
Unemployment: 5.9 percent
> Agriculture: 31 percent
> Industry: 27 percent
> Services: 42 percent

Languages: The official language is Portuguese, which is spoken by approximately 97 percent of the population.

Ethnic mix: Brazil's population is primarily of African and European (chiefly Portuguese) origin, plus about 200,000 indigenous Indians (mainly Guaraní). Sizable numbers of Arab and Japanese immigrants and their descendants also live in the area extending from Rio to São Paulo. The 1980 census found 54 percent of the population to be of European origin, 38 percent of mixed race, 6 percent of African origin, and one percent Japanese.

Literacy and Educational levels: Literacy rates increased from 50 percent in 1950 to 77 percent in 1990, but most Brazilians still do not complete primary school. Brazil is the worst performer on an index that compares expected educational levels given a country's per capita income and actual figures: just 39 percent of Brazilian children complete the fifth grade, compared to 88 percent that ought to do so, given the country's riches, says a UNICEF report.

Climate: Mainly tropical and sub-tropical; mild on the southern coast and in the higher lands.

Best times to visit: Anytime is good to visit for business except during vacation periods. A rule of thumb is to avoid the summer period between Christmas and the pre-Lenten Carnival. The date of Carnival changes every year according to the Roman Catholic Church calendar, but it generally takes place during the month of February. Another vacation period takes place during June.

Natural Resources/Chief Agricultural Products: Brazil is rich in both mineral resources and agricultural production. It has bauxite, iron ore, nickel, manganese, tin copper, silver and gold. Brazil is a leading producer of coffee, cocoa, soybeans, orange juice, sugar, alcohol, cotton and tobacco for export. The country produces beans, rice, manioc, and a large variety of vegetables and fruits for domestic use and is a substantial cattle raising country.

Land area: 8,511,965 square kilometers.

Economic Statistics:

> GDP: $447 billion (1993)
>
> Per capita GDP: $2,809 (1993)
>
> Economic growth rate: 5.7 percent (1994)

Exports: $43.5 billion (fob, 1994). Main products: iron ore, coffee, footwear, orange juice, soybean bran, motor vehicle parts.

Imports: $33.2 billion (1994). Main products: Crude oil, capital goods, coal, chemical products, foodstuffs.

Import duties: The current average duty is 14 percent, with a 35 percent maximum for selected products, including assembled computers and automobiles. Many consumer durables, capital goods and processed foodstuffs have 20 percent tariffs. In 1995, the maximum tariff for all but one-tenth of imports drops to 20 percent as part of the Mercosul accord.

Repatriation of profits: According to *Doing Business in Brazil* by Ernst & Young: "No restrictions are imposed on the amount of dividends distributable to shareholders domiciled abroad. The penalty tax on excess dividend remittances was eliminated with effect on 1 January 1992. Before earnings may be distributed, corporations must allocate 5 percent of annual net income to a reserve. This annual allocation is required until the reserve equals 20 percent of total capital."

When You Go to Brazil

Visas: A valid passport and business visa (obtained from a Brazilian consulate in the traveler's home country) are officially required, although in practice many business visitors travel on tourist visas, which involve less expense and red tape. U.S. citizens should be aware of a simmering dispute between the Brazilian Foreign Ministry and

U.S. State Department. Recently enacted legislation in the United States requires U.S. consulates to employ norms and fees for foreign nationals that are at least as rigorous as those employed for U.S. citizens applying for visas in the respective country. As a result, rules for Brazilians wishing to travel to the United States have been tightened and fees increased. Instead of having the desired effect of encouraging easier rules for Americans wishing to visit Brazil, the U.S. policy has engendered a reaction from the Brazilians that can now cause greater delays and complications for Americans applying for Brazilian visas.

Airlines: Foreign carriers flying to Brazil include United, American, Swissair, British Airways, Ibéria, Aerolineas Argentinas, Air France, Alitalia, JAL, KLM, LAB, Ladeco, Lan Chile, LAP, Lufthansa. Brazilian carriers Varig and Vasp also have regular service to many parts of the world. Travelers to São Paulo should be aware that Varig customarily sells tickets for what it claims are direct service flights to that city; however, passengers are invariably required to change planes in Rio de Janeiro and are generally subject to several hours of delay in the Rio de Janeiro airport.

Miscellaneous Tips:

● Money can be changed on arriving at the airport. It would be advisable to change enough to have some walking around cash for a day or two. Then ask local contacts to suggest a money changer.

● Taxis from the São Paulo and Rio de Janeiro international airports should be hired and paid for at a kiosk inside the airport. Charges vary according to destination, but are clearly displayed at the desk. Do not hire an independent cab at the airport.

● Because of the inflationary environment, where retailers invariably lose on the float, credit cards are still less widely accepted than in most countries; most upscale restaurants and other business-oriented establishments accept them (but this is not always the case: ask first before having to fork over all your cash on hand to pay for a dinner.).

● Specific issues regarding samples should be discussed with a local contact in Brazil before leaving home. It would be advisable to have the local contact refer you to a customs agent (*despachante*) and to ask that person to help prepare any required documentation. In general, all persons entering the country can bring in up to $500 worth of goods duty free.

Urban transportation:

Rental car services are available in all major cities, although prices tend to be higher than in many countries. Many rental companies also offer limousines or vans. Drivers can be hired along with the vehicles. Some firms offer bilingual drivers.

Taxis can be hailed on the street or through the concierge at your hotel. Those called by the hotel personnel are normally more expensive. Taxi meters operate according to a *unidade taxímetro,* which corresponds to a price on a chart (*tabela*) that the driver carries in the vehicle. Do not pay the price shown on the meter, which is not registered in currency. If the driver does not consult the chart, ask him or her to do so. Radio taxis can be called without the assistance of the hotel staff and charge normal prices. The best service in São Paulo is Coopertaxi (phone 941-2555).

Hotels

SÃO PAULO

All of the following are world class hotels with good infrastructure for business travelers.

Near Avenida Paulista (main business district):

Maksoud Plaza.
Alameda Campinas, 150
Tel: (55-11) 253-4411.
Rooms start at $180.

Caesar Park
Rua Augusta, 1508
Tel: (55-11) 253-6622.
$180 and up.

Sheraton Mofarrej
Alameda Santos, 1437
Tel: (55-11) 253-5544.
$180 and up.

Santo Amaro neighborhood (manufacturing center and growing center for offices, especially for multinationals)
Transamérica
Avenida das Nações Unidas, 18591
Tel: (55-11) 523-4511.
$132 and up.

Downtown
Grand Hotel Ca'd'Oro
Rua Augusta, 129
Tel: (55-11) 256-8011.
$132 and up.
São Paulo Hilton.
Avenida Ipiranga, 165
Tel: (55-11) 256-0033.
Over $180.

RIO DE JANEIRO
Personal attention is generally less efficient in Rio hotels than in São Paulo, but the facilities in the following are world class unless otherwise stated.

Near Downtown
Hotel Glória.
Rua do Russell, 632
Tel: (55-21) 205-7272.
$35-$100.
An older hotel popular when the capital was in Rio de Janeiro and government offices were located nearby. Doesn't offer the comfort or ser-

vice level of hotels in the southern zone of the city, but has an advantageous location near government agencies, state-owned companies, and most leading businesses still located in Rio. Staying at the Glória means you can avoid fighting traffic to get to appointments.

Southern Zone of Rio (Leme, Copacabana, Ipanema, Leblon)
Rio Othon Palace.
Avenida Atléntica, 3264
Tel: (55-21) 521-5522. Business center.
$132 and up.
Caesar Park.
Avenida Vieira Souto, 460
Tel: (55-21) 287-3122.
$132 and up
Rio Palace.
Avenida Atlántica, 4240. Business center.
Tel: (55-21) 521-232.
$132 and up.
Le Meridien.
Av. Atlântica, 1020
Tel: (55-21) 275-9922. Business center.
Over $180.
Copacabana Palace.
Avenida Atlántica, 1702
Tel: (55-21) 255-7070.
$132 and up

Farther south in Rio:
Sheraton Rio Hotel & Towers.
Av. Niemeyer, 121
Tel: (55-21) 274-1122. Business center.
Over $177.
Inter-Continental Rio
Avenida Pref. Mendes de Morais, 222

Tel: (55-21) 322-2200. Business center.
$132-$177.

BRASÍLIA

NOTE: All hotels in Brasília are located in the "hotel sector." They are conveniently located in relation to government offices, but trying to do anything else (jog, find a restaurant or bar, or do shopping) can be complicated for anyone not familiar with the city. Cab drivers are a good source of information, and they can often be hired cheaply for the day.

Naoum Plaza.
Setor Hoteleiro Sul, QD5
Tel: (55-61) 226-6494.
$132 and up.
Kubitschek Plaza.
Setor Hoteleiro Norte, QD2
Tel: (55-61) 316-3333.
$100-$180.

MANAUS
Tropical Manaus.
Estrada da Ponta Negra, kilometer 18
Tel: (55-92) 658-5000.
$132 and up.

PORTO ALEGRE
Plaza São Rafael.
Avenida Alberto Bins, 514
Tel: (55-51) 221-6100.
$75-$130.
Center Park.
Rua Cel. Frederico Link, 25

Tel: (55-51) 221-5320.
$75-$130.

CURITIBA
Grand Hotel Rayon.
Rua Visconde de Nacar, 1424
Tel: (55-125) 322-6006.
$132-$177.

RECIFE
Sheraton Petibu.
Avenida Bernardo Vieira de Melo, 1624
Tel: (55-81) 361-4511.
$100-$177.
On a beach, a bit outside of town.
Recife Palace Lucsim.
Avenida Boa Viagem, 4070
Tel: (55-81) 325-4044.
$100-$177.

SALVADOR
Meridien Bahia.
Rua Fonte do Boi, 216
Tel: (55-71) 248-8011.
$98-$131.
Bahia Othon Palace.
Avenida Presidente Vargas, 2456
Tel: (55-71) 247-1044.
$98-$177.
Tropical da Bahia
Praça 2 de Julho, 2
Tel: (55-710 321-3699.
$73-$98.

Contacts

Selected Foreign Embassy Commercial Sections (commercial sections tend to be located in São Paulo and not in Brasília):

ARGENTINA
Avenida Paulista, 1106 - 9th floor, São Paulo, SP.
Tel: (55-11) 284-1355.

UNITED STATES
Rua Estados Unidos, 1812, São Paulo.
Tel: (55-11) 853-2011. Fax: 853-2744.

UNITED KINGDOM
Avenida Paulista, 1938 - 17th floor, São Paulo.
Tel: (55-11) 287-7722. Fax: 287-7637.

CANADA
Avenida Paulista, 854 - 5th floor, São Paulo.
Tel: (55-11) 287-2122. Fax: (55-11) 251-5057.

JAPAN
Avenida Paulista, 475, São Paulo.
Tel: (55-11) 287-0100.

SOUTH KOREA
Avenida Paulista, 37 - 9th floor, São Paulo.
Tel: (55-11) 288-3455.

Business Organizations:

AMCHAM BRASIL SÃO PAULO (American Chamber of Commerce)
Rua Alexandre Dumas, 1976, 04717 São Paulo, SP.
Tel: (55-11) 246-9199. Fax: (55-11) 246-9080.
Executive Director: John Mein

ARGENTINE-BRAZILIAN CHAMBER OF COMMERCE
Avenida Brigadeiro Luiz Antonio, 2367 - 20th floor, São Paulo, SP.
Tel: (55-11) 289-8655. Fax: (55-11) 288-7212.
Executive Director: Felix Larrañaga

**BRAZIL-MEXICO CHAMBER OF INDUSTRY
AND COMMERCE**

Avenida Brigadeiro Faria Lima, 534 - conjunto 601, 01452 São Paulo, SP.

Tel: (55-11) 280-2881. Fax: (55-11) 64-7819.

Executive Director: Adolpho Guilherme Luce Neto

**BRAZILIAN-GERMAN CHAMBER OF
INDUSTRY AND COMMERCE**

Rua Verbo Divino, 1488 - 3rd Floor, 04719-904 São Paulo, SP.

Tel: (55-11) 247-0677. Fax: (55-11) 524-7013.

President: Cláudio Fonder

JAPANESE CHAMBER OF INDUSTRY AND COMMERCE

Avenida Paulista, 475 - 13th floor, 01311-908 São Paulo, SP.

Tel: (55-11) 287-6853. Fax: (55-11) 284-9424.

AMERICAN CHAMBER OF COMMERCE IN RIO DE JANEIRO

Mail: Caixa Postal 916

Street address: Praça Pio X-15, 5th Floor, 20040 Rio de Janeiro.

Tel: (55-21) 203-2477. Fax: (55-21) 263-4477.

Manager: Augusto de Moura Diniz

AMERICAN CHAMBER OF COMMERCE IN SALVADOR

Rua de Espanha, 2 - salas 604-606, 40000 Salvador, Bahia.

Tel: (55-71) 242-0077. Fax: (55-71) 243-9986.

**BRAZIL-U.S. CHAMBER OF COMMERCE FOR
NORTHEASTERN BRAZIL**

Rua José Bonifácio, 944 - Torre, 50710-900 Recife, Pernambuco.

Tel: (55-81) 412-7377 or 412-8616. Fax: (55-81) 227-3251.

SÃO PAULO INDUSTRIAL FEDERATION (FIESP)

Avenida Paulista 1313, 14th floor, 01311-923 São Paulo, SP.

Tel: (55-11) 280-8120 or 287-3322. Fax: (55-11) 284-3971.

Assistant to the President: Luis Antonio Martinez Vidal

RIO GRANDE DO SUL INDUSTRIAL FEDERATION (FIERGS)

Av. Assis Brasil, 8787, 91140-001 Porto Alegre, RS.

Tel: (55-51) 344-4655. Fax: (55-51) 344-4757.

BAHIA INDUSTRIAL FEDERATION (FIEB)

Rua Edístio Pondé, 259 STIEP, 41760-310 Salvador, BA.

Tel: (55-71) 371-4611. Fax: (55-71) 371-3593.

President: José de Freitas Mascarenhas

NATIONAL INDUSTRIAL CONFEDERATION (CNI)

Avenida Nilo Peçanha, 50 - 34th floor, 20044-900 Rio de Janeiro, RJ.

Tel: (55-21) 292-7766.

NATIONAL GRASSROOTS BUSINESS ASSOCIATION (PNBE)

Rua Zaíra, 294, 01252 São Paulo, SP.

.Tel: (55-11) 65-5972. Fax: (55-11) 262-5247.

Emerson Kapaz, coordinator

TIETÊ PARANÃ DEVELOPMENT AGENCY (ADTP)

Rua Jerônimo da Veiga, 164 - 15th Floor, 04536-900 São Paulo, SP.

Tel: (55-11) 282-2100. Fax: (55-11) 282-2464.

John Prier de Saone, manager

Government Agencies:

FINANCE MINISTRY (overall regulation of the economy)

Esplanada dos Ministérios, Bloco P - 5th floor, 70048-900 Brasília, DF.

Tel: (55-61) 223-6959.

MINISTRY OF INDUSTRY, COMMERCE AND TOURISM (promotion and regulation)

Esplanada dos Ministérios, Bloco J - 6th floor, 70056-900 Brasília, DF.

Tel: (55-61) 225-8808.

FOREIGN MINISTRY

Esplanada dos Ministérios, Palácio do Itamaraty, 70170-900 Brasília, DF.

Tel: (55-61) 211-6100.

Lawyers (*listing here does not constitute a recommendation*):

Noronha Advogados

Durval de Noronha Goyos Jr., senior partner

Avenida Brigadeiro Faria Lima, 2100 - 3rd floor, 01452-919 São Paulo, SP.

Tel: (55-11) 816-6609. Fax: (55-11) 212-2495.

Albino Advogados Associados

Fernando Albino, senior partner; Santiago Marin Gallo, attorney.

Alameda Gabriel Monteiro da Silva, 2069, 01440 São Paulo, SP.
Tel: (55-11) 883-7788. Fax: (55-11) 280-4160.

Fischer & Forster Advogados
Georges Charles Fischer, attorney
Avenida Cidade Jardim, 377 - sobreloja, 01453-900 São Paulo, SP.
Tel: (55-11) 881-2100. Fax: (55-11) 282-6629.

Pinheiro Neto Advogados
Fernando B. Pinheiro, partner
Rua Boa Vista, 254 - 9th floor, 01414 São Paulo, SP.
Tel: (55-11) 232-5022. Fax: (55-11) 36-5011.

Mattos Filho e Suchodolski
Rua Jose Maria Lisboa, 41, 01423-000 São Paulo, SP.
Tel: (55-11) 885-6922. Fax: (55-11) 885-0903.
Ary Oswaldo Mattos Filho, senior partner

Interpreters/Translators:

Roberto Raposo
Rua Alice 175 - number 401, 22241 Rio de Janeiro, RJ.
Tel: (55-21) 225-0071.

Peter Lenny
Rua Redentor 156 - number 302, Rio de Janeiro, RJ.
Tel/Fax: (55-21) 521-1339.

Stanley Lehman
Rua Major Quedinho 111, sala 707, 01050-030 São Paulo, SP.
Tels: (55-11) 256-0520, 256-4135, 280-8216.

Roberta Barni Summa
Rua Augusta 434, number 22, 01304 São Paulo, SP.
Tel/Fax: (55-11) 256-5578.

Maria de Lourdes Botelho
Rua Inhambu, 873 - number 41, São Paulo, SP.
Tel/Fax: (55-11) 241-7206.

Julio Fischer
Rua Dr. José de Queiroz Aranha, 32 - number 225, São Paulo, SP.
Tel: (55-11) 571-9775.

Consultants and Other Business Contacts:

Boucinhas & Campos
Rua Barão de Itapetininga, 140 - 7th floor, São Paulo, SP.
Tel: (55-11) 231-3011. Fax: (55-11) 255-0343.

CLA
Rua Dante Cararo, 94, 05422 São Paulo, SP.
Tel: (55-11) 815-3988. Fax: (55-11) 815-3856.
Director: Mario Ernesto Humberg

Simonsen Associados
Avenida 9 de Julho, 5017 - 12th floor, 01407 São Paulo, SP.
Tel: (55-11) 853-4733. Fax: (55-11) 883-4958.
Harry Simonsen, director

Fundamental Research
Rua Dr. Rubens de Azevedo Marques, 379, 04646-071 São Paulo, SP.
Tel: (55-11) 524-4321. Fax: (55-11) 524-3018.
Márcio Orlandi, director

Piereck & Luce Business Consultants
Avenida Brigadeiro Fria Lima, 534 - conjunto 601, 01452 São Paulo, SP.
Tel/Fax: (55-11) 280-2881 or 64-7819.
Adolpho G. Luce Neto and Edmyr de M. Piereck, directors

Early Warning
C.P. 0-2941, 71609 Brasília, DF.
Tel: (55-61) 245-4795. Fax: (55-61) 245-4350.
Contact: Alexandre Barros

IMF Editora
Avenida Almirante Barroso, 63 - sala 409, 20031-001 Rio de Janeiro, RJ.
Tel: (55-21) 240-4347. Fax: (55-21) 262-7570.
Ronaldo Nogueira, director

Vendor
Avenida 9 de Julho, 5345 - conjunto 52, 01407-908 São Paulo, SP.
Tel: (55-11) 280-0366. Fax: (55-11) 852-9807.
Contact: Geraldo G. da Rocha Azevedo

Shigeaki Ueki
Avenida Paulista 949, 22nd floor, 01113 São Paulo, SP.
Tel: (55-11) 283-0833. Fax: (55-11) 251-4940.
Emplarel
Avenida Odilon E. do Amaral Souza, 140, 04671-360 São Paulo, SP.
Tel: (55-11) 246-7033. Fax: (55-11) 246-8568.
Ferdinando Farah Netto, director
Folio MKT
Rua Ptolomeu, 650, 04762-040 São Paulo, SP.
Tel: (55-11) 524-6117. Fax: (55-11) 523-1100.
Bernardo Giacometti, president
SLM & Lopes Filho Consultants
Rua México, 98 - 11th Floor, Rio de Janeiro, RJ.
Tel: (55-21) 210-2152.
Multiport Export & Import
Rua Jesuino Arruda, 878, 04532 São Paulo, SP.
Tel: (55-11) 881-7030. Fax: (55-11) 282-6356.
Alberto J. Alzueta, director
Brasilpar Financial Services
Alameda Santos 1357, 2nd floor, 01419 São Paulo, SP.
Tel: (55-11) 285-1222. Fax: (55-11) 285-6582.
Roberto Teixeira da Costa, director-president

Travel Agent:

KATUR
Avenida Brigadeiro Faria Lima, 1483 - conjunto 1303, 01451 São Paulo, SP.
Tel: (55-11) 815-1900 or 815-1828. Fax: (55-11) 814-8771.

Useful Publications:
Village News (expatriate biweekly) and *Update* (American Chamber of Commerce newsletter) are both published by: Mini-Max Editora Especializada, Caixa Postal 4997, 01051 São Paulo, SP. Brian Nicholson, director

Industrial Equipment News
Grupo Lund
Rua Brigadeiro Tobias, 356 - 5th floor, 01032-901 São Paulo, SP.
Tels: (55-11) 227-1022, 228-8248, 228-8162. Fax: (55-11) 228-9373.
Christopher Lund, director

Doing Business in Brazil
Ernst & Young Sotec
Avenida Presidente Juscelino Kubitscheck, 1830, Torre I, Floors 5-8, 04543 São Paulo, SP.
Tel: (55-11) 820-8277. Fax: (55-11) 820-6840.

Business in Brazil: Legal Guide
Noronha Advogados
Durval de Noronha Goyos Jr., senior partner.
Avenida Brigadeiro Faria Lima, 2100 - 3rd floor, 01452-919 São Paulo, SP.
Tel: (55-11) 816-6609. Fax: (55-11) 212-2495.

Yearbook
Amcham Brasil São Paulo (American Chamber of Commerce)
Rua Alexandre Dumas, 1976, 04717 São Paulo, SP.
Tel: (55-11) 246-9199. Fax: (55-11) 246-9080.

Brazil Business & Investment Guide
Arthur Andersen
Rua Alexandre Dumas, 1981, 04717-906 São Paulo, SP.
Tel: (55-11) 524-2444. Fax: (55-11) 521-2911.

In Case of Illness:

SÃO PAULO
U.S. Consulate Health Unit
Marita Leite, RN
Tel: (55-11) 881-6511.
U.S. Consulate Post Medical Adviser
João Jorge Leite, MD
Tel: (55-11) 887-7722.

João Jorge Leite
Rua Bela Cintra, 746 - 6th floor, 01415 São Paulo, SP.
Tels: (55-11) 259-3129, 259-3481, 259-7195.
Dr. Thomas Muller Carioba
Tel: (55-11) 542-6577

RIO DE JANEIRO
Dr. Claudio Souza Leite
Rua João Afonso, 62, Rio de Janeiro.
Tel: (55-21) 246-1788.
Dr. Marcos Moraes
Rua Lauro Miller, 116 - Room 3306, Rio de Janeiro.
Tel: (55-21) 541-3343.
Dr. Octávio P. Vaz
Rua Sorocaba, 477 - Room 1101, Rio de Janeiro.
Tel: (55-21) 286-2898.

BRASILIA
Dr. Cesar Thomas de A. Vieira
Centro Medico de Brasília, Bloco E, room 209.
Tel: (55-61) 245-3276.
Dr. Geraldo Benicio de Carvalho
Hospital Santa Lucia, Brasília.
Tel: (55-61) 245-7441.

RECIFE
Dr. Fernando Sabova
Rua da Hora, 892, Recife.
Tel: (55-81) 221-2823.
Dr. William Stamford
Hospital Portugues, Av. Portugal, 163, Recife.
Tel: (55-81) 222-1444.
Dr. Jose A. Queiroga
Av. Conselheiro Aguiar, 1092, Recife.
Tel: (55-81) 325-3686.

5

CENTRAL AMERICA

From the Eighteenth Hole:
Coups and Other Palace Intrigues

By Scott Norvell

rent Holmes, a pioneer of Guatemala's clothing assembly
drawback industry, was golfing with a friend one weekday
morning in1993 when radios reported that the then President,
Jorge Serrano Elias, after three years in office, had dissolved congress
and declared martial law. Accustomed to tumultuous politics after six
years in Guatemala, Brent Holmes did that day what most Guatemalans
do when they hear news of such political upheaval — nothing unusual. "We finished our game," he said.

Images of Guatemala City being beamed overseas at the time
— of police patrolling the streets in open jeeps, sweeping the barrels
of their M-60s across the sidewalks — left many outside Guatemala
with the impression that chaos reigned. Holmes immediately began
getting calls from suppliers and customers abroad. Some wondered
whether he was barricaded in his home or office, others why he wasn't
fleeing the country. Most asked whether their orders would be filled.

To Holmes and most others like him on the scene, the concern
was unjustified. "We finished our game and I went to work, just like

always," he remembers of that spring day. "Everyone else was there, just like always. Frankly, I spent more time convincing people that everything was okay than even thinking about what Serrano was doing."

Since Holmes moved to Guatemala in 1987 and opened one of the country's first clothing assembly, or *maquila,* plants, there have been several such days. In addition to Serrano's so-called self-coup, which failed and led to his eventual exile, there were a couple of failed coup attempts against former President Vinicio Cerezo and literally dozens of days when Guatemala City's rumor mill kicked into overdrive in response to the latest machinations in the country's gothic National Palace. Each time, Holmes says, life in the city went on pretty much as normal. "We had almost no absenteeism at the plant," he recalls of those days. "Hell, the bus strikes cause more problems than the coups, but even then — let's face it — people have to come to work to get paid, so they find a way."

It is ironic, say Holmes and many others with experience in Central American business, that the political turmoil for which Guatemala and the rest of the region is best known to foreigners is also the least troublesome aspect of actually doing business in the area. Barring wholesale revolutions, most old Central America hands agree, it is the day-to-day minutiae — the endless quests for rubber stamps, the hours waiting on the musty couch of some ministerial antechamber, the haggling with corrupt customs officials — that prove far more problematic.

Recent events in Guatemala notwithstanding, the seven-nation Central American region is currently in an unprecedented period of economic and political stability and the skeptics are starting to take another look. The guerrillas of El Salvador have traded their olive-drab uniforms for Armani suits, and the Nicaraguan Sandinistas have taken to petty bickering over outdated Marxist political theory. A salsa singer took third place in the 1994 Panamanian elections, and air bases in Honduras once used to arm the anti-Sandinista Contras now are being used to ferry cantaloupes and frozen shrimp to northern wholesalers.

With the political bloodletting largely over, leaders in the region have turned their attention to economic concerns and have generated impressive results. Out are the import-substitution models of the 1970s that favored triple-digit import duties and artificial exchange rates; in are tariff ceilings and export incentive programs. Fiscal conservatives and ardent free-traders hold the presidential reins in most countries of the region, and young technocrats with degrees from such places as Wharton or Texas A&M or Stanford occupy the ministries. If the 1980s were the "Lost Decade" in Central America, then the 1990s are shaping up as the decade of its rediscovery.

Per capita GDPs in most of Central America rose consistently in the first half of the 1990s, and unemployment fell. Inflation was under control, and exchange rates stabilized without government intervention. Exports grew at double-digit clips in some cases — El Salvador and Costa Rica, most notably — and imports rose at an even healthier rate. Guatemala's $111 million market for agricultural equipment, for example, rose at 20 percent a year, Costa Rica's computer software imports at 30 percent a year.

For foreign investors and traders the structural changes accompanying this economic revitalization represent a monumental shift. While not without its perils and frustrations, the Central America of the 1990s is a much more accommodating place for foreign investors. They are usually steered to "one-stop" windows for paperwork processing and massive export processing zones where taxes are almost non-existent. Changes in the restrictive import regulations of the past have come slower, but are evident nevertheless.

Reams of legislation and scores of well-intentioned politicians have not been able, however, and will likely never be able, to create a fret-free operating environment in Central America. Red tape is still a nightmare, and transport costs are astronomical. Rock-bottom wages can be offset by low productivity, high training costs, and constant employee turnover. Importers often find that the reality of low tariffs can be offset by the surrealism of some non-tariff barriers, both formal and informal. Still, they are coming to Central America, and many are managing to make money.

While traditional commodities such as coffee, bananas, and sugar still generate the bulk of export revenues, the most dynamic aspect of Central American economies in recent years has been the so-called non-traditional sector. Encompassing products ranging from shrimp and clothing to blackberries and baby vegetables, it accounted for nearly a quarter of the $5.7 billion in exports from Central America in 1993 and is likely to continue gaining share.

For the moment at least, investors like Holmes represent the most common form of direct investment in Central America's non-traditional sector. With wages and operating costs increasing in Asia, and Mexico uncertain, many makers of labor-intensive products, such as clothing and simple electronics, are turning to Central America to fill the void. Exports of goods produced under such drawback regimes, in which U.S.-made parts are shipped abroad to be assembled and re-exported, have increased dramatically in the past five years. Those from the Caribbean Basin, which includes all of Central America plus the Dominican Republic and Jamaica, rose from $2.27 billion in 1991 to $3.57 billion in 1993.

Holmes, who arrived in Guatemala with a decade of experience in the U.S. textile industry behind him, scouted the local industry and sank $100,000 into a small sewing machine shop that produced inexpensive cloth for the Guatemala City market. Heeding the advice of others to find both a good lawyer to help with the incorporation paperwork and a knowledgeable local partner, he was up and running almost immediately. The first arrangement worked out; the second didn't.

A good lawyer, Holmes says, is vital when starting out, not just in Guatemala but throughout Central America. The lawyer shepherded Holmes' paperwork through the Guatemalan Internal Revenue Service and into the Mercantile Registry. He filled out the stamped fiscal sheets required for all official communications, rounded up the various stamps needed, and filed applications with the ministries of labor, economy and finance, as well as with the attorney general's office.

Without the lawyer's network of personal contacts and familiarity with the system, Holmes now says, his company, **Fantastika, S.A.**, would have died before it was born. In addition to incorporation advice, the lawyer provided invaluable introductions to both government and private sector leaders, aided in drawing up a labor agreement, steered Holmes away from unreliable customs brokers and freight forwarders, and helped set up a network of *tramitadores* (a Spanish term for bureaucratic fixers) that Holmes still uses.

Holmes' second initial arrangement, with the local partner, didn't fare as well. Inexperienced and unconnected, the partner almost drove the business into the ground. Forced to step in, Holmes says he learned quickly the key to successfully operating in Central America: making and maintaining personal contacts. In Guatemala, much as in the rest of Latin America, business is built on personal relationships and mutual trust, relationships that always precede, and frequently take precedence over, contractual arrangements.

Holmes learned to make small talk about family and sports with the director of customs so if spare parts or raw materials were held up, he had someone from whom to seek help. He learned to pay friendly calls on bureaucrats in the Labor Ministry periodically to keep up with the constantly changing labor codes, and he learned to network within the *gremiales,* or industry associations, that dominate private sector activity in the region.

Executives accustomed to the unbridled ambition, rock-hard deadlines, and participatory management style of the more developed world must make major adjustments when dealing with Central American labor pools. "Everyone doesn't live by the clock down here," says James Stanley, who has manufactured industrial textiles in Costa Rica for nearly two decades. Manufacturing deadlines almost always come and go without event, he says, but "if you are insistent and you stay on top of everything, the work will get done. You just have to keep hammering at the parameters."

Because familial obligations and personal relationships often take precedence over work, employee turnover rates in Costa Rica run as high as 30 percent a year, hindering productivity. Stanley has managed to keep half of his 60 employees for more than 20 years by conforming to the paternalistic nature of employee-supervisor relations in Costa Rica. The law gives employees 12 days of vacation a year; he gives them

20 days. The law requires social security contributions and Christmas bonuses; to this he adds free uniforms and subsidized lunches.

Stanley's labor costs balloon by 50 percent — including 26 percent in cash outlays — by the time such fringes are added to the base payroll. Labor laws throughout the region, in fact, mandate a series of benefits that are often overlooked in cost analyses of operating in Central America. El Salvador's benefits are typical of the area, and add an average of 30 percent to total payroll costs. An annual Christmas bonus, called an *aguinaldo,* equal to one month's salary must be paid each year, and two weeks paid vacation is standard. Severance packages that must, in essence, be paid to all departing employees are equal to one month's salary for each year of employment. And in addition to social security contributions, employers are required to make regular payments to a government housing plan.

Holmes also found that the government minimum wage was an impractical indicator of labor costs in Guatemala. "People are clearly not motivated by minimum wage," he says. "You can pay them 20 or 30 percent more and it won't affect them. Fifty percent, and they still won't care. You pay double, you start catching their attention. You pay two to three times minimum, you catch their attention and they start responding." Applying these concepts helped Holmes reduce defect rates among the Nike shorts and Jansen slacks his plant assembles from 30 percent to 0.5 percent over the past five years.

The proliferation of free zones and *maquilas* in Central America has a down side for later-comers to the region. The shortage of technical and managerial help has always been acute, but now employers are facing scarcities of unskilled manual labor as well. Buses operated by the *maquilas* in Guatemala City are now seen venturing farther and farther into the countryside to pick up employees each morning.

The patience required in dealing with the work force is also essential in coping with government. The bureaucracy and its protocol are taken very seriously, no matter how absurd the process or seemingly irrelevant the document. "If they want you to deliver an application or request on the third Tuesday of the month after a full moon, you have to do it," advises Henry Nicols, a former U.S. commercial attache in Guatemala now consulting for foreign investors in the region.

While forbidden now in some Latin countries, bribery is still a common way around the tangled bureaucracy in Central America. Because customs has traditionally served as a cash cow for loyal government cronies or retired military officers, it is there that both exporters from and importers to Central America will likely encounter the most blatant corruption. Operators in Honduras, for example, insist that despite laws exempting most free zone-bound machinery from import duties, bribes are often required to get it through customs.

Often the bribe is little more than a bottle or two of Johnny Walker or the equivalent of a few hundred dollars in national currency, so most folks accept it as a cost of doing business and let local partners or *tramitadores* handle it. Nicols advises clients that excessive bribes can sometimes be avoided by circumventing the offending official — just one example of a time when personal relationships can prevent sticky hassles — or selecting freight forwarders carefully.

Grounded in the Napoleonic Code of French civil law, courts in Central America provide little recourse for wronged foreigners, in bribery cases or any other. With the exception of Belize, Central American judicial systems are based on code instead of the precedent of common law and generally lack the option of jury trials. Overworked and underfunded, the courts are easily manipulated by local elites and usually incapable of rendering clear and timely decisions. "A deal for my friends; the law for my enemies," is all too true in Central America.

With the chances of judicial or police reprisal slim and thousands of weapons unaccounted for following the peace agreements of the early 1990s, the security situation in Central America has worsened considerably. Kidnapping for ransom is increasingly common in Guatemala and El Salvador, and petty crime is common throughout the region. Most direct investors rent only on short-term leases and limit in-country capital to insured machinery.

Some of the world's highest transportation costs — whether shipping into the region, by sea or air, or moving goods around among the countries of Central America — add considerably to operating costs. There are frequent delays, caused by bottlenecks at the overburdened ports or border crossings and the precarious state of roads in the area, which force many companies to maintain huge inventories of spare parts, raw materials and components as a fallback. For the same reasons, the just-in-time logistics so touted by economic development officials in the region are often easier planned than executed.

Air cargo service to Costa Rica and Guatemala from outside the area is relatively good, taking one to two days, but poor in the rest of the region, and seabound cargo takes three to five days between ports in Central America and Miami or New Orleans. Because all sea rates are set by the Central American Liner Freight Association, they vary little among the carriers and are extremely high. Generally, shipping a container to the Far East from Central America costs no more than sending one the much shorter distance to Miami.

For many of the same reasons that ports and roads in Central America are in disastrous shape, the rest of the infrastructure vital to industry is also in bad shape. Governments have invested little in their state-run utilities, and service reflects the neglect. Generally, telephone service is erratic, a constant struggle with inexplicably dead lines and overloaded circuits, and water and electricity supplies are not much better, although they cost about twice as much as in the more developed world.

The region's dependence on hydro-electric power has caused widespread rationing during periods of drought in recent years, forcing rolling blackouts for periods of up to 12 hours a day. Almost all industrial concerns require independent sources of power, usually diesel generators.

For those brave or hearty enough to withstand these and other unforeseen hassles, there are opportunities in Central America. Steadily dropping tariffs and steadily rising incomes have contributed to a boom in local sales of everything from car stereos to breakfast cereals. Costa Rica's import of consumer goods, for example, rose more than 70 percent between 1992-94 and automobile imports increased ten-fold between 1991-92 after tariffs were reduced. Demand for capital machinery and raw materials also has risen dramatically as the capital flight of the 1980s has reversed and local industry gears up for foreign competition.

Those importing goods into Central America will find that fees to local distributors are high, direct sales are time-consuming, and financing options are limited. Rules about exclusive supplier-distributor relationships vary from country to country, and many of the arrangements are covered by draconian local laws that make it practically impossible to fire distributors without considerable cost. Ideally, the arrangement is structured so that all disputes are settled in the home judicial systems of foreign firms, but that is not always possible.

There are many who believe that Central America, from an off-shore manufacturer's standpoint, is in the same position that Mexico was two decades ago when the *maquiladora* boom began there. Central America's proximity and preferential access to two huge markets (Mexico and the United States), low wages and government incentives have contributed to the boom in piece work, primarily clothing. The "Assembled in Guatemala," or Costa Rica or Honduras stamp is becoming increasingly common on goods carrying such well-known labels as Gitano, Hanes and Hagar.

Much of the labor-intensive industry has been concentrated in the growing network of free trade zones popping up all along the isthmus. All of the Central American countries now have laws formally establishing industrial parks and offering tenants exemptions from income taxes, import duties on both raw materials and machinery, and virtually unrestricted movement of capital and foreign exchange. Guatemala and El Salvador also offer the option of creating so-called bonded areas almost anywhere in the national territory, where individual companies on their own sites enjoy many of the same tax benefits that are available to those gathered in industrial parks.

Also falling under the non-traditional label and enjoying many of the same benefits, both in terms of access to the U.S. market and local government incentives, are agricultural products outside the range of traditional commodities, such as coffee, sugar, and bananas. Central America's year-round growing season allows exporters to supply U.S. and European markets with fresh fruit, exotic vegetables, cut flowers, ornamental plants and spices. Aquaculture projects, mainly shrimp farms, have also attracted considerable foreign investment.

Government procurement and contracting are still beyond the purview of all but the most masochistic foreign executives. Governments are opening such areas to foreign investment for the first time, but the bidding process, while ostensibly public, is far from transparent. Bid specifications are often changed without notice, public notification is scant, favored companies are allowed to change bids after deadlines and "extra-official goodwill" (as the diplomats refer to bribes) are common.

Outright privatization of government monopolies, all the rage elsewhere in Latin America, is occurring far more slowly in Central America. With revenues scarce, the governments have been loath to lose the money generated by these enterprises and shown little of the political will needed to push privatization past strident public unions. So far, the sell-off has been restricted to minor enterprises, such as cement companies in Honduras, railroad yards in Guatemala, and hotels in Nicaragua.

An outgrowth of the recent liberalization efforts of benefit to importers is the increasingly open borders in the region. The Central American Common Market, which broke down in the late 1960s, has been revived with measurable success. Common external tariffs, ranging from 5-20 percent for most goods, are now in place throughout the region, and the border-crossing formalities — notoriously tedious in the past — have eased substantially among the so-called C-4 countries (Guatemala, Honduras, El Salvador, and Nicaragua). Costa Rica, while signing on to the bloc in spirit, has so far resisted integration with the rest of Central America, hoping instead to negotiate bi-lateral treaties with other countries. Belize, Panama and Mexico are also likely to sign on to the economic integration system.

A flurry of bilateral treaties signed in recent years is cementing Central America's access to markets elsewhere in Latin America, as well. Fully 70 percent of El Salvador's exports enjoy duty-free access to markets in Mexico, Colombia, and Venezuela. Costa Rica's bilateral agreement with Mexico is the most comprehensive free trade agreement signed to date in Latin America. The agreements have made it easier for multi-national manufacturers to consolidate production for much of Central America's domestic market in one or two countries. Guatemala's position abutting the largest economic bloc in the world, North America, would seem to offer great potential, but historical animosities between the two countries make selling to Mexico from Guatemala difficult in spite of any existing or forthcoming trade pacts.

The preferential access to the U.S. market of the Caribbean Basin region, including Central America, is codified in legislation initially set to expire in 1996 but extended indefinitely in 1990. Under that, products from local materials, or products with at least 35 percent of their value added locally, are allowed duty-free access to the United States. Exceptions include apparel and textiles, petroleum products, footwear, most leather products and canned tuna. Many of the same benefits are provided to all developing countries under the General System of Preferences, or GSP, but the Caribbean Basin Initiative is typically more lenient than the former.

Apparel producers like Holmes are still subject to fluctuating quotas in the United States, but he has found — in spite of these and other limitations — that making money is not as difficult a task as he had anticipated. After floundering for three years, losing almost all his $400,000 savings, Holmes recovered and recouped all of his losses in the following two years. By staying on top of the business, leaving nothing to subordinates, he now nets between $200,000 and $300,000 a year.

"I believe you can make a lot more money in Central America than you can in the United States on a percentage basis," Holmes insists. "The economies of these countries are growing. The business people are starting to work. There's a sense of optimism for the first time in a while, a sense that things are starting to happen."

Tinker, Tailor, Lawyer, Salesman
Our Man in San Salvador

When the talk in El Salvador turns to American businessmen who have managed to prosper in the tiny country through war and peace, one name comes first to everyone's lips: Ramsey Moore.

Moore has gone from lone salesman — trundling auto parts in the tropical backwaters — to head of a diversified, privately owned empire topping $40 million in annual sales. He has directed his rise slowly, steadily, stressing solid, unspectacular values such as paying bills on time, being true to his word, and above all, eschewing ostentation.

The chairman's office is a cubbyhole in a nondescript warehouse in one of the older, lower middle-class neighborhoods of San Salvador, the capital city. Fluorescent lighting casts a greenish pall, and a noisy air conditioner grinds away in the window that gives onto the clogged street and the roar of diesel bus engines.

The office furniture is Salvadoran Everyman, the walls adorned with inexpensive art — mostly line drawings of cows — and a hodgepodge of certificates from various business organizations. Almost lost in all this is a letter from former President Ronald Reagan, thanking him for his concern and efforts to stem the tide of Marxist revolution in Central America during the 1970s and 1980s.

Buried behind a desk piled a foot high with file folders, annual reports, regulations, and other esoterica sits a 79-year-old native Texan. Straining a teabag, he dismisses his success with the explanation that "I've probably been here longer than the others."

After graduating from the University of Texas with degrees in business administration and law, Moore accepted a U.S. government job in 1940 that took him to El Salvador. He met and married a Savadoran woman and went home in 1945. In 1948 he returned to El Salvador and set up a one-man operation as a sales representative for various U.S. manufacturers, selling processed food, auto parts and clothing throughout Central America. He eventually tired of traveling and decided to concentrate on El Salvador. Later he began doing importing himself, gradually increasing the number of items to include agricultural chemicals and more food products.

Moore has since expanded into a manufacturing operation that processes many imported products for local sale. For example, the company elaborates feed for poultry, beef and dairy cattle, horses and swine. It formulates agricultural chemicals and certain commercial food products under license, including **Lea & Perrin** worcestershire sauce. His empire also includes retail stores, dairy farms, cattle ranches, coffee and citrus groves, and a worldwide export market for ornamental plants grown locally.

Various corporations are privately owned by Moore and his family, and all are organized under and managed by one umbrella holding company. A son, a daughter and her husband all work in the company, along with Moore's wife. **Moore Commercial** now has nearly 500 full-time employees.

In the 1970s, revolutionary fervor began to sweep the land. Fledgling guerrilla groups carried out extortion campaigns against landowners and wealthy businessmen to finance their planned armed rebellion. At the same time, armed gangs of police and military officers took advantage of the chaos to run their own criminal rings, often making it appear that their actions were committed by leftist groups.

By the early 1980s, many businessmen, both Salvadorans and foreigners, had packed up and fled to avoid attacks or kidnappings for ransom. Moore says he never considered following suit. "Practically everything I have is invested down here. If I weren't willing to stay and defend what I have, I couldn't very well ask somebody else to do it," he says.

With the war over, development and democracy have become the ubiquitous slogans. Former leftist guerrilla leaders are sounding, in the words of one U.S. trade official, "just like Milton Friedman." Highway robberies and other banditry seem to be as high or higher than ever, but Moore thinks a new national police force still in formation will reduce lawlessness, adding: "I don't think it's any worse than in many cities in the United States."

The man who started at the bottom and weathered the ups and downs of both the market and political upheaval believes the future is bright for foreign investors in El Salvador. He sees opportunities in the privatization of services traditionally owned and delivered by government: the telephone and telecommunications network, the port system, electrical generation and distribution, and the sugar processing mills. The Salvadoran state even owns a movie theater chain that will likely be sold off.

His advice to those considering doing business in El Salvador: The key thing is to know the conditions, the laws and regulations regarding the market you want to get into. For that, maybe it is good to have a local partner.

–Thomas Long

–Thomas Long is a free lance journalist based in El Salvador since 1988. He has reported for *Newsweek*, CBS News, *The New York Times*, *The Miami Herald*, Christian Science Monitor Radio, and other news organizations.

Sewing Up a Storm Where Political Prisoners Once Languished

James Scott Vaughn and Nelson Vidal, both from the United States, are among a relative handful of clothing manufacturers who have brushed aside nervousness about Nicaragua's chaotic politics and its unresolved property rights disputes to set up operations in the sprawling Las Mercedes Free Zone near the Managua international airport.

Vaughn has found the challenges of manufacturing in Nicaragua a little daunting, including spotty electricity and water services, and the unwanted privilege of "continually hearing other conversations while I'm on the telephone." Vidal is more sanguine, with nothing but good things to say about the government officials who facilitated the startup of his operation.

Both, however, say they met their initial production goals within a relative short time, and both are in the process of expanding or planning to expand soon. Vaughn said his firm, **Rocedes, S.A.,** manufacturers of pants, jeans, and tee shirts, would increase from 525 workers to about a thousand. Vidal, whose firm, **Varon's Internacional,** began making jackets, shirts and other men's clothing items in July 1994 with 325 workers, is also doubling his work force.

The increased hiring is sweet music to the ears of a government grappling with double-digit unemployment and one of the world's highest population growth rates.

The duty-free assembly area was created during the era when the Somoza family still ruled Nicaragua, but was quickly converted to a political prison after foreign firms pulled out in the wake of the 1979 insurrection victory by the leftist Sandinista Front. With Violeta Chamorro's defeat of the Sandinistas in presidential elections in 1990 it became a manufacturing center again, and foreign manufacturers are now actively courted.

So far, firms have come from Italy, Taiwan, and South Korea, in addition to the United States and Nicaragua itself. Besides clothing, they make shoes and aluminum products.

Both Vaughn and Vidal said they began their efforts to set up operations in Nicaragua by contacting officials of the Corporación de Zonas Francas (Free Zone Corporation), who in turn helped each of them with other steps in the process. The Free Zone Corporation will also coordinate access to the privately financed El Aguila Free Zone under construction a few miles east of Las Mercedes.

–**Carmen Chavarria**

–**Carmen Chavarria, a Nicaraguan journalist, has worked for** *La Prensa* **and** *The New York Times.*

Through Central America
Country by Country

By Scott Norvell

BELIZE

The youngest independent nation in the Western Hemisphere, Belize is more Caribbean than Latin American. A British Colony until 1981, Belize avoided the political and economic turmoil suffered by its Central American neighbors through the 1980s and remains a part of the English Commonwealth.

For the foreign investor, Belize stands out from its neighbors as a place where the laws are transparent, the bureaucracy minimal and the politics mundane. In addition, it is the only country on the Central American mainland that enjoys preferential access to both the European and U.S. markets, and the only with English as its official language.

Several areas of the economy have attracted foreign interest in recent years, the most dynamic of which has been tourism. With the second largest barrier reef in the world and hundreds of palm-fringed islands sitting off its coast, Belize has blossomed into one of the premiere diving and sport fishing destinations in the Americas. Because it is sparsely populated, the forests of rural Belize are remarkably wild compared to those of its neighbors and are attracting increasing numbers of ecology-minded tourists. About a third of existing U.S. investment in Belize is concentrated in the tourism sector.

The export economy is focused largely on natural resources — shrimp farming, tropical fruits, citrus, and forestry-related projects have all been given the green light in recent years — and light assembly. Any land purchases involving more than 10 acres for either export-related agriculture or tourism projects must receive ministry approval, but such requests have rarely been refused.

Belize's export incentive program revolves around so-called Development Concessions, valid for up to 25 years for export industries and 10 years for all others. Usually granted within 60 days, the concessions offer tax holidays, exemptions from import duties on both equipment and materials, and favorable lease terms on factory shells or industrial space for a period of time that depends largely on the local value-added and the employment opportunities created for the country's citizens.

Foreigners are forbidden from investing in certain areas, including fishing within the barrier reef, internal transport, restaurants and bars, souvenir manufacturing, diving and sightseeing operations, accounting services, and insurance. Belize's investment code also prohibits foreign companies from selling at the retail level within the country or engaging in merchandising, so importers must hire local representatives.

Belize at a Glance

Population: 243,000.

Labor force: 60,000.

Languages: English is the official language, but many people know Spanish as well.

Ethnic Mix: African, European, Mayan and other indigenous groups, and East Indian.

Literacy: 91 percent.

Education Levels: School is compulsory to age 14, but only 60 percent go on to secondary schools and a tiny elite to universities.

Climate: Hot and humid, tempered by trade winds. The rainy season runs from May to February.

Natural Resources: arable land, timber, fish.

Chief Agricultural Products: sugar cane, bananas, cocoa, citrus, fruits, lumber, farmed shrimp.

Land Area: 22,800 square kilometers.

Economic Statistics:

> GDP: $458 million (1993)
>
> Per capita GDP: $2,255
>
> GDP growth rate: 4.5 percent (1993)

Exports: sugar, clothing, seafood, molasses, citrus, wood and wood products.

Imports: Machinery and transportation equipment, food, manufactured goods, fuels, chemicals, pharmaceuticals.

Import duties: 5 percent to 45 percent.

When You Go to Belize

Visas: Citizens of the United States and Canada are allowed entry for up to 30 days without a visa.

Airlines: American Airlines from Miami and Washington; Taca from Miami and New Orleans; Continental from Houston, New Orleans, New York, Chicago and Denver; Delta from Montreal and Toronto; Air Canada from Montreal.

Hotels

Radisson Fort George.

2 Marine Parade, Belize City.

Tel: (501-2) 77-400, Fax: (501-2) 73-820.

Rates start at $104, plus 16 percent tax and service. U.S. reservations number: (800) 333-3333.

Belize Biltmore Plaza.

Mile 3 North Highway, Belize City.

Tel: (501-2) 32-302, Fax: (501-2) 32-301.

Corporate rate of $70 plus 16 percent tax and service.

Ramada Royal Reef and Marina.

Newton Barracks, Belize City.

Tel: (501-2) 32-677, Fax: (501-2) 32-660.

Corporate rate of $105 plus 16 percent tax and service. U.S. reservations number: (800) 854-7854.

Contacts

Commercial Section, U.S. EMBASSY.
Gabourel Lane and Hutson St., (PO Box 286), Belize City.
Tel: (501-2) 77-161, Fax: (501-2) 30-802.
Commercial Officer, EMBASSY OF BELIZE.
2535 Massachusetts Ave. NW, Washington, D.C. 20008.
Tel: (202) 332-9636, Fax: (202) 332-6888.
BELIZE EXPORT AND INVESTMENT PROMOTION UNIT.
6 Regent St., Belize City.
Tel: (501-2) 73-148, Fax: (501-2) 74-984.
MINISTRY OF ECONOMIC DEVELOPMENT.
38/40 Unity Boulevard, (PO Box 42), Belmopan, Belize.
Tel: (501-8) 22-526, Fax: (501-2) 23-111.

In case of illness:
International Association for Medical Assistance to Travelers Clinic.
99 Freetown Rd., Belize City.
Tel: (501-2) 44-368.

COSTA RICA

Much like Belize, Costa Rica belongs in a category by itself in any discussion of Central America. Home to one of Latin America's longest standing democracies and one of its most developed middle classes, the West Virginia-sized country escaped the turmoil of the 1980s with only minor political scars. Its economy, while bludgeoned like the rest, bounced back quickly, and now Costa Rica is one of the most promising locales in the Americas for foreign investors.

The opportunities are vast and varied. Almost one million tourists a year now flock to Costa Rica, spawning construction projects of all scales at every turn. A spate of new free trade zones is luring investment in the exotic (biotechnology) and the ordinary (apparel and

electronics). Long established as a healthy market for foreign consumer goods, an improving economy and lower tariffs in the 1990s
have pushed demand for both durables and non-durables to new
heights. Automobile imports, for example, increased ten-fold between
1991-92 when tariffs were reduced.

An influx of resident foreigners, principally retirees from the
United States, has added another dynamic to the domestic market. A
society that was already accustomed to consumer goods has become
even more so under the influence of 30,000 *pensionados,* as the retirees
are known.

Through most of the 1980s and into the 1990s, Costa Rica
enjoyed positive economic growth and improving worker productivity.
Along with the rest of his colleagues in Latin America, former President Rafael Angel Calderon began economic reform efforts in 1990.
Also as occurred with many of his colleagues, however, the structural
reform program proved politically unpopular and his party, the Christian Social Unity Party, lost the 1994 presidential election to José Maria
Figueres of the National Liberation Party.

Bowing to political pressure soon after taking office, Figueres
began backing away from the reform efforts by re-establishing some
price controls and halting plans to deregulate the insurance and banking industries. Later, he went even further, resisting pressure from
holders of Costa Rica's $3.5 billion in foreign debt to curtail public
spending (the deficit shot up to 8 percent of GDP in 1995, an eight-
fold increase over 1993) and instead proposing to raise taxes considerably. Even with an opposition-controlled congress blocking his way in
some areas, Figueres' actions set a clear precedent for economic policy at least through the 1998 elections.

For all the hype about its being a "tropical paradise," Costa
Rica is still very much a part of the developing world. The capital, San
José, is becoming increasingly polluted and overcrowded, and successive social-democratic governments have left a legacy of heavy-hand-
ed bureaucracy that has survived the recent wave of deregulation. The
customs system is still notoriously corrupt and inefficient. Also, des-

perately needed infrastructure improvements have been slow coming in this era of government austerity, so the logistics of business in Costa Rica can be troublesome.

Most investment incentives offered by the Costa Rican government center on exemptions from import duties on equipment and on material to be assembled and re-exported outside of Central America. This Export Contract program, however, is winding down, and the exemptions will be restricted to companies operating within the dozen or so free trade zones. On the whole, in fact, Costa Rica has been reducing the tax subsidies designed to encourage investment as a means of tackling a persistent budget deficit and appease international lenders.

Still, industries in Costa Rica's free trade zones enjoy exemptions of between 50 percent and 100 percent from the taxes on gross or net profits, in addition to on-site customs inspections and restricted access to domestic markets. Minimum employment levels must be met to qualify for the tax breaks. There are additional perks, including government-sponsored training programs and employee bonuses totaling 7-15 percent of annual wages, for investments that create jobs in rural areas.

Costa Rica, a pioneer of the Central American drawback industry, under which U.S. made components are shipped abroad for assembly, then sent back to the United States as finished products, continues to attract export-minded foreigners. This is despite relatively high wages and transportation deficiencies. Because the Ticos, as Costa Ricans refer to themselves, are better educated and trained than their neighbors, training time is less and output is immediately higher than in the other countries. While apparel is still a common product for such undertakings, the government's current emphasis is on more sophisticated labor intensive industries, such as electronics and data processing.

The birthplace of the solidarity movement, Costa Rica has little traditional union activity outside the public sector. Most multinational firms and medium-sized employers have solidarity groups that typically own 10-20 percent of the company's stock and negotiate amicably with management through member-elected boards.

As elsewhere, however, labor codes can be daunting. Required benefits, including social security contributions, Christmas bonuses, and paid vacations, can total as much as 40 percent of payroll. Salaries in urban areas are usually higher than minimum wage (about $1 an hour in 1994, adjusted bi-annually with the cost-of-living index), and wages for white collar and clerical workers in some industries approach those of the United States and Canada.

Outside of manufacturing, tourism-related projects and exotic non-traditionals also offer potential. Demand for hotel rooms has out-stripped supply for several years running, and resort projects are eligible for, in some cases, exemptions from property taxes and import duties on products and materials used in their development or mainte-nance. The red tape involved in receiving the latter, as well as securing permission to build near the ubiquitous national parks and on the coasts, can be long and cumbersome.

In the past, Costa Rica's agricultural production has mirrored the rest of Central America in its reliance on coffee, bananas and other traditionals. Exports of non-traditionals, ranging from orchids and ornamental plants to spices and macadamia nuts, have boomed in recent years. Forestry also remains strong, but environmental pressures have limited the growth more recently to commercial tree farms such as those initiated by Chicago-based **Stone Container Corp** in 1989. Oil exploration efforts, a monopoly of the state-owned refinery, **RECOPE**, until 1994, have in the past been unfruitful.

Those trying to export to Costa Rica will find that "selected consumption taxes" on many luxury imported goods, such as cars and stereos, can considerably hamper price advantages. An 8 percent hike in import duties, introduced by Figueres in 1995, and a proposed increase in the national sales tax, from 10 percent to 15 percent, will exacerbate the problem even further.

Exporters to Costa Rica must contract with a local representa-tive or agent, one who has been in business for at least 10 years (most are members of CRECEX, the Chamber of Representatives of Foreign Firms), on an exclusive basis. Forming a local subsidiary is the only way around this rule. The easing of foreign exchange regulations in 1992, along with increased tourism and export earnings, have considerably improved local buyers' financing options, so sight drafts and open letters of credit are common. New players in the market are strongly advised, however, to deal only in confirmed letters of credit until they are well-established.

Costa Rica at a Glance

Population: 3.3 million.

Labor Force: 1 million.

Languages: Spanish, with Caribbean English spoken in pockets around Limón on the Caribbean coast.

Ethnic Mix: 96 percent European, two percent West Indian.

Literacy: 93 percent with generally high levels of education.

Climate: Tropical, though cooler in the central highlands around San José, the capital. May-October rainy season.

Natural Resources: Hydropower potential .

Chief Agricultural Products: coffee, beef, bananas, sugar.

Land Area: 50,660 square kilometers.

Economic Statistics:

GDP: $6.3 billion (1994)

Per Capita GDP: $1,958

GDP Growth Rate: 5 percent (1994)

Principal Exports: Coffee, bananas, textiles, sugar, flowers and ornamental plants, melons and papayas, dates, figs, pineapples, avocados, textiles and apparel.

Principal Imports: Industrial raw materials, machinery and other capital goods, consumer goods, fuels and lubricants, oil, paper and paperboard, autos and auto parts, and corn.

Import Duties: 5-20 percent on most goods.

When You Go to Costa Rica

Visas: For stays of up to 90 days, only a valid passport is required.

Airlines: Direct, non-stop flights to San José by American Airlines from Miami and Dallas; United from Miami; Continental Airlines from Houston; Lacsa from Miami.

Hotels

Aurora Holiday Inn

Avda. 5 y Calle 5, San José.

Tel: (506) 233-7233, Fax: (506) 255-1036.

A business class hotel on a quieter side of the normally noisy downtown with full health facilities. On-site business center offers secretarial service.

Rates start at $111 plus 13 percent tax. U.S. reservations: (800) 465-4329.

Gran Costa Rica

Avda. 2 y Calle 1/3, San José.

Tel: (506) 221-4000, Fax: (506) 221-3505.

The grand old hotel of downtown San José, everyone you want to meet seems to linger in its terrace coffee shop at some time. Rooms have direct-dial telephones, and the business center offer computer terminals, presentation facilities and secretarial services.

Rates start at $71 plus 13 percent tax.

Herradura

Cuidad Cariari, San José.

Tel: (506) 239-0033, Fax: (506) 239-2292.

Near the airport and duty-free zones, a new hotel and the main convention center. Full business center, as well as golf and tennis facilities.

Rates start at $110 plus 13 percent tax.

Camino Real San José

New resort hotel in the suburb of Escasú about 10 minutes from downtown San José. Has a nightclub, casino, pool, and lighted tennis courts.

Rates begin at $150 plus 13 percent tax.

Reservations from the United States: (800) 722-6466.

Contacts

COSTA RICAN COALITION FOR DEVELOPMENT INITIA-TIVES (CINDE).
Complejo San José 2000, La Uruca, Edificio CINDE, San José.
Tel: (506) 220-0036, Fax: (506) 220-4750.
   CINDE also has two contact points in the United States at:
   108 Flat Rock Road, Easton, Connecticut, 06612,
   Tel: (203) 374-5588, Fax: (203) 374-5396.
   1600 NW LeJeune Rd., Suite 303, Miami, Florida, 33126,
   Tel: (305) 871-1019, Fax: (305) 871-0791.
CENTER FOR THE PROMOTION OF EXPORTS AND INVESTMENT (CENPRO).
Edificio Centro de Comercio Exterior, Costada Noroeste del Centro Colón, San José.
Tel: (506) 221-7166, Fax: (506) 223-5722.
COSTA RICAN-AMERICAN CHAMBER OF COMMERCE.
Mail: Apartado 4946-1000, San José.
Tel: (506) 220-2200, Fax: (506) 220-2300.
   The Chamber also has a more reliable U.S. mail drop at:
   Aerocasillas, Dept. 1576, PO Box 02-5216, Miami, Florida, 33102.
Commercial Section, U.S. EMBASSY.
Mail: Apartado 10053-1000, San José.
Tel: (506) 220-3939, Fax: (506) 220-2305.
CHAMBER OF REPRESENTATIVES OF FOREIGN COMPA-NIES (CRECEX).
Mail: Apartado 3738-1000, San José.
Tel: (506) 253-0126, Fax: (506) 234-2557.

In case of Illness:

Clinica Biblica
Calle Central/1, Avda. 14, San José
Tel: 223-6422.

Clinica Catolica
Calle Guadalupe, San José
Tel: 225-9095.

EL SALVADOR

The civil war in El Salvador had barely ended in early 1992 before business executives in other Central American countries began grumbling. The war, which devastated El Salvador, had been something of a boon to them. The region's most ambitious private sector, and what is known as its most industrious work force, had been sidelined for 12 years, allowing Honduras, Guatemala and Costa Rica to siphon off what little foreign investment entered the region during the 1980s and early 1990s.

With the conflict over, El Salvador is poised to regain its pre-war status as the industrial heart of Central America. Concern about the course of post-war politics has kept much of the investment concentrated in low-capital assembly, but the re-election of the conservative Nationalist Republican Alliance, or ARENA, party in 1994 allayed any immediate fears of a government led by former rebels and heightened the pace of foreign investment.

The opportunities of the moment in El Salvador are similar to those elsewhere in Central America, but perhaps more acute. Sabotage and neglect during the war — the government spent nearly half its budget on security and defense during the 1980s — left the country's infrastructure in disrepair.

With help from international lenders, El Salvador is racing to catch up. Ports at Acajutla and Cutuco near La Unión are being upgraded and expanded. **ANTEL,** the state-owned telephone company, is doubling the country's roughly 150,000 telephones lines and inviting foreign participation in almost all areas of the telecommunications sector. Water treatment and power generating facilities are being rebuilt or started from scratch.

Participation in these public projects, as usual in Central America, requires an on-the-ground agent with good contacts in government, as bids are solicited on short notice and the red tape is trying. Perhaps even more so than in the rest of Central America, in fact, El Salvador's private sector remains a tight-knit group that can be cracked by foreigners only with time and personal contacts.

While the groundwork for El Salvador's pro-business environment was laid in 1986 with an Investment Guarantee and Promotion Act that permitted profit remittances and repatriation of capital, the economic reforms of former President Alfredo Cristiani created the macroeconomic framework that is fueling the country's current boom.

Reversing the populist policies of the Christian Democrats, who maintained a tenuous hold on the presidency during the tumult of the early and mid-1980s, Cristiani embraced the neo-liberal ideal with gusto. Import duties were slashed and non-tariff barriers virtually eliminated. State-run marketing boards controlling the sugar and coffee crops were dismantled, government price controls were eliminated and the banking sector was completely privatized. Cristiani was also an unabashed free-trader, pursuing commercial pacts with — in addition to neighboring Guatemala, Honduras, and Nicaragua — México, Venezuela, and Colombia.

The policies proved auspicious. Economic growth has remained robust in the face of modest prices for El Salvador's major export, coffee, and drastic electricity shortages caused by drought in the early 1990s. Non-traditional exports are growing at more than 25 percent a year. A growing middle class with higher purchasing power now craves the consumer goods it missed out on under the wartime economy.

Industrial activity by foreigners is concentrated in duty-free zones dedicated largely to drawback production, where companies are exempt from import tariffs and from income taxes for 10 years, renewable for a total of 20 years. Exporters are also entitled to duty-free import of machinery and materials, which can be arranged through government-run "one-stop" windows set up to ease the inevitable red tape.

Despite its dense population, pre-war El Salvador also maintained a healthy agricultural sector that the government is now attempting to steer in non-traditional directions. Aquaculture investments (primarily shrimp farming in the Gulf of Fonseca) is also being encouraged.

El Salvador has little organized trade union activity to speak of (most union leaders were killed off during the right-wing terror campaigns of the early 1980s). Mandatory fringe benefits, such as bonuses, vacation pay, social security contributions, and a required set-aside of severance pay, add 28-30 percent to total payroll costs. The work force of two million is growing at a rate of 100,000 workers a year, many of them coming through new industrial training programs.

El Salvador's caveats are daunting. It will take years of effort to bring the war-ravaged infrastructure up to par with other countries in the region, and in the meantime energy shortages will likely persist and the supply of industrial space will remain tight. Importers have also reported delays processing customs documents, and damage or robbery of goods during the wait is not uncommon.

And for all the talk of their being such an industrious work force, most Salvadorans remain relatively uneducated and require extensive training. With time and patience, however, foreign investors will find that the pro-business climate makes it one of the better stepping stones to doing business in Central America.

El Salvador at a Glance

Population: 5.82 million.

Labor Force: 2 million.

Language: Spanish.

Ethnic Mix: 89 percent Ladino (mixed Spanish and indigenous), 10 percent indigenous, one percent European.

Literacy/Educational Level: 73 percent literacy, but half the work force has, at best, a third-grade education.

Climate: Tropical with May-October rainy season.

Natural Resources: Hydro and geothermal power.

Chief Agricultural Products: Coffee, sugar, cotton, shrimp.

Land Area: 20,720 square kilometers.

Economic Statistics:

GDP: $8.7 billion (1994)

GDP Growth Rate: 5.5 percent (1994)

Per Capita GDP: $1,647

Principal Exports: Coffee, sugar, cotton, shrimp.

Principal Imports: Petroleum products, consumer goods, foodstuffs, machinery, construction materials, fertilizer.

Import Duties: 5-20 percent.

When You Go to El Salvador

Visas: One-time business visitors may enter El Salvador with tourist cards, available for U.S. $10 on arrival at the airport. Those doing regular business in El Salvador or coming to invest should apply for a multiple-entry visa at the nearest Salvadoran consulate before leaving home.

Airlines: Direct flights to San Salvador by American Airlines from Miami; Continental from Houston and Los Angeles; Taca from New Orleans, Miami, New York, and San Francisco.

Hotels

Camino Real

Boulevard Los Heroes, San Salvador.

Well situated, efficient, and long the favorite of business travelers.

Tels: (503) 223-3344, 279-3888. Fax: (503) 223-5660.

Rates start at $110 plus 10 percent tax, corporate rate of $135 plus 10 percent for executive floor.

Presidente

Final Avda. de la Revolución, San Salvador.

Tel: (503) 279-4444. Fax: (503) 279-2020.

Corporate rate of $99 including tax.

Contacts

SALVADORAN FOUNDATION FOR ECONOMIC AND SOCIAL DEVELOPMENT (FUSADES)

Edificio FUSADES, Boulevard y Urbanización Santa Elena, Antiguo Cuscatlán.

Tel: (503) 278-3366, Fax: (503) 278-3356.

FUSADES also has two contact points in the United States at:

Interamericana Center, 396 Alhambra Circle, Suite 602, Coral Gables, Florida, 33134.

Tel: (305) 529-2255, Fax: (305) 529-9449.

500 Fifth Ave., Suite 1850, New York, New York, 10110

Tel: (212) 840-7050, Fax: (212) 840-7106.

COEXPORT

Tel: (503) 224-4019.

Commercial Section, U.S. EMBASSY.

Final Blvd. Santa Elena, Antiguo Cuscatlán, San Salvador.

Tel: (503) 278-4444

U.S. AGENCY FOR INTERNATIONAL DEVELOPMENT

Tel: (503) 298-1666

Commercial Counselor, EMBASSY OF EL SALVADOR

2308 California St. NW, Washington, D.C.

Tel: (202) 265-9671.

Attorneys:

Roberto Romero Pineda and Associates.

Tels: (503) 223-1622, 223-9179, 223-0344, 224-2953.

Piero Rusconi and Benjamín Valdez.

Tels: (503) 223-2493, 279-0163.

Jaime Roberto Vilanova

Tels: (503) 273-2524, 273-4525.

Simultaneous Interpreters:

Frida de Garcia

Tels: (503) 274-7503, 223-0858.

Bert Pacas
Tel: (503) 225-6369.

In case of Illness:

Clinicas Medicas, 21 Calle Poniente 1605, San Salvador. Tel: 225-8325.

GUATEMALA

The most populous country in Central America, Guatemala is at once economically promising and politically troubled. Now bordering the largest economic bloc in the world because of its frontier with Mexico, the country of 10 million people has a solidly pro-business history. At the same time, it is home to Central America's only remaining civil war and is the only country in the region that has breached the constitutional order during the 1990s.

As the Nineties began, Guatemala seemed headed down the right path. After nearly four decades of military rule, the presidential baton was passed from one elected civilian, Vinicio Cerezo Arévalo, to another, Jorge Serrano Elias, for the first time in the country's history. Policy-wise, Serrano immediately began falling in line with the rest of Latin America, stabilizing and liberalizing the economy. Peace talks to end the 33-year-old civil war began, and the macroeconomic outlook, while not exemplary, was healthy.

Not one known for his patience and deference, however, Serrano threw a hatchet into the picture by dissolving congress and the Supreme Court in mid-1993, ostensibly to end corruption. Wildly popular at first, the plan backfired when he lost the support of both the military and the private sector and was forced into exile. Chosen in his place was the country's human right ombudsman, Ramiro de Leon Carpio, an inexperienced and disorganized administrator with no political base.

De Leon managed to hold the country together, but the sort of stability that lures investment was elusive and seemed likely to remain so, at least until presidential elections scheduled for November 1995.

Largely because of its powerful and influential private sector, Guatemala has always been friendly to business interests, in legal terms anyway, a fact that has never changed with the politics of the moment. Foreigners are afforded the same treatment as nationals in most areas, and there are no local participation requirements. Nor are there restrictions on remittances of assets, profits or capital gains.

The barriers that do exist to both trading and investing in Guatemala are largely informal and bureaucratic. A registration and incorporation process that used to take up to nine months has been winnowed considerably with the addition of a "one-stop" window for foreign investors, but delays are still common, especially for those without local contacts.

The customs system continues to be a problem for both importers and investors. Attempts to bring in machinery or inputs under duty-free rules established for exporters are often stymied by customs officials who feign ignorance of the rules or falsely classify the goods as a means of soliciting bribes. Importers will find themselves battling such arbitrary classifications almost constantly, as well as dealing with delays at the borders and corruption from other corners.

Otherwise, importers will find a much more open trade environment than only five years ago. With very few exceptions, duties on capital goods now range between 5 percent and 15 percent, those on consumer goods between 5 percent and 20 percent. A value-added sales tax of 7 percent is also levied on the c.i.f. value of all imports, and legalization of all commercial invoices and bills of lading by Guatemalan consuls abroad is still required. Import licenses have been eliminated for all products except milk, wheat, sugar, flour and some other basic grains.

Corporations in Guatemala are taxed at a flat 25 percent of income, as are profits of branches in the country. Branch profits are also subject to a remittance tax of 12.5 percent. Property taxes total 0.1 percent of net assets to a maximum of 20,000 Guatemalan quetzals (about $3,500).

The main incentives for direct foreign investment are codified in two laws passed in 1989, both intended to promote the production of non-traditional exports. One allows for the creation of export processing zones, with benefits including exemptions from import tariffs for inputs and capital goods and from income taxes for up to 15 years. The two private free zones and one public one, however, have not attracted much investment because free-standing *maquiladoras* are offered the same tax benefits as those within the zones.

Guatemala has been most successful at luring apparel manufacturers under the export incentive programs. The industry, drawn by the large pools of unskilled labor and low wages, has grown from a handful of operators five years ago to more than 300 now. The boom has been so pronounced that labor shortages are beginning to be seen in and around Guatemala City, adding to the existing shortages of managerial and skilled labor.

Labor codes are consistently cited as the most problematic aspect of doing business in Guatemala. Employees are entitled to two annual bonuses, one in July and another at Christmas, equivalent to one month's salary each. After a two-month probationary period, dismissing employees, even with just cause, is difficult and costly. Overall, mandatory benefits add an estimated 62 percent to the employer's average wage costs.

Tourism, one of Guatemala's greatest potentials, has been hampered considerably by political and social events in Guatemala. After rising steadily through the late 1980s and early 90s, even surpassing coffee as the primary foreign exchange earner in 1993, it plunged in 1994 following a series of attacks on tourists by rural Indians who feared local babies were being kidnapped and sold for their organs. Because the industry is so fickle, little direct foreign investment has been steered into tourism despite a number of tax incentives offered through the Guatemalan National Tourism Commission, known as INGUAT.

Guatemala's most productive natural resource has been the low quality crude oil discovered in the northern Petén region. Bahamas-based **Basic Resources International** has been drilling for nearly a decade, despite constant sabotage by guerrillas in the region, and plans a refinery for the Atlantic coast. Exploration concessions are continually being offered, but the solicitation process is protracted and royalty payments are high. By law, all subsurface minerals (including oil) are property of the government, so concessions in these areas are usually in the form of production-sharing contracts.

In agriculture, the production of traditional exports such as coffee, sugar and bananas is dominated by local elites and presents little room for growth. Non-traditional products are another matter. Exports of melons, berries, roses, exotic vegetables and other such products have grown from nothing 10 years ago to a $100 million-a-year business, and is likely to continue the 25 percent-a-year growth of the last several years. The U.S.-based **Chestnut Hill Co.**, for example, is investing $40 million in strawberry production in Guatemala.

Agri-business also represents a healthy market for imported machinery and equipment. While many agricultural products are being shipped out of the country fresh, an increasing number are being frozen and packaged locally. Imports of agricultural machinery grew 16 percent in 1993 to $111 million.

Another area with considerable potential for foreign investors is electrical production. Previously a state monopoly, Guatemala's electrical generation system has been hobbled by shortages and has begun buying power from foreign companies. Demand is growing by 7 percent a year (only a third of the country's residents now have electricity) and the government's antiquated grid cannot cope. Contracts have been signed to purchase power from a dozen foreign companies, one of which is now producing a fifth of the country's operating capacity from a ship off the Pacific Coast.

Guatemala at a Glance

Population: 10.2 million.
Labor Force: 2.6 million.
Languages: Spanish, with 18 Indian dialects (Quiche, Cakchiquel and Kekchi are the most prominent).

Ethnic Mix: About half Ladino (mixed Spanish and Indian) and half Indian, with a very small percentage of people of entirely European ancestry.

Literacy/Educational Levels: 55 percent literacy, with a third of the population having no formal schooling at all and 20 percent completing only primary school.

Climate: Crisp and cool in central highlands, including the Guatemala City region; tropical heat elsewhere. May-October rainy season.

Natural Resources: Crude oil, nickel, tropical hardwoods, fish, chicle.

Chief Agricultural Products: Sugarcane, corn, bananas, coffee, beans, cardamom.

Land Area: 108,430 square kilometers.

Economic Statistics:

> GDP: $12 billion (1994)
>
> Per Capita GDP: $1,163
>
> GDP Growth Rate: 4 percent (1994)

Main Exports: Coffee, sugar, bananas, non-traditional items (including snow peas and baby vegetables), beef.

Main Imports: Fuel and petroleum products, machinery, grain, fertilizers, motor vehicles.

Import Duties: 5-20 percent.

When You Go to Guatemala

Visas: Multiple entry business visas are available for U.S. $10 from the nearest Guatemalan consulate upon presentation of two photographs and a letter (in duplicate) on company letterhead. Tourist visas, available from the airlines or on arrival, are acceptable for short trips where no legal business will be conducted.

Airlines: Direct flights to Guatemala City by American Airlines from Dallas and Miami; United Airlines from Miami and Los Angeles; Continental from Houston and New Orleans; Aviateca Airlines from Houston, Miami, New Orleans and Los Angeles.

Hotels

El Dorado

7a. Avda. 15-45, Zona 9, Guatemala City.

Tel: (502-2) 31-7777, Fax: (502-2) 32-1877.

Direct-dial telephones, business center and close to the airport on the newer side of town. One of two main business hotels in the city.

Corporate rates begin at $95 plus 17 percent tax.

Camino Real

Avda. Reforma y 14 Calle, Zona 10, Guatemala City.

Tel: (502-2) 33-4633, Fax: (502-2) 37-4313.

The second main business hotel, also on the new side of town, with pool and health club, business center and meeting facilities.

Rates start at $140 plus 17 percent tax; corporate rates on request.

Hotel Las Americas

Avda. Las Americas 9-08, Zona 13, Guatemala City.

Tel: (502-2) 39-0676, Fax: (502-2) 39-0690.

The newest in Guatemala City, with business center, direct-dial telephones and meeting facilities.

Rates start at $120 plus 17 percent tax; corporate rates on request.

Radisson Suites Villa Magna.

1a. Avda. 12-46, Zona 10, Guatemala City.

Tel: (502-2) 32-9797, Fax: (502-2) 32-9772, Toll-free from the United States: (800) 333-3333.

Rates beginning at $95. Secretarial services, translations, facsimile and computers.

Contacts

BUSINESS CHAMBER OF GUATEMALA

Edificio Cámaras de Indústrias, Nivel 8, Ruta 6, 9-21, Zona 6, Guatemala City.

Tel: (502-2) 31-6513, 34-6878, Fax: (502-2) 34-6879.

AMERICAN CHAMBER OF COMMERCE

Tel: (502-2) 35-3355, Fax: (502-2) 35-3372.

Commercial Attache, EMBASSY OF GUATEMALA

2220 R Street N.W., Washington, D.C., 20008.
Tel: (202)-745-4952, Ext. 113. Fax: (202) 332-7393.
Commercial Attache, U.S. EMBASSY
Avda. Reforma 7-01, Zona 10, Guatemala City. (Mail: APO Miami 34024).
Tel: (502-2) 34-8479, Fax: (502-2) 31-7373.

In Case of Illness:

Hospital Herrera Llerandi
Tel: 36-6771. Drs. Mario Duarte Flores, Rodolfo Herrera-Llerandi, Carlos Pérez Avedaño.

HONDURAS

The quintessential Latin American technocrat, former Honduran President Rafael Callejas both looks and plays the part. The ascendance of this bespectacled graduate of Mississippi State University to the presidency of Honduras in 1990 marked a sea change for Central America's least developed country. True to form, Callejas immediately set out dismantling a bloated public bureaucracy and unraveling the protectionist policies of the previous two decades.

During Callejas' four-year term, the government lifted restrictions on profit remittances and reduced the heavy tax burden levied on foreign companies operating in Honduras. The young president lobbied hard on behalf of free trade throughout the Americas and followed through at home by lowering import duties and shelving non-tariff barriers. By floating the currency and introducing periodic devaluations, the Callejas government endeared itself to foreign lenders and aid money began pouring in again.

While a boon for foreign investors, the changes ending up costing Callejas' National Party the next election. After an acrimonious 1993 campaign filled with denunciations of the reforms, the opposition Liberal Party was swept into office with Carlos Roberto Reina at its head.

The anti-free market rhetoric of the campaign waned quickly after Reina took office in early 1994, however, and the new president continued down the path of his predecessor. During the first months of his presidency, Reina devalued the currency, cut government spending by 10 percent and announced his intention to sell the military-run telecommunications company, **HONDUTEL.**

Faced with a limited local market, foreign business in Honduras in recent years has been concentrated in the export sector. Honduras has what many consider the best port in Central America, plus four international airports, and it lived in relative political stability while most of its neighbors were at war in recent years.

San Pedro Sula, the country's second-largest city and its business capital, is now ringed with export processing zones (known locally by their acronym, ZIPS) employing more than 30,000 of the 1.4 million-strong Honduran work force. Low development levels require extensive training of local employees, so much of the investment so far has been in simple assembly such as clothing.

Aside from the usual impediments, such as an inefficient legal system and unreliable utilities, the biggest drain on business activity in recent years has been a shortage of foreign exchange. For firms wanting to export to Honduras, it means local importers rarely have the credit needed to make purchases; for foreign manufacturers operating in Honduras, it has led to delays in the remittance of profits abroad. The country's improved standing with international lenders has opened up some lines of credit for local buyers of foreign goods, but only prolonged increases in the country's balance of trade will fully remedy the situation.

There are other business-related hassles in Honduras. Its trade union movement is the strongest in Central America, even within the private sector, and the unions have a history of being quite combative. Corruption is still rampant, and while tariffs on most consumer products are within the 5-20 percent range of the rest of Central America, they are offset by a customs administrative fee of 5 percent and selective taxes on "luxury goods" that are applied to many imports. Other impediments are on the nit picky side. All commercial invoices, for example, must be legalized (for a fee, of course) by Honduran consulates abroad.

With few deal-making advantages to speak of, Honduras goes out of its way with tax breaks and investment guarantees. A 1992 investment law reduced government intervention in the private sector, guaranteed foreigners' ability to ship their profits abroad, mandated equal treatment for foreign and national investors and codified the same sort of tax breaks for exporters being implemented in the other Central American countries.

The bulk of the investment under these rules has migrated toward the ZIPs on and near the Atlantic coast near Puerto Cortez and San Pedro Sula, many of which are private. Operators in the zones — about a third of whom are American, a third Korean, and a third involving some mix of foreign and domestic capital — are allowed duty-free import of all machinery, equipment and supplies.

While corporate tax rates for those outside the ZIPs, whether foreign or domestic corporations, run on a sliding scale from 15 percent to 40 percent, companies inside the zones are exempt from income taxes indefinitely. Exporters of such non-traditional products as shrimp and melons, other areas of considerable growth in recent years, enjoy the same tax holidays for up to 10 years.

Most pre-1992 restrictions on imports, with the exception of those covering a few agricultural products, have been lifted in Honduras. Importers must still register with commercial banks before each batch of merchandise clears customs, but the import registration process of before has been replaced with a relatively straightforward customs declaration.

The distribution network in Honduras also deserves note. Provisions in the agent-distributor law make it very difficult for a foreign manufacturer to end an exclusive relationship with a Honduran distributor or agent without paying the hefty severance and other benefits normally due regular employees. This has resulted in local distributors who operate on a non-exclusive basis, and their inventories are often low, a situation that has forced many retailers to develop networks of wholesalers and brokers in U.S. gateway cities such as Miami and New Orleans from whom they buy directly.

Honduras at a Glance

Population: 5.4 million.

Labor Force: 1.4 million.

Language: Spanish

Ethnic Mix: About 90 percent Ladino (Spanish and Indian), with small percentages of indigenous, African, and European.

Literacy/Educational Levels: 73 percent literacy, with one-third of population having no formal schooling.

Climate: Tropical in lowlands; temperate highlands. May-October rainy season.

Natural Resources: Timber, gold, silver, copper, lead, zinc, iron ore, antimony, coal, fish.

Chief Agricultural Products: Bananas, coffee, timber, beef, citrus fruit, shrimp.

Land Area: 111,890 square kilometers.

Economic Statistics:

> GDP: $3.4 billion (1993)
>
> GDP Per Capita: $630
>
> GDP Growth Rate: Negative 1.9 percent (1994)

Main Exports: Bananas, coffee, shrimp, lobster, minerals, lumber.

Main Imports: Machinery and transport equipment, chemical products, manufactured goods, fuel and oil, foodstuffs.

Import Duties: 5-20 percent.

When You Go to Honduras

Visas: Tourist cards, valid for up to 30 days, are available on arrival at airports and may be used by business travelers as well.

Airlines: Direct flights to Tegucigalpa on American Airlines from Miami; Continental from Houston and Denver; Sahsa from Miami or Houston. To San Pedro Sula on Ibéria from Miami; Lacsa from New York, Los Angeles, Atlanta and New Orleans; American Airlines from Miami; Taca from Miami.

Hotels

Hotel Gran Sula

1 Calle entre 3/4 Avdas., San Pedro Sula.

Tel: (504) 52-9999. Reservations fax: (504) 53-2176. Guest fax: (504) 52-70-00.

Rooms start at $100 plus 7 percent tax.

Hotel y Club Copantl

Colonia Las Mesetas, San Pedro Sula.

Tel: (504) 53-0900. Fax: (504) 57-3890.

Corporate rates start at $85 plus 7 percent tax.

Honduras Maya

Colonia Palmira, Tegucigalpa.

Tel: (504) 32-3191, Fax: (504) 32-7629.

Rates start at $124 plus 7 percent tax; corporate rates on request.

Contacts

FOUNDATION FOR INVESTMENT AND DEVELOPMENT OF EXPORTS (FIDE)

Tel: (504) 32-9345, Fax: (504) 31-1808.

FIDE also has two contact points in the United States at:

Airport Corporate Center, 7200 19th St. N.W., Miami, Florida, 33126. Tel: (305) 592-3166, Fax: (305) 592-3969.

170 Hamilton Ave., Suite 211, White Plains, New York, 10601.

Tel: (914) 761-4233, Fax: (914) 761-4389.

CHAMBER OF COMMERCE AND INDUSTRY of San Pedro Sula

Tel: (504) 53-2490, Fax: (504) 31-1808.

Commercial Attache, U.S. EMBASSY

Tegucigalpa, Tel: (504) 32-3120, Fax: (504) 32-2888.

Commercial Attache, EMBASSY OF HONDURAS

3007 Tilden St. NW, Washington, D.C.

Tel: (202) 966-7702, Fax: (202) 966-7751.

In case of Illness:

Hospital and Clinica Viera
5 Calle, 11 y 12 Avdas., Tegucigalpa, Tel: 37-7136.
Hospital La Policlinica
3 Avda., 7 y 8 Calles, Comayaguela, Tel: 37-3503.
Centro Medico Hondureño
3 Avda., 3 Calle, Barrio La Granja, Comayaguela, Tel: 33-6028.

NICARAGUA

By far the most troubled country in Central America, post-Sandinista Nicaragua is a place for the only the fleetest and most patient of foreign investors. Property rights can be tentative, the union movement can be strong and antagonistic, and the infrastructure is almost medieval.

It's not that the government of President Violeta Chamorro, which took over following a surprise election victory over the Sandinistas in 1990, hasn't tried. Considering what she inherited — a debilitated private sector, rampant hyperinflation and a foreign debt seven times as large as the national GDP — and the tumultuous politics of her tenure, the government deserves some credit.

A holding company formed to sell off more than 350 state companies completed two-thirds of its work in the first two years. Inflation has dropped almost into the single digits, and economic growth climbed back into the black in 1994 for the first time in a decade. A trickle of foreign investment also began, estimated at between $40 million and $50 million total. In addition, Chamorro signed an agreement to unite the country's macroeconomic policies with those of Honduras, El Salvador and Guatemala, reduce tariffs and simplify both the structure of the customs system and trade policies.

The Chamorro government has also virtually rewritten the anti-business laws of the Sandinista government, dramatically improving the legal framework for foreign investors. The 1991 Foreign Investment and

Export Promotion laws allow for free repatriation of capital and profits and guarantee, ostensibly, indemnity in cases of expropriation.

That same year, Nicaragua established the legal framework for duty-free zones, a program that has met with only minimal success, despite 100 percent exemptions from income taxes and duties on most raw material and equipment imports. By the end of 1994, 14 firms — including a subcontractor of **Sara Lee** knit products and a Taiwanese concern assembling apparel for **Sears, J.C. Penney Co.,** and **Kmart** — had set up shop in the state-run Las Mercedes Free Zone near Managua's international airport. Several others were preparing to begin operations in 1995. A second duty-free manufacturing zone, this one privately owned, was under construction at Tipitapa to the east of the airport.

Political instability is one of the main factors keeping people away from an otherwise promising place. The conservative Chamorro's continuing struggle with leftist Sandinistas for control of the army and police, as well as policy wrangling within her own administration, have lent an air of uncertainty to Nicaragua that is likely to remain at least through the 1996 presidential elections.

Day-to-day working conditions can also be tough. The telephone system is abysmal even by Central American standards, and electricity and water services are unreliable. Despite legal guarantees that income generated locally may be freely remitted, foreign exchange shortages are chronic and can delay such transfers considerably.

Preferential access to the U.S. market is more tentative in Nicaragua than it is elsewhere in Central America. Squabbling over payment for property expropriated by the Sandinistas has at times soured relations between the United States and Nicaragua to the point of jeopardizing Nicaragua's trade privileges.

There are, nevertheless, considerable opportunities in Nicaragua. A decade of economic stagnation left the industrial infrastructure decimated and capital that accompanied returning exiles is still being spent to upgrade. The fire sale of government assets, including hotels and resort properties, has added to that demand.

The domestic consumer market is limited because of both size and purchasing power. Tariffs have dropped considerably, but a 5 percent stamp tax is still on the books and duties on imported luxury goods remain high. Import licenses are required, but are said to be easy to obtain.

Nicaragua at a Glance

Population: 4.1 million.
Labor Force: 1.2 million.
Languages: Spanish, Caribbean English on the Caribbean coast.
Ethnic Mix: 69 percent Ladino (mixed Spanish and indigenous); 17 percent European; 9 Caribbean-African; 5 percent indigenous.
Literacy/Educational Level: 57 percent literacy.
Climate: Tropical, May-October rainy season.
Natural Resources: Gold, silver, copper, tungsten, lead, zinc, timber, fish.
Chief Agricultural Products: Coffee, bananas, sugar cane, cotton, dairy and animal products, citrus.
Land Area: 120,254 square kilometers
Economic Statistics:
>   GDP: $1.8 billion (1994)
>   Per Capita GDP: $410
>   GDP Growth Rate: 2 percent (1994)

Main Exports: Coffee, sugar, cotton, bananas, seafood, meat, chemicals.
Main Imports: Petroleum, food, chemicals, machinery, clothing.
Import Duties: 5-20 percent.

When You Go to Nicaragua

Visas Required: Business visitors and tourists need only a passport valid for at least six months and an onward ticket to enter. Entry is granted for 30 days.
Airlines: Direct flights to Managua on American Airlines from Miami; Continental Airlines from Houston; Taca from Miami; Nica Airlines from Miami.
Urban Transportation: Managua, Nicaragua, may be the only national capital in the world without names for its streets. Nicaraguans have

invented a system of giving addresses that makes liberal use of descriptions and proximity to landmarks or sites of former landmarks. They've even created their own directions: *Abajo* (down) for west, *arriba* (up) for east, *al lago* (toward the lake) for north, and *a la montaña* (toward the mountain) for south. It's a system that makes perfect sense to anyone whose ancestry dates back at least 200 years in Managua, and to outsiders it seems quaint and colorful — until they get behind the wheel of an automobile.

That's why renting a vehicle with a driver makes a lot of sense in Managua if you are interested in reaching your appointments on time and getting back to your hotel in time for a good night's sleep. The following agencies can rent you an auto with or without a driver and have locations at the Managua airport as well as the Hotel Intercontinental and in some cases the Camino Real:

Budget. Reservations: (505-2) 66-6226 and 66-7222.

Targa. Reservations: (505-2) 22-4881 and 4882.

Toyota Rent-a-Car. Reservations: (505-2) 66-1010, ext. 210.

In addition, there are private drivers available who can drive a rented vehicle or, in some cases, arrange for a vehicle themselves. Two who have done a lot of work for foreign organizations in Managua and are highly reliable and knowledgeable (although they speak only Spanish) are:

Guillermo Marcia.Tel: (505-2) 78-2699.

Luis López Acuña. Tel: (505-2) 89-7513.

Hotels

Inter-Continental Managua

Tel: (505-2) 28-3530 through 3539. Fax: (505-2) 28-3087. Reservations: (505-2) 28-6991. Rooms $166 and up.

Camino Real

Tel: (505-2) 63-1381 through 1387. Fax: (505-2) 63-1380. Reservations: (505-2) 63-1410. Rooms $115 and up.

Las Mercedes

Tel: (505-2) 63-1011 through 1028. Fax: (505-2) 63-1083. Rooms $55 and up.

Contacts

CENTER OF EXPORTS AND INVESTMENTS

Important place to begin investigation of business possibilities in Nicaragua. Has representatives of Ministry of Economy and Development, the Superior Council of Private Enterprise, the Nicaraguan Investment Financing Co., Association of Private Banks, and the American Chamber of Commerce. Located in Oscar Pérez Cassar building on the highway to Masaya.

Tel: (505-2) 78-3075 through 3079. Fax: (505-2) 78-3129, 78-3087, and 78-3085.

The investment center also has a reliable maildrop in the United States at:

Nicabox 285, PO Box 52-7444, Miami, Florida, 33152-7444.

CORPORATION FOR FREE ZONE.

This organization manages the Las Mercedes duty-free manufacturing zone and will also provide services for the El Aguila duty-free zone when it opens.

Tel: (505-2) 63-1530. Fax: (505-2) 63-1700.

MINISTRY OF ECONOMY AND DEVELOPMENT

General Directorate of Foreign Investments, Alejandro Carrión, director.

Tel: (505-2) 67-0150. Fax: (505-2) 67-0095.

NICARAGUAN INVESTMENT FINANCING CO.

Rodolfo Delgado, director.

Tel: (505-2) 78-5810 through 5815. Fax: (505-2) 78-5800.

CHAMBER OF INDUSTRY

Gilberto Solís, executive secretary.

Tel: (505-2) 66-8847 through 8851. Fax: (505-2) 66-1891.

AMERICAN CHAMBER OF COMMERCE OF NICARAGUA

Susan de Aguerri, executive director.

Tel: (505-2) 67-3099, 67-3633, and 78-1665. Fax: (505-2) 67-3098.

U.S. EMBASSY Commercial Section

Tel: (505-2) 66-2291.

Lawyers (listing here does not constitute endorsement):

Guy José Bendaña - Guerrero and Associates
Tel: (505-2) 66-5696 and 5697. Fax: (505-2) 66-8863.
Buffette Carrión, Morales and Associates
Tel: (505-2) 67-1020.
Buffette Hueck, Manzanarez, Delaney, Ortega and Sanchez
Tel: (505-2) 78-3820 and 3821.
Dr. Rafael Solís Cerda
Tel: (505-2) 22-5419 and 66-8510. Fax: (505-2) 66-8652.

Simultaneous Interpreters:

Carolina Zapata Ruiz
Tel: (505-2) 69-6159.
Jackeline Vargas
Tel: (505-2) 22-2895.
Jackeline Altamirano
Tel: (505-2) 60-1265.
Carolina Navarro (Spanish-French)
Tel: (505-2) 66-7948.
Daniel Rivera
Tel: (505-2) 66-6226.
Carlos Humberto Martínez
Tel: (505-2) 7-2924.

In case of Illness:

Clinica Plaza España
Tels: 66-5852 through 5856.
Clinica Tiscapa
Tels: 67-1425, 78-2561, 78-2683, 78-2798.

PANAMA

Panama of the late 1990s offers foreign investors some of the most interesting opportunities in all of Latin America. Despite its potential and advantages, however, Panama has had little success attracting the attention of North American executives outside the banking industry. A long history of commerce and industriousness has been overshadowed by a recent past checkered with military strongmen and populist economic policies.

As Panama prepares to take over the 50-mile waterway for which it is famous on Dec. 31, 1999, the country is desperately attempting to diversify an economy heavily dependent on services and attract the hard investment needed to help it compete. Tax incentives are being offered in areas such as tourism, and export processing zones are popping up to take advantage of the best infrastructure in the region.

On the whole, Panama is probably the easiest place in the region to do business. Although it is officially a Spanish-speaking nation, English is widely spoken, and the cultural influences of the United States are apparent in everything from consumer purchasing patterns to the prevalence of breakfast business meetings. While the domestic market is, at about 2.6 million, small, its use of the U.S. dollar as legal tender allows easier and less-risky financing options.

Much of the interest of the moment centers on the Colón Free Zone, the world's second-largest with nearly $10 billion a year in goods passing through. With Latin America now one of the hottest markets in the world, North American exporters of all sizes are discovering what Asian entrepreneurs have known since the 1950s, that posting sales staffs and showrooms in Colón is an inexpensive and easy alternative to setting up distribution agents in several countries. Companies in the zone may move goods freely, with no import or export duties, and pay less than half the income taxes of companies outside the zone, 22 percent compared to 46 percent, following a five-year tax holiday.

For the medium to long term, much talk is centered on the status of the old Canal Zone. A government commission is drafting master plans for managing the remaining warehouses, roads, buildings and land that make up the zone, a plan which will likely include selling or leasing portions of the property for manufacturing plants, tourist resorts and other export-oriented industries.

To further attract export-oriented industries, the government offers exemptions from import duties, export sales taxes, production levies and income taxes for such companies. Tourism is also a high priority, but even new tax breaks and a marketing blitz to promote its unspoiled rain forests and gorgeous offshore islands haven't been enough to overcome Panama's reputation and this sector has yet to yield many results.

The tenuous politics of the period after the United States invaded in December 1989 and deposed the former military ruler, Gen. Manuel Antonio Noriega, slowed economic reform efforts in Panama, so it has yet to lower its tariffs on imports in line with those of its Central American neighbors. Duties on items for which the government is trying to encourage local production can run as high as 50 percent, and import licenses are still required for some products — clothing, luggage, soaps, toiletries and 200-odd other items. Legalized consular invoices are required on all incoming shipments.

The 1994 election may have been the turning point for further liberalization efforts. President Ernesto Pérez Balladares, a pro-business millionaire and graduate of Pennsylvania's Wharton School, beat out four other major candidates on a reformist platform and immediately appointed a pro-reform economy minister. Privatization of public utilities is on the table for the first time.

Panama at a Glance

Population: 2.6 million.

Labor Force: 800,000.

Languages: Spanish, English.

Ethnic Mix: 70 percent mestizo; 14 percent West Indian; 10 percent European white, 6 percent indigenous.

Literacy/Educational Levels: 88 percent literacy with generally high level of schooling; 90 percent has at least completed elementary school.

Climate: Tropical, hot, humid, cloudy. Prolonged rainy season from May to January.

Natural Resources: Copper, mahogany forests, shrimp.

Chief Agricultural Products: Bananas, rice, corn, coffee, sugar cane.

Land Area: 75,990 square kilometers

Economic Statistics:

>   GDP: $6.45 billion (1993)

>   GDP Per Capita: $2,500

>   GDP Growth Rate: 6 percent (1993), 5 percent (1994)

Main Exports: Bananas, shrimp, sugar, clothing, coffee.

Main Imports: Capital goods, crude oil, foodstuffs, consumer goods, chemicals.

Import Duties: 5-50 percent.

When You Go to Panama

Visas: Business visas valid for up to one year are available at Panamanian consulates in the United States and other countries. Most occasional business visitors, however, enter on tourist visas available upon arrival.

Airlines: American Airlines from Miami; United Airlines from New York; Aviateca from Los Angeles; Continental from Houston.

Hotels

Westin Caesar Park

Via Israel y 77th Calle, Panama City.

Tel: (507) 26-4077, Fax: (507) 26-0116, Reservations Fax: (507) 26-4262.

A favorite of many foreign visitors, has full line of business facilities; located five minutes from downtown and across from the Atlapa convention center. Rates begin at $135 plus 10 percent tax.

The Executive

Calle Aquilino De La Guardia y 52ndo Calle, Panama City.

Tel: (507) 64-3333, Fax: (507) 69-1944.

Direct dial telephones, in-room computers, business center, presentation facilities. Rates begin at $85 plus 10 percent tax.

Plaza Paitilla
Punta Paitilla, Panama City.
Tel: (507) 69-1122, Fax: (507) 23-1470.
Former Holiday Inn located a mile from downtown in pleasant residential area. Rates start at $78 plus 10 percent tax.

Washington
Avda. del Frente Final, Colón.
Tel: (507) 41-7133. Fax: (507) 41-7397.
A restored art-deco behemoth in Colón near the Atlantic side entrance to the Panama Canal. Rates start at $45 plus 10 percent tax.

Contacts

PANAMA TRADE DEVELOPMENT INSTITUTE
Banco Exterior Building, Floors 3-4, Paitilla.
Tel: (507) 25-7244, Fax: (507) 25-2193.
The TRADE DEVELOPMENT INSTITUTE also has a contact point in the United States at:
1477 South Miami Ave., 2nd Floor, Miami, Florida, 33130.
Tel: (305) 994-8101. Fax: (305) 374-1933.

NATIONAL ASSOCIATION FOR ECONOMIC DEVELOPMENT (ANDE)
This umbrella organization formed by various private enterprise groups promotes trade and foreign investment.
Avda. Cuba y Ecuador #33-A, Edificio Cámara de Comércio e Industria, Panama City.
Tels: (507) 27-1233, 25-4615. Fax: (507) 25-3653.

AUTHORITY OF THE INTEROCEANIC REGION (ARI)
Carlos Mendoza, president.
This new agency, operating from an office in the former Canal Zone, will approve investment projects in the zone, which is now referred to as the "reverted areas" because the United States has handed over control to the government of Panama.
Tels: (507) 32-5411, 32-5565. Fax: (507) 32-6665.

Commercial Section, U.S. EMBASSY
Tel: (507) 27-1777.

In case of Illness:

Clinica San Fernando.
Via España between Calles 66 and 69 Oeste, Las Sabanas.
Tel: 61-6666, 61-3471.
Centro Medico Paitilla.
Avda. Balboa and Calle 52.
Tel: (507) 63-6060, 69-4643.

6

CHILE

Lured by Andes and the Pacific, Marine Biologist Joins Revolution

By Holly Johnson

On a clear morning, landing at Chile's international airport on the outskirts of Santiago is an unforgettable experience. Coming in from the north or the east, the aircraft glides close by the perpetually snow-capped peaks of the Andes, then makes a vertical dive over green, fertile valleys planted with grapes and fruit trees up to the sides of the mountains. Santiago itself, like most of Chile, lies stretched out on the floor of a valley tucked between the Andes and the coastal range.

The airport is a clue to what Chile holds in store for the business traveler. Inaugurated in March 1994 to replace the cramped building from which domestic flights now depart, the international terminal offers the most modern of services, as well as bagels and New England clam chowder at the **Au Bon Pain** deli.

A combination of the ageless beauty seen from the sky and the economic transformation apparent on landing has made Chile appealing to those looking for promising business frontiers, whether they be mining and other corporate giants, portfolio managers, or adventuresome Baby Boom entrepreneurs like Deborah Mogelberg, who came and loved and stayed.

Trained as a marine biologist at the University of California at Berkeley and with experience in restaurant ventures in the San Francisco Bay Area, Mogelberg jumped at an offer to move to Chile in 1984 to oversee what was then a pioneering aquaculture project for South America — scallop farming and exporting. She moved to Pisagua, a tiny fishing village on the edge of the Atacama desert in far northern Chile, and set up a partnership with local seafood processors who held the marine concession for the Pisagua bay.

The arrangement seemed straightforward: her backers in the United States would provide the capital and know how; and the Chilean partners the concession and divers. The unpolluted and productive waters around Pisagua provided the perfect conditions for farming the delicious Chilean scallop, which is similar to the U.S. and Canadian versions. Mogelberg's backers, who financed a laboratory to provide scallop seed, hoped that by using the latest technology, they could take advantage of Chile's natural conditions and lower costs of production to complement the company's other operations.

But the venture didn't function as successfully as Mogelberg and her backers had hoped. She says her local partners' lack of commitment with time and capital was a deterrent to continuing to do business with them. She also had problems with the middle-management, and had mistakenly assumed that working with small-town business people in the middle of nowhere didn't require the same legal and business formalities as anywhere else. "We had never formalized the joint venture, and I didn't have my own legal counsel," she recalled. So, after a few years she sold out to a Chilean conglomerate with major holdings in the mining and fishing sectors.

Lessons for the Future

Even though she abandoned the scallop-farming business, Mogelberg walked away with a love for her adopted country that gave her enthusiasm for finding another novelty business to get into and a handful of lessons that would prove invaluable in her future dealings in Chile. She moved on to set up a successful limousine rental service, which she sold four years later to a banking and tourism conglomerate, and began scouting for a new project, probably in restaurants.

Mogelberg says that there are many pros to doing business in Chile, and that the cons are easily avoided by the careful businessperson. In her experience, the pros include: a highly trainable working class, untapped natural resources and pristine conditions of nature practically unmatched anywhere else in the world, straightforward regulations and minimal bureaucracy; and the chance to create your own opportunity in a robust economy.

The biggest setbacks, she says, are caused by inefficient middle-management or yes-men who fail to do their job or let the boss know when something is going wrong.

"It helps to be a generalist, and be able to cover all aspects of your business or at least recognize problems before they get too big to be solved," she says, adding that "you can't presume that labor is cheap, or that things in general are cheaper here. My experience shows that you aren't necessarily going to save money."

It is also extremely important to have good legal counsel and keep things formal and clear from the beginning. Chilean society is very legalistic, and places a great deal of emphasis on written contracts, notarized signatures, and the like. Gentlemen's agreements between top executives are swiftly formalized by the staff underneath, often behind the scenes.

"Get a good lawyer who can check on everyone you plan to work with," Mogelberg advises. "Don't feel that because Chile is the host country that you don't have to investigate the people you are going to work with."

She kept this in mind when she set up and ran her second business here, and feels it made a difference in both the success of the limousine service and her business relationships. Mogelberg set up the limousine service, called **Executive Cars Limousine Services,** with a Chilean partner who had experience in importing cars. Organizing things in 1988, they wanted to be sure they had a business that would succeed no matter what happened in the national plebiscite held that year. Chileans were to vote on whether to keep Gen. Augusto Pinochet in power for eight more years by marking the "yes" box, or to proceed with a transition to a democratic government by marking the "no" box. The partners thought a victory for the "no" vote could mean increased international exposure and that an upscale transport service would complement the growing luxury hotel market and airline coverage.

The "no" vote did win, and General Pinochet stepped down in early 1990 when the country inaugurated an elected civilian president, Patricio Aylwin. The economy had already been growing under the Pinochet government and continued to do so throughout the surprisingly smooth transition period, allowing the limousine service to benefit from being the first in the market. It was bought out a few years later by a banking group interested in strengthening its presence in the tourism and hotel sector.

Ski Trip Led to Successful Tex-Mex Venture

Mogelberg's verdicts on setting up and doing business are shared by Vern Fry, a Canadian who's lived in Chile for 18 years. He says the upside of working in Chile is that "it is easy to start a business here — if you have a good lawyer." Fry first came to Chile to ski, and ended up staying. His first job was in forestry exports, but eight years ago he got into restaurants.

He started out with a concession to run the mid-mountain snack bar and cafe at La Parva ski area, one hour from downtown Santiago, and then added a trendy Tex-Mex restaurant called **Cafe Santa Fe** that is booked every night of the week. The restaurant business meant swapping the dry powder and blue skies of the Andes ski slopes for the mundane world of leases and liquor licenses.

"It can be pretty bureaucratic," he says, "but if you get all the paperwork together and get the right government stamps, it can be done," adding that "cycles tend to be shorter here, and it is hard to nail things down for longer terms. For example, a five-year lease is a big deal."

It took him between four and five months to set up his restaurant, and another four or five months until it caught on. Fry says the

Cafe Santa Fe, which opened in 1993, came at just the right time. As Chile's international exposure increased with the end of the isolation brought about by 17 years of a military dictatorship, people were turned on to new flavors and trends. And people's spending habits began to change once the economic recovery of the mid-1980's seemed permanent. There was suddenly a demand for fun and exotic things to do at night. Tex-Mex with a friendly bar and imported beer caught on fast.

"Chileans are relaxing more," says Fry. That feeling set him to looking for new ventures to undertake, and during the 1995 summer season he opened another **Cafe Santa Fe** in the Pacific beach resort town Viña del Mar. It proved very popular, especially among Argentine tourists.

Fruit Exporter Tested the Ups and Downs

While Mogelberg and Fry have had the basically good experience of setting up businesses in the flourishing economy of the past decade in Chile, Bill Lewis is with a firm that has been here long enough to have experienced the ups and the downs, and now the ups again. Lewis oversees operations in Chile for **Pandol Bros. Inc.,** of Delano, California, which markets and distributes fruit throughout the United States and the Far East. His is one of many such firms that have made Chile a major exporter of fruit to northern countries, where growing seasons are the reverse of those in Chile. **Pandol** first came to Chile in the 1960's, attracted by optimal fruit growing conditions, but lost money because of changing laws and economic policy. The firm came back in the mid-1970s, and "took on the best legal counsel available," according to Lewis. It also took on a number of farming partners as part of a strategy to line up fruit to market in the United States.

Pandol's operations have grown since then, along with the dynamic impulse of Chile's export sector. **Pandol** expected to write off its first investments here as marketing costs, but instead the initial undertakings developed into solid partnerships with growers and export companies. The Californians helped their partners buy land, securing the loans with contracts for future production. Today the group produces and exports table grapes, raspberries and melon balls for freezing, kiwis and apples and other tree fruits. It sends more than 4 million boxes of Chilean fruit a season to the United States.

Given this successful experience, Lewis recommends working with joint ventures. "Chileans are entrepreneurial, and with the right partners, you can go further than alone. You should use their expertise," he says. There is no need to import a managerial staff, either. "It is expensive, and you can find top notch people here," he says.

Good lawyers are the best contacts for relations with regulators and the government in general, as long as they come from a reputable firm, Lewis says, adding that even a mid-level attorney with some international law expertise is often enough, and it's not always necessary to hire the largest firms. One of the reasons to hire local legal representation is that the legal system, as in most of Latin America, operates under the Napoleonic Code and is completely different from the Common Law-based system in the United States. Lewis says it is important to understand that the burden of proof is on the individual in Chile, which is why even a simple document has to be notarized and paperwork always takes more time than you expect.

Regardless of the legal complications, Lewis, who has been in Chile since 1985, finds doing business in the country to be straightforward. Chileans are friendly on the whole, he says, and "so far we've not had to be involved with bribery." Lewis has had good experiences with all levels of management, but agrees that you have to be on top of things, and follow through. "Don't assume anything."

Business and pleasure can mix in Chile, often in a prelude to the real business at hand. "American executives tend to make the mistake of diving into business and not taking the time to enjoy getting to know the individual," Lewis says. "Here a company is judged by the quality of the individuals working for it, rather than vice versa." But he's also found that there are certain aspects in which Chileans don't mix business and pleasure, such as the matter of punctuality. It isn't a virtue of Chileans in their social lives, but business appointments are usually kept on time. Lewis calls Chileans "the most punctual in Latin America."

Chile Overview

Setting the Pace for Region's Economies

Chile used to mean copper to the outside world, plus a certain politically sophisticated Third-World view that intrigued foreign journalists and intellectuals and discouraged private enterprise, both foreign and domestic. Today, after having tried almost every political current known to the Western world over recent decades, it is the country that has plowed the ground, set the pace, and given birth to innovative concepts for Latin America's swing toward free-market economies. As any visitor can attest, after riding in from the airport past beat-up, smoke-spewing buses and even a horse cart or two, Chile still has many of the contradictions typical of the Third World. But it is working hard to leave that world behind, and with an average economic growth rate of six percent for the past 10 years, it has a good chance of doing so. While some of its neighbors have produced more spectacular economic results in the past two or three years, Chile has held the course the longest and is judged to have the firmest footing.

Many of today's successes are the product of the sweeping transformations made to Chile's economy during the 1980s, although the framework for the economic changes was put together starting in the mid-1970s. Foreign business played an important role in many of these changes. Except for a period of Chile's history from the mid-1960s to the mid-1970s, foreign business has been welcome in the country. During those conflictive years, in which a Marxist, Salvador Allende, was elected President, major foreign holdings in natural resources, mainly copper mines, were expropriated. By 1975, two years after the armed forces under General Pinochet ousted the Allende government, foreign business began investing again. In the 20-year period prior to June 1994, foreign investment brought in more than $10 billion.

Chile is going through a period of consolidation of both its political and economic systems. In March 1994, President Aylwin, the first democratically elected leader to follow General Pinochet, handed over the presidential sash to Eduardo Frei. The new president's father, Eduardo Frei Montalva, led the nation between 1964-70, and was succeeded by Allende. Both Aylwin and the younger Frei were elected with more than 50 percent of the vote, and both are from the Christian Democratic party and were supported by a coalition of center and center-left political parties called the Concertation for Democracy.

The Concertation's electoral platform was based on consolidating economic growth with greater social equity. Frei promised to define a national plan for eradicating extreme poverty and is increasing government resources available for education, health, housing and infrastructure.

The private sector perceives Frei's government as being more pro-business than Aylwin's was, although this has not been proved true in the practice. Both administrations have been keen on allowing the private sector to become involved in areas and industries dominated by the State, and several state-owned companies have been privatized. In large measure, the Concertation governments are continuing to push the economic model imposed by the military government. The model is aggressively export-oriented, and the idea is to move away from purely natural resources into non-traditional exports and those with higher value added. But today, exports are still dominated by copper, fish meal, forestry products and fruit.

Chile's economic model is considered by economists and the international banking community to be one of the purest neo-liberal regimes ever devised The high growth rate of the past 10 years came after a difficult period in the second half of the 1970s when entire industries, such as textiles, failed after protective tariffs were lifted or reduced. Unemployment reached 25-30 percent, and labor unions were first illegal and then strictly limited. Since 1990, the labor code has been modified to give unions more clout, but some tension is mounting between workers and management because further reforms have been slow in coming about.

Growing and More Sophisticated Capital Markets

Chile is putting a lot of faith in its growing capital markets, and the possibilities of incorporating domestic and foreign private savings into the task of leaving the Third World behind. Most workers under contract, which is the case with most people employed in long-term jobs, are required to pay 13 percent of their monthly wages into privately managed pension funds known as AFPs, and these have accumulated more than $20 billion, which is invested in a mixture of instruments, including certificates of deposit, Central Bank and commercial paper, and the stock market. A slight percentage is being invested abroad. New financial instruments will allow these and other private funds to finance such things as housing, public works concessions, and small businesses. Chilean capitalists are also expanding their operations abroad, investing in neighboring countries, including Argentina and Peru. In general, Chile's economy is becoming increasingly globalized.

But not everything is rosy. Both public education and health are undergoing crises of quality and service, and the situation has not improved, even with increased government spending. Bulky, centralized administration is inefficient and costly, and the government is desperately looking for solutions. Some ideas include handing part of the administration over to the private sector.

Despite the current crises, public education and health in Chile do produce good results in many ways. The traditional universities, particularly the University of Chile and the Catholic University, have always been well respected throughout Latin America. More than a dozen private universities have sprung up over the past decade, as well, and Chile produces fine professionals, especially doctors, lawyers, economists, and agronomists. There is adequate technical training as well, and both the government and the private sectors have vowed to invest in it to guarantee the next generation will have the skills and flexibility to confront new technical developments.

Public health statistics, such as infant mortality (14.6 deaths for every 1,000 births) and life expectancy at birth (72.17 years) show that Chile is one of the most advanced nations in Latin America. The

—*An unlikely alliance of General Pinochet and two of his long-time critics, former President Aylwin and President Frei, has built the sturdy foundation of Chile's free-market system.*

crisis in public health has more to do with productivity, and the patients' satisfaction. The waiting time for medical attention in the public clinics can be hours, and elective surgeries have months-long waiting lists.

Private health care is another story, and excellent care is available to those who can pay. There are several private hospitals where most modern procedures can be done. Private clinics and the private practices of well-trained specialists have developed along with the growth of the ISAPRES, private health insurers. These have been institutionalized since 1980, and are now responsible for the health care of almost one-third of Chileans. Another one-third pays into FONASA, the national health fund, which covers care at the public or private facilities. The remaining one-third receives free health care, except for the million or so people covered by the military health system.

Real wages rose by 3.9 percent in 1993, accompanied by increased productivity. National unemployment averaged just 4.6 percent during the same year, but rose to 5.9 percent in 1994. Laborers are becoming scarce for seasonal jobs, such as picking and packing fruit, and wages and benefits for those workers are rising accordingly. Many fruit growers are mechanizing their production to keep ahead of the shortage of unskilled labor.

Employees pay for their own pension plan and disability insurance as well as health insurance, which is deducted from their monthly paychecks. Funds for workers' compensation insurance and rehabilitation are paid by the employer, based on the level of risk the job entails, about 0.9 percent of the worker's salary. Funds are administered by three non-profit workers' compensation organizations. Employees under contract have the right to paid vacations of 15 working days per year. They also receive a severance fee of one month's salary per year of service up to a maximum of 11 months, unless they are fired for non-compliance. Employees on certified sick leave cannot be fired, nor can women making use of maternity leave. The health insurers, either FONASA or an ISAPRE, pay the worker's salary during sick leave, and the national health system pays for maternity leave.

Women are eligible for maternity leave for 42 days before the expected date of delivery, and 84 days after the birth. They are also eligible to take leave in the case of serious illness of a child under one year of age or adoption of a child under six months old. New mothers may also take two breaks during the day to breastfeed their babies, and may not be fired during the first full year after returning to work.

Any company that employs more than 19 women must provide childcare or reimburse childcare expenses. The work week may be up to 48 hours long, and overtime must be paid extra, with a 50 percent surcharge. The minimum wage is about $125 per month, but the percentage of the workforce that earns only minimum wage is shrinking.

Few Restrictions on Foreign Investment

Chile's foreign investment statute, Decree Law 600, known as DL600, guarantees non-discriminatory treatment to foreigners, and the right to remit profits immediately, once tax obligations have been met. Capital may be repatriated one year after the date of entry. Investments must be approved by the Foreign Investment Committee. Small investments, meaning less than $5 million, require just a 30-day waiting period and approval by the head of the committee.

There are few restrictions on direct foreign investment. Large investments and those in public utilities and mass communications must be approved by the entire ministerial committee. Majority national control has been required in those sectors as well as in fishing, shipping and hydrocarbons, but such restrictions are being done away with in practice. There are some regional incentives for investment available, and foreign investments for more than $50 million have unlimited access to local credit.

DL600 allows the investor to choose to lock in a fixed tax rate of 42 percent for 10 years or be taxed at the same rate as Chilean companies, 15 percent, with an additional tax of 35 percent on remitted profits and dividends. In both the foreign investor rate and the domestic rate, companies pre-pay a 15 percent withholding tax on a monthly basis, which is used as credit toward the total effective rate.

Investors not wishing to make their investments under DL600, which gives the protection of a contract with the State, can bring in capital under the Central Bank's foreign exchange regulations, Chapter 14, which currently has the same rules on profit remittance and capital repatriation as DL600.

Companies from the United States and Canada operating in Chile are too numerous to name, but a short list of the most recent direct investors includes: **Gerber Foods, BellSouth, Southwestern Bell, Ralston Purina, Placer Dome,** and **J.C . Penney.**

Chile provides more than adequate business conditions for foreign business. Telecommunications are excellent; the **Chilean Telephone Company,** the main local carrier, was the first in South America to totally digitalize the network, and as of September 1994 half a dozen long-distance companies began to compete under Latin America's first multi-carrier service. Fax, telex and data-transmission services are widely available in Santiago, and available on a limited basis in other large cities. Cellular telephones can be used from La Serena in the north to Puerto Montt in the south, and rentals are easily obtained.

The national postal system isn't always reliable or fast, but there are private postal services, and all major international courier services have operations in Chile. The network of ports and highways gives relatively easy access to most of the country. Land transport between the more important cities and towns is fluid and frequent.

Growth Puts Pressure on Ports

There are 13 major ports, most of which are owned and run by Emporchi, the state port authority. Because of the country's rapid economic growth, the ports are generally crowded, and delays are common. The U.S. Embassy recommends that exporters to Chile use appropriate weatherproof and pilferage-proof containers.

Emporchi is considering allowing the private sector to invest in state-owned ports in an effort to enlarge them and improve conditions. Several ports have already been developed by the private sector, mostly in response to specific projects, such as one in Corral, in the forestry district, or Puerto Ventanas, developed by **Chilgener,** a thermal-electrical firm. Some private ports are opening up for commercial cargo as well, in competition with Emporchi. More than $300 million will be spent on ports between now and the year 2000, with $200 million to be spent by the private sector. Investors are toying with the idea of establishing dry ports to ease congestion and reduce delays at the most troubled ports, particularly San Antonio and Valparaiso, which are still rebuilding from damage caused by the 1985 earthquake.

Santiago is the main distribution center by far, as more than one-third of the country's population lives in the greater Santiago area. But Concepción, the second largest city and hub for the growing petrochemical, forestry, fishing and metal-working industries, is taking on increased importance.

There are two free trade zones, the ZOFRI at Iquique in the far north, and PARANEZON at Punta Arenas in the far south. They are reputed to have relatively low labor costs, and good quality production.

Chile's industrial property law, passed in 1989, gives 15 years' protection to industrial patents. Despite being one of the region's most advanced laws, it is considered insufficient by the U.S. Trade Representative because it does not provide pipeline protection for pharmaceutical products with patents filed before the law came into force, and because of other shortcomings regarding foreign pharmaceutical patents. The copyright law protects copyrights for 50 years, but there is considerable piracy, especially for computer software.

The Central Bank sets the official, or *acuerdo,* exchange rate for the peso by a complicated calculation based on a basket of currencies, including the dollar, yen and mark. The official market rate is allowed to move within a range of 10 percent above or below the set rate. The Central Bank can step in to buy or sell dollars when it perceives the dollar-peso rate will move out of the band. During 1994, the average dollar/peso exchange rate was US$1 = 420 pesos. But after taking inflation into account, the peso has been appreciating relative to the dollar for the past few years, sparking complaints by Chilean exporters. Currency traders say the Central Bank, trying to prevent appreciation, bought more than $1 billion in U.S. currency in 1994, but the strong economy and inflow of investment money continued to put pressure on the exchange rate in 1995.

There are no restrictions on the amount of foreign or domestic currency that may be taken in or out of the country. The Central Bank does, however, require a 30 percent cash reserve requirement, known in Spanish as *encaje,* on foreign credits to keep a leash on "hot money" coming in because of the high local interest rates. Banks charge their best business borrowers about 6.25 percent a year above the inflation rate.

Imports Get Largely Uniform Treatment

Imports are levied a flat 11 percent duty on CIF value, with relatively few exceptions. Imports from a handful of other Latin American countries pay less in some cases. Free trade agreements with Mexico, Venezuela, and Colombia are in force, scheduling zero duties for the end of the century, and there are more narrow agreements with Bolivia and Argentina. About two dozen luxury products, including whiskey, fine jewels, and cars with engines larger than 1500cc, are hit with an additional surcharge, ranging from around 15 percent to 70 percent. There are also non-tariff barriers in place to protect the domestic production of wheat, wheat flour, sugar and vegetable oils. An additional surcharge is made if the import price falls below a pre-set price band.

Duties can be deferred on imports of capital goods if the production is for export, and reduced by the percentage of production actually exported. Imported goods are then subjected to the same value-added-tax, or VAT, as domestically produced items. The VAT is currently set at 18 percent of the CIF value plus the 11 percent duty. Those importing items for more than $3,000 must obtain a registration certificate within 120 days prior to shipment. The certificate is issued by the Central Bank, a commercial bank, or the Chilean Copper Commission, in the case of copper imports. The registration process takes five days. Importers need the certificate in order to access the official foreign exchange market.

Imports take two days to clear customs, but can be pre-cleared by a customs broker by presenting four copies of the commercial invoice, two copies of the bill of lading and the insurance receipt, if insured. Imports can remain just 90 days in customs warehouses. The original copy of a health clearance from the country of origin is obligatory for live animals and foodstuffs. Temporary import permits are available for exhibits and demonstrations, and temporary export permits are available to allow the re-entry, duty-free, of imported goods shipped back to the foreign supplier for replacement or repairs. Imported goods must show the country of origin on the label and require Spanish-language labels before being sold for consumption, although they can be relabeled in Chile.

The U.S. Commerce Department can provide to U.S. firms wishing to export to Chile a list of interested agents and distributors through its Agent/Distribution Service and can identify potential representatives through its Comparison Shopping Service.

What's Coming?

Chile's economy is clearly taking on new directions, and will present an entirely different picture by the turn of the century. One development that will affect U.S. and Canadian business people is the incorporation of Chile into the North American Free Trade Agreement, NAFTA.

President Clinton has announced several times that Chile is the next country in line for a free trade agreement with the United States. Both U.S. Trade Representative Mickey Kantor and the Secretary of Commerce, Ron Brown, have made official visits to the country. The currency and reserve crisis that hit Mexico, the third country already in NAFTA, at the end of 1994 raised some concerns that Chile's membership might be delayed, although officials of the Clinton Administration said negotiations would proceed on schedule in 1995.

The FTA isn't expected to increase trade between Chile and the United States by much, but the American Chamber of Commerce in Chile, AMCHAM, estimates that an FTA would save U.S. exporters more than $200 million in tariffs and could increase total U.S. exports to Chile by nearly one-fourth. The United States exported almost $2.5 billion worth of goods to Chile in 1993. SOFOFA, the manufacturers' association, estimates that Chile's exports to the United States would probably increase only a quarter of a percent over the $1.7 billion worth exported there in 1993, but another study predicts that Chile's exports to the entire three-country NAFTA region would rise almost 13 percent over the long term.

But an FTA would help Chile's economy by serving as a stamp of approval, which could strengthen foreign investment in Chile. It will also protect Chilean products from future protectionist measures in the United States.

Whatever the outcome of the trade negotiations, Chile's economic potential represents real opportunities for foreign businesses. Some of the fastest growing sectors of the economy, and those which could be the best bets for North American suppliers are: telecommunications, as companies upgrade services and provide new ones, such as satellite links and data transmission; aviation, as air travel and cargo shipments increase; computers and software, as personal income increases and business takes on a more modern appearance; and pollution control equipment, as environmental standards are raised and the government goes ahead with plans to invest more than $2 billion for such equipment by 1997.

Infrastructure Needs Offer Opportunities

Infrastructure could be the largest single industrial sector to pose new opportunities for both suppliers and those interested in setting up operations in the country. The Public Works ministry has approved eight new highways to be built under private concessions by 1996 at a cost estimated at more than $600 million. A $1.2 billion gas pipeline from Argentina will need pipeline engineering and management services, as well as equipment. There are major investments to be made in ports and ports services, as well as in railways, where **Ferrocarriles del Estado,** the state-owned railway company, is spinning off its cargo line for privatization.

The planned investments in public works are meant to address transportation shortcomings that could become a bottleneck for Chilean development in the next few years. For instance, 80 percent of domestic cargo moves by truck, and the highway network is rapidly deteriorating. Only half of the basic road system, the 56,000 kilometers where 90 percent of traffic is concentrated, is paved. The Congress passed a law in 1993 allowing private companies to bid for what are called "Build, Operate and Transfer" (BOT) concessions for major public works projects. Over the next 25 years, the private sector could invest about $3.5 billion to finance new projects and operate some 10,000 kilometers of new or improved roads. There are no restrictions on foreign participation in the tenders.

The Health Ministry is working to improve infrastructure in its existing hospitals, and is building four new hospitals in the Santiago area alone. And private-sector building, while growing less rapidly than during the boom years of 1992 and 1993, still requires imported building products and machinery and equipment.

Franchising has already proved to be a successful way for foreign companies to get into the Chilean economy. Over the past five or six years, Santiago and other major cities have been practically invaded by U.S.-based fast food chains, including **McDonald's, Pizza Hut, Burger King, Kentucky Fried Chicken, Domino's Pizza,** and **Taco Bell. Au Bon Pain, Arby's** and **Chuck E Cheese's** are the latest to arrive. Clothing stores such as **Esprit** and **Benetton** have been around a little longer, and are equally successful. Mini-markets and fitness centers seem to be the next wave of franchises. It is important to note that royalty contracts must be approved by the Central Bank, and can only be expressed as a percentage of sales.

The U.S. Embassy in Santiago rates Chile as very receptive to U.S. products and services. The same can be said for several other supplier countries, particularly Canada, Japan, and much of western Europe. Chile's economy is bound to continue growing at a pace of 5-6 percent a year through the end of the century, and Chileans have already proved that they are hungry for goods and services from abroad.

Chile at a Glance

Population: 13.25 million (1992 census), of whom nearly 40 percent reside in Greater Santiago.

Labor force: 5.24 million.

Language: Spanish.

Ethnic mix: Most of the population is considered mestizo, a mix of European with indigenous races. However, Chile's population is relatively more homogeneous, at least on the surface, than most other Latin American countries; only about one million people claimed to be of an indigenous race in the 1992 census.

Literacy/Educational levels: 93.4 percent literacy (1992); 98 percent enrollment rate for primary school.

Climate and best times to visit: Chile's climate is temperate, with marked seasons, especially in the central part of the country where Santiago is located. The far south is very rainy, and the far north is very dry. The best time to visit is Spring and early Summer, September through December.

Natural resources/Chief agricultural products: Copper and other metals, forestry products, pelagic fish for fish meal, and agricultural products: most fruits (except tropical), wheat, corn and barley, legumes and other vegetables.

Land area: 2,006,626 square kilometers.

Economic statistics:

>   GDP: $52.153 billion (1994)
>   Per Capita GDP: $3,950
>   GDP Growth Rate: 4.2 percent (1994)

Main exports: Copper, fruit, forestry products, fish meal and salmon (fresh and frozen).

Main imports: Capital goods, including mining and other heavy equipment, computers, building products, construction equipment.

Duties on imports: In most cases, 11 percent on CIF value.

Repatriation of profits: May be repatriated immediately once tax obligations are met. Foreign investment made under Decree Law 600, the foreign investment statute can choose between a fixed tax rate for 10 years of 42 percent or the regular Chilean tax rate, 15 percent plus 35 percent on repatriated profits and dividends. Capital may be repatriated one year after date of entry.

When You Go to Chile

Visas: Travelers from most countries may enter the country without a visa, using the tourist card handed out on the plane. The card is good for 90 days, and may be renewed once. It must be presented upon leaving the country, so don't lose it. It does not allow the traveler to work or engage in commerce. If business travelers plan to do business while in the country, they should obtain a business visa from the Chilean Consulate in their area.

Airlines: From Miami, the U.S. flag carriers United and American fly direct to Santiago, or with stops in Buenos Aires. The two principal Chilean carriers, LanChile and Ladeco, which are competitive with the U.S. lines in schedules, prices and service, also fly from Miami, direct or with stops in Lima or Buenos Aires. Lan Chile also has a flight twice a week from Los Angeles, with stops in Mexico City and Lima. Most major European lines also fly to Chile, mainly with stops in Brazil.

Urban Transportation:
- Most hotels offer airport pick-up, otherwise there are taxis waiting. The fare into downtown Santiago runs about $25.
- There are also minivans that can be reserved ahead of time and cost about $15. Two minivan services are: Navett, tel: (562) 695-6868, fax: 672-2645; Transfer, tel: (562) 204-5840.
- There is a bus that takes you downtown for the equivalent of $6.
- Executive Cars Limousines Service, Avda. Vitacura 2937, Tel: (562) 232-2780, provides limousine service from the airport or for traveling around the city.
- The main international auto agencies have offices at the airport.

Hotels

NOTE: The number and quality of hotels in Santiago has increased substantially over the past five years. There are nearly a dozen four and five-star quality places of lodging, but business people still seem to favor the international chains and a traditional Chilean-owned hotel downtown. All of them have business centers, minibars in the rooms, restaurants, swimming pools, spas and excellent service at the front desk. All add an 18 percent tax to the bill and offer corporate discounts.

Holiday Inn Crowne Plaza
Located on the Alameda Bernardo O'Higgins on the eastern edge of downtown Santiago.
Tel: (562) 638-1042. Fax: 633-6015.
Rates start at $180.

Hyatt Regency Santiago
Located uptown near residential and shopping areas as well as the new office towers.
Tel: (562) 218-1234. Fax: 218-2513.
Rates start at $265.

Hotel Plaza San Francisco Kempinski
Also downtown on the Avenida Bernardo O'Higgins.
Tel: (562) 639-3832. Fax: 639-7826.
Rates start at $210.

Hotel Sheraton San Cristóbal
Located across the river from downtown.
Tel: (562) 233-5000. Fax: 234-1729.
Rates start at $240.

Hotel Carrera
Old favorite facing plaza across from presidential palace and ministries.
Tel: (562) 698-2011. Fax: 696-5926.
Rates start at $160.

Contacts

Governmental:

U.S. EMBASSY Commercial Section
Avda. Andrés Bello 2800
Tel: (562) 330-3316, fax: 330-3172.
Mail from United States: US and FCS
                        AMEMBASSY Santiago
                        Unit 4111, APO AA 34033
FOREIGN INVESTMENT COMMITTEE
Teatinos 120, 10th floor
Tel: (562) 698-4254, fax: 699-1025.
Eduardo Moyano, executive vice president.
Registers and approves all investment made under the foreign investment statute, DL600. It works as a liaison between the potential investor and other government agencies and promotes Chile abroad.
PROCHILE
Avda. Bernardo O'Higgins 1315, 2nd floor
Tel: (562) 696-0043, fax: 696-0639.
Contact: Carlos Mladinic, director.
The Foreign Ministry's trade promotion arm.
FUNDACIÓN CHILE
Avda. Parque Antonio Rabat 6165, Las Condes
Tel: (562) 218-5211, fax: 242-6900.
Anthony Wylie, director
A non-profit agency dedicated to the transfer of technology to Chile and its use in the promotion of business startups.
MINISTRY OF PUBLIC WORKS (Ministerio de Obras Públicas)
Oficina de Partes, Dirección General de Obras Públicas
Morandé 59
Tel: (562) 671-0854, fax: 672-6609.
Handles public works concessions.
Contact: Carlos Cruz, coordinator of concessions

Business Organizations:

SOCIEDAD FOMENTO FABRIL (SOFOFA)
Andrés Bello 2825, Providencia
Tel: (562) 203-3100, fax: 203-3101.
Manufacturers' association and lobby group
Contact: Pedro Lizana, president

CONFEDERACIÓN DE PRODUCCIÓN Y DEL COMERCIO (COPROCO)
Mons. Nuncio S. Sanz de Villaba 182
Tel: (562) 231-9764, fax: 231-9808.
Business association and lobbying group
Contact: José Antonio Guzman, president

AMERICAN CHAMBER OF COMMERCE
Americo Vespucio Sur 80, 9th floor, Las Condes
Tel: (562) 208-4140, fax: 206-0911.
Contacts: Claudio Garcia, president; María Isabel Jaramillo, general manager

CHILEAN-BRITISH CHAMBER OF COMMERCE
Suécia 155-C, Providencia.
Tel: (562) 231-4366, fax: 231-8211.
Contact: David Turner, president; Paulina Carvajal, general manager

CHILEAN-CANADIAN CHAMBER OF COMMERCE
El Retiro 4892.
Tel: (562) 228-7563, fax: 219-2551.
Contact: Jorge Carey, president

Lawyers:

Law firms handling a lot of international business include the following, whose listing here does not constitute a recommendation:

Claro y Compañia
Avda. Gertrudis Echeñique 30, 13th floor, Las Condes

Tel: (562) 206-1230, fax: 206-0658.
Contact: Cristián Eyzaguirre, administrative manager
Carey y Compañia
Miraflores 222, 24th floor.
Tel: (562) 639-3801, fax: 633-1980.
Contact: Claudia Blanche, administrative manager
Cruzat, Ortuzar y Mackenna, Abogados
Miraflores 222, 19th floor.
Tel: (562) 632-3686 fax: 633-8011
Contact: León Larraín, partner
Arturo Alessandri, Estudio
Amunátegui 277, 8th floor.
Tel: (562) 696-5185, fax: 672-6263.
Contact: Blanca Molina, administrative manager
Guerrero, Olivos, Novoa y Errázuriz
Augustinas 1350, 2nd floor.
Tel: (562) 698-5860, fax: 698-4197.
Contact: Hernán Felipe Errázuriz, partner

Accountants and Market Consultants:

Adimark Ltda
Luis Thayer Ojeda 1106, Providencia
Tel: (562) 698-1972, fax: 699-3634.
Contact: Veronica Edwards, general manager
Langton Clarke (Coopers & Lybrand)
Huérfanos 812, 5th floor
Tel: (562) 638-1320, fax: 638-2850.
Contact: Vivian Clarke, managing partner, Diego Valdes, partner
Search Marketing
Avda. Bilbao 2841
Tel: (562) 204-5103, fax: 204-7466.
Contact: Juan Carlos Sanjul, general manager

Price Waterhouse
Huérfanos 863, 2nd floor.
Tel: (562) 638-1320, fax: 633-3329.
Contact: Luis Carlos Costa and Steven Bartley, partners

Useful Publications:

Guia Silber is an indispensable listing of government offices, businesses, business and professional groups, and political organizations, including names and telephone numbers. Issued twice a year, it can be obtained
by mail or in person from: Silber Editores Ltda, Pérez Valenzuela 1520,
Oficina 401, Providencia, Tel/Fax: (562) 235-0662. Price: $70 for one
copy by airmail, or $120 for a year's subscription of two issues.

Potentially Useful: Santiago hosts a number of trade fairs that have
become regional fairs, providing the business person an important
opportunity to reach a numerous public. The most important are:
● FIDAE (Every even-numbered year in March) - Air and space,
  moving away from mostly military to civil aviation and airports.
● Expomin (May) - mining.
● Exposalud (May) - health industry.
● Softel (July) - computers and data processing.
● Expoagro (September) - agribusiness.
● FISA (October) - general.
● Hotelga-Alimenta - food services, hotels.

In case of illness:
Most hotels have doctors on call, but here are two English-speaking
doctors who are highly regarded:

Dr. Ricardo Gacitua, internist
Apoquindo 3990, Of. 609
Tel: 207-0561.

Dr. Juan Vargas, gynecologist
Apoquindo 3990, Of 308,
Tel: 207-0325
or Miguel Claro 373
Tel: 235-8401.

7

COLOMBIA

Trading Swedish Style for Colombian

By Ruth Sánchez and Steven Gutkin

After setting up his own business selling air-purifying systems in Bogotá, Colombia, Jan Marklund is not without regrets. He spent hundreds of thousands of dollars purchasing a building, furniture and computers when he could have rented. He gave customers long-term credit with low interest rates when he could have asked for cash. He imported merchandise from the United States by ship when airplanes could have saved valuable time. As a result, he tied up much of the capital needed to run his new operation. Yet despite these mistakes, Marklund expected to turn a profit of $65,000 during his first 12 months in business. If you know the right people and you have the right product, says this tall, fair-skinned Swede, you can't go wrong in Colombia.

In April 1994, Marklund became the exclusive distributor in Colombia for **Health-Mor Co.,** a firm based in Cleveland, Ohio, that manufactures an air-purifier called Princess. The product, which doubles as a dust-free vacuum cleaner, is not for everyone. At $1,300, it appeals to affluent people who have qualms about breathing Colombia's increasingly polluted air. It's the only machine of its kind in the country. Working together with his Colombian wife, Amparo, and 50 local employees, Jan planned to sell 1,500 Princess machines during the company's first year. By the second year, the sales goal is 10,000 machines. The company has also begun to sell an industrial version of the Princess and a sophisticated electronic horse-grooming system.

Being a Swede in Bogotá has its advantages. "People trust foreigners more," Marklund explained. "The doors are wide open." When his employees want to get something done — such as obtaining a new telephone line or a meeting with a company president — they invariably mention his Swedish-sounding name. Even errands as seemingly simple as reserving a hotel room, he says, are easier when conducted in his Scandinavian-accented Spanish. Yet he admits that compared to Stockholm, Bogotá may as well be Mars. In Colombia, it's the personal touch — the lunches, the impromptu office chats, the cocktails at a local tavern — that makes the difference.

"You have to have good contacts here," he explains. "If you don't, you're out."

A member of the American Society and the Bogotá Country Club, Jan says he was able to obtain a $420,000-loan from **Lloyds** bank because he likes to play golf. Every Saturday morning he and 10 other businessmen hit the country club's lush golf course and then retire to the bar to discuss deals. That's how he met the president of **Lloyds** Colombian subsidiary — the **Banco Anglo-Colombiano** —who recognized the potential of the Princess machines. The golf course is also where he met the president of his insurance company, Seguros Andino, and the director of the Colombian-American Chamber of Commerce, Joseph Finnin, who helped guide him through the process of starting a business.

"If you live the Swedish style — arriving at the office at seven in the morning and going straight home at five — I don't think you would succeed here," Jan says.

A construction engineer by trade, Marklund came to Colombia in 1987 as the managing director of **Electrolux A.B.,** the Swedish vacuum maker. During his initial years in the country, Colombia was still very much a closed economy, based on a traditional Third World import substitution model. Most imports were prohibited outright. The few items that could come in paid tariffs starting at 40 percent. Foreign investment was seen as a threat.

Things began to change by the late Eighties. The government initiated an economic liberalization program similar to those sweeping through the rest of Latin America. In Colombia there was a fundamental difference, however. The other countries, plagued by hyperinflation and crushing debt burdens, were more or less forced to free their economies of excessive protectionism and state bureaucracy. Colombia, which avoided the debt crisis of the 1980s, did so by choice. Unlike their counterparts almost everywhere else on the continent, the country's conservative economic managers had no catastrophes with which to contend. The economy was stable, vital and relatively well-diversified. Yet the leaders concluded that growth could be sustained only by joining the regional movement toward free-trade and outward looking economies.

Colombia was the only country in Latin America to post a steady growth rate during the past two decades, always avoiding wild fluctuations in its exchange and inflation rates. The country's economic opening program - begun by President Virgilio Barco and expanded by his successors, Cesar Gaviria and Ernesto Samper - vastly reduced import tariffs and eliminated obstacles to foreign investment. For Jan Marklund, who knew the Colombian market and had access to new products abroad, this meant opportunity.

It was when **Electrolux** wanted Marklund to accept a transfer back to Sweden, from which he was to travel regularly to Latin America, that he decided to resign and make his own opportunity with the Princess. A former colleague at **Electrolux,** who had taken a job as the general manager of **Health-Mor** in Mexico, told Marklund about Princess' potential in Colombia. The company was selling machines in 45 countries, though it owned its own franchise only in Mexico.

Economy Finally Opened to Foreigners

By then, 1992, the rules of the game in Colombia were largely the same for foreigners as they were for locals. With few exceptions, virtually all sectors of the economy were open to foreigners. Restrictions on remitting profits abroad were eliminated. There was no longer any requirement to export products abroad, or to use a certain percentage of domestic raw materials in production. Import red tape was vastly reduced. Marklund resigned from **Electrolux** at the end of 1992 and spent the next year preparing to sell Princess air purifiers in Bogotá.

Like most people starting a business, Marklund needed money. In March 1993 he found the man he believed would finance his project: Jaime Gilinski, one of Colombia's most renowned and wealthiest industrialists. Based in the southwestern city of Cali, the Gilinski family manufactures more than two dozen products, including steel wool, crackers, leather and coffee. It recently purchased Colombia's second largest bank, the **Banco de Colombia.** Jaime took an immediate interest in Marklund's Princess idea, and offered to put up the cash. First, he wanted to check out the credentials, talent, and even the personal life of this soft-spoken Swede with a Colombian wife.

"He invited me out to breakfast at least 20 times," recalls Marklund, who was struck by Gilinski's energy and persistence. "He was a real tiger." The two men spent an afternoon enjoying a sauna together at a five-star hotel in Bogotá's plush northern sector. Gilinski even showed up unannounced at Marklund's home one evening. "He wanted to see what my apartment looked like and meet my wife," Jan says. Eventually, Gilinski had a change of heart. He decided Jan was not the man to run Princess sales in Colombia and proceeded to hire a friend from Cali to take charge. He sent the friend to Puerto Rico for a course on direct sales. Jan saw his dream slipping out of his hands.

Marklund said Gilinski traveled to Cleveland to make a deal with **Health-Mor,** offering to buy 250 machines for $100,000 and proposing to pay in 90 days without a letter of credit. "We don't do business like that," the **Health-Mor** executive reportedly told him. The deal fell through and Marklund's prospects revived.

He put together a financial proposal and delivered it to his golfing friend at the **Banco Anglo Colombiano.** When the loan was approved, he hired a lawyer to register the business legally. That process took two weeks and cost less than $200, including the legal fees. Given the government's interest in promoting foreign investment, Jan says it's easy to do things by the book. "I'm trying to be legal, legal, legal," he says.

When necessary, though, Marklund is willing to play hardball. Since his business does only direct sales — nothing is sold to stores for resale — Marklund knew he needed a seasoned expert to run the sales department. He set out to get the sales manager of his former employer, **Electrolux.** To convince the man to quit his job and join the Princess experiment, Marklund paid him a one-time bonus of $62,500.

Learning About Interest Rates the Hard Way

Marklund learned the hard way to avoid tying up capital and merchandise in a country with interest rates that reach 50 percent a year. His first shipment of 600 Princess air purifiers took a month and a half to arrive. Jan had them sent by train to Miami, from where they were taken by ship to the Colombian coastal city of Cartagena. A friend told him Cartagena was a better destination than the nearby town of Barranquilla, whose port was supposedly plagued by robbery and corruption. But there was a problem. Colombian law doesn't allow merchandise to be flown out of Cartagena. So Marklund had to truck the 600 machines to Barranquilla anyway, from where they were flown to Bogotá. On the second shipment, the machines were shipped directly to Barranquilla from Miami.

Now, Marklund has given up ships completely. Although freight costs are somewhat higher, he airlifts the merchandise directly from Cleveland to Bogotá through a private airline called **Stair Cargo,** which obtains the necessary import licenses and pays the 20 percent import duty. In the end, shipping 30 to 50 machines at a time by plane has saved Marklund money.

Marklund has also decided to end what is considered cheap, long-term credit in Colombia. In his first few months in business, he allowed customers to pay off the machines in 18 months at 2.5 percent interest per month. Now, there's a maximum of 12 months at 3.8 percent interest per month.

Making some mistakes is to be expected when starting a business in Colombia. But Marklund insists most can be avoided by talking to the right people. He suggests getting a good lawyer, a good banker, and having close contacts with other foreign investors who've been through the trial-and-error process. Another important contact is **Coinvertir,** a joint private-public organization that provides advice and guidance to foreign investors.

And what about the supposed robberies in Barranquilla and other security risks in Colombia? The country still hosts the world's most powerful and violent drug mafia, as well as the oldest remaining Marxist insurgency in the Western Hemisphere. If you're not willing to subject yourself to a certain amount of risk, Colombia is not the place for you. In addition to the drug and guerrilla problems, common crimes such as burglary, muggings, kidnappings and street murders have skyrocketed in recent years. However, most foreigners in Colombia do not live in fear. Life in Bogotá is very similar to life in any other major metropolitan area. Jan Marklund says he's never had a security problem during his seven years in the country. He does, however, have a rifle-toting guard standing outside his north Bogotá headquarters. "Most companies treat the security issue as just another business cost," says Armando Vegalara, the director of **Coinvertir.**

Colombia's economic opening — known as *la apertura* — has had its share of winners and losers. To succeed, it's important to carve out a solid market niche with a convincing product. Marklund says **Electrolux**'s sales have plummeted in recent years because of cheaper vacuums from Asia. Princess, on the other hand, is no ordinary vacuum cleaner. It looks like R2D2, the glitzy robot of *Star Wars,* with a hose protruding from his nose. It's silver, shiny and can make your bedroom smell like fresh eucalyptus. Bogotá's army hospital bought 15 machines for its asthma patients. Most of Princess's customers, however, are wealthy Colombians thrilled to have clean air and a vacuum that doesn't emit any dust. The fact that it's expensive, says Marklund, is an advantage. "People like to tell their friends they bought a machine that cost over a million pesos. It's like having a **BMW** or a **Mercedes.**"

At the beginning of each work day, Marklund convenes his 34 salespeople in a conference room to discuss strategy. One morning he asked them what their most fruitful sales argument was when approaching potential Colombian customers. The group's reply was as simple as it was unanimous: "It's made in the USA."

Colombia Overview

A Land of Surprising Opportunities

Despite its ongoing problem of drug- and guerrilla-related violence, Colombia remains one of Latin America's most solid investment opportunities. The 1980s are often referred to as the Lost Decade in the rest of the continent, where shrinking economies, growing poverty, hyperinflation, debt burdens and economic instability were the norm. None of this occurred in Colombia. Over the past two decades the country has maintained a steady growth rate every year. It has never missed a single payment on its $18 billion- foreign debt. Colombian companies are not among Latin America's largest; only 20 of the top 500 firms in the region are Colombian, according to the regional business magazine *América Economía.* But what they lack in size they make up for in performance. Of Latin America's 50 most profitable companies, 11 are Colombian, the magazine reported.

Unlike neighboring Venezuela, Colombia is not dependent on a single export product; its economy is well diversified by Latin America standards. Cocaine is the largest business, although Colombia is also a major exporter of oil, coffee, coal, nickel, cut flowers, and emeralds. Firms specializing in risk analyses such as the Economist Intelligence Unit, Standard and Poor's, and Duff and Phelps have recommended Colombia and Chile as the best investment risks in Latin America. Colombia is also something of a political paradox in South America. With only one brief exception this century, political parties, not the military, have ruled.

Yet such advantages have not translated into a foreign investment boom. Largely because of the country's violent image, companies are often afraid to do business in Colombia. Unfortunately, many of the fears are well founded. The country is home to the world's most powerful drug mafia, the Cali cartel, as well as three active leftist guerrilla movements. There are about 30,000 murders reported each year. The United States, with a population eight times as large, registers about 24,000 murders per year. In Colombia, crimes such as kidnapping and robbery have spiraled out of control in recent years. Yet most foreign businessmen say the security issue is manageable. Extra money is set aside to hire guards, and business goes on as usual.

Cultural Riches, Bloody Crime

Colombia is a contradiction: a civilized, prosperous land where killing knows no bounds. Its cities are famed for their rich cultural life; there is a plethora of theaters, art exhibits, universities, concerts, and coffee houses. Bogotá has the feel of a genteel European city. Colombians are excruciatingly formal. They dress in suits, always say thank you and engage in an elaborate ritual just to say hello: phrases such as *qué hubo, cómo me le va, como está, qué hay, qué tal* and *qué más* are exchanged for several minutes before any business is conducted. Yet the people of Colombia never quite learned to live with each other in peace. On any given day, you can open the newspaper and read about the massacre of three, four, five or more people, or police being shot to death on the streets of Bogotá, Cali, or Medellín. Such news would make front-page headlines in any other country. In Colombia, it's relegated to the back pages.

Amazingly, the bloodshed has not seriously affected Colombia's economic or political stability. Despite the prevalence of a violent, get-rich-quick ethic, Colombia is characterized by a hard-working populace that eschews the *mañana* mentality often associated with Latin America. When possible, things are done today, not tomorrow. This helps explain Colombia's vibrant economy. The Gross National Product grew by 4.3 percent in 1990, 2.1 percent in 1991, 3.5 percent in

1992 and 5.2 percent in 1993. Inflation has been declining slowly, from 26.8 percent in 1992 to 22.6 percent in 1994. Exchange rates have likewise been steady, hovering around 800 pesos to the dollar for the past two years. The left of center Liberal Party and the center-right Conservative Party have spent the past century alternating power. Foreigners doing business in Colombia know they are safe from most of the ills that have plagued the rest of the region: wild fluctuations in the economy, military coups, arbitrary expropriation of property.

Colombia has initiated an ambitious program to promote foreign investment. The country has never been more open to international businesses, ranging from chemical manufacturers and banks to food franchises and cellular phone companies. Foreign investment in non-oil sectors went from $101 million in 1991 to $350 million in 1992 to $437 million in 1993, according the **Bank of the Republic.** Oil investment by foreigners stands at about $500 million a year. Colombia has made foreign investment an integral part of its move to an open economy. The country's leaders believe economic participation from abroad will aid Colombia's development by transferring technology and expertise, improving its infrastructure, giving Colombians greater access to world markets and increasing competitiveness. New foreign investors in Colombia include **Kentucky Fried Chicken, BellSouth, Bell Canada** and **Barclays. McDonald's** is also opening franchises in Colombia.

Government Agency Aids Investors

Major obstacles to foreign investment — such as restrictions on profit remittances and requiring foreigners to export a percentage of their production or to utilize a set amount of domestic raw materials — have been eliminated. In 1992, the government and a host of private Colombian companies together set up an organization specifically designed to promote foreign investment. The new organization, **Coinvertir,** provides information and advice to anyone interested in doing business in Colombia. The entity guides foreigners through the process of setting up, financing and operating a business. Luckily, the paperwork needed to do so has now been vastly reduced. Investors are permitted to bring capital into Colombia through a financial intermediary. Within three months (which can be extended to six) the capital must be registered at the International Technical Department of the Bank of the Republic, which functions as Colombia's central bank. In the case of portfolio investments, the term for registering capital is 30 days after the sale of the currency on the exchange market. Foreigners still complain of a certain amount of red tape and corruption when setting up businesses or importing goods into Colombia. Yet by all accounts the situation has improved in recent years.

The rules governing foreign investment in Colombia are now essentially the same as those governing local businesses. The government has set out to modernize the legal framework for investment and to negotiate international agreements to protect foreign business interests in Colombia. The country is a member of the Multilateral Investment Guarantee Agency, which insures foreign investors against noncommercial risks such as expropriation and civil disorder.

Foreign investment used to be prohibited in many economic sectors. Today, only those related to defense, national security or the processing of dangerous toxic waste are excluded. In a few sectors, including large-scale mining, foreigners must receive prior government authorization before investing. The approval can be obtained at the National Planning Department through its Foreign Investment Division, the Office of the Superintendent of Banking, the Ministry of Mines and Energy, and the National Superintendent of Bonds and Securities. Once installed in Colombia, foreign companies must pay a 30 percent tax on their Colombian-generated income. In addition, there is a tax on profits remitted abroad. In 1994, this tax was set at 10 percent, but was slated to go down to eight percent in 1995 and seven percent in the following years.

In 1994, newly elected President Ernesto Samper instituted an additional restriction on foreign participation in an effort to curb the influx of Colombian narco-dollars disguised as foreign investment. Offshore money can no longer be used to purchase real estate that has no productive or commercial purpose.

The laundering of at least $2 billion of drug profits per year, while bringing some financial benefits, has distorted Colombia's economy. The most damaging consequence has been to overvalue the peso, contributing to an influx of cheap imports and putting exporters at a disadvantage. From 1990 to 1992, exports exceeded imports by between $1 billion and $3 billion. But in 1993, imports totaled $8.7 billion compared to exports of $7.6 billion. The government's National Planning Department estimated that imports totaled $10.5 billion for 1994, with exports reaching $8.3 billion. Drug traffickers launder huge amounts of money by smuggling in inexpensive Asian clothing and electronic equipment, which are then sold in open markets known as San Andresitos.

With 36 million people, Colombia has Latin America's third largest population, slightly ahead of Argentina, though well behind Brazil and Mexico. There is a large and accessible market for all kinds of products. The country's principal imports, by order of value, are gasoline, telecommunications equipment, utility vehicles, airplanes, computers, passenger cars and motorcycles. Given the fact that Colombia's economy always seems to be booming — even in the midst of a worldwide recession — the sale of practically any imported consumer item (sunglasses, watches, costume jewelry, baby goods, kitchen appliances, office supplies, etc.) stands a good chance of success. The *apertura* has reduced import tariffs from an average of 40 percent to an average of 11 percent. Imports destined to produce export goods pay no duty at all. In 1984, 99.5 percent of all imports required licenses to enter Colombia. Six years later, only 3.3 percent needed import licenses.

Colombian industry had a strong year in 1993, despite low international coffee prices, which depressed the sector that employs 10 percent of Colombia's people. According to the National Industrial Association (ANDI), sales of consumer goods grew by 4.8 percent and capital goods sales increased an impressive 27.8 percent. Largely because of drug money, Colombia has also experienced a construction boom. The sector grew by 10.6 percent in 1993, ANDI reported. Sectors related to construction also posted impressive growth rates in

1993: cement (10.1 percent); glass (13.7 percent); and ceramic and porcelain goods (13.6 percent). In 1993, sectors that experienced sales difficulties were textiles, clothing, leather and shoes, according to ANDI.

Two Booms Underway: Coffee and Oil

Prospects for a bright economic future have been greatly enhanced by two booms: oil and coffee. A massive oil field recently discovered in the country's eastern plains — containing at least two billion barrels of proven reserves — is expected to generate some $14 billion in the coming years. And coffee prices skyrocketed in recent years following a prolonged frost in Brazil that destroyed much of that country's crops. Coffee prices on the New York Stock Exchange went from 68 cents a pound in June 1992 to 2.05 dollars a pound in July 1994. The problem for Colombia's leaders has not been whether there will be enough money, but how to avoid the inflationary effects of windfalls.

The government plans to use much of the money to ease poverty (which remains rampant, especially in the countryside) and improve Colombia's shoddy infrastructure, the country's biggest obstacle to economic development. Roads, highways, power generation, telephone lines and other public services are in serious decay. Infrastructure improvement forms an integral part of Colombia's privatization program and affords excellent opportunities to foreign investors. Unlike most of its neighbors, Colombia has decided to privatize state companies not out of necessity, but because of a belief that the state should avoid activities where it is least efficient and instead concentrate its efforts on areas of social benefit such as justice, health care, education and defense. The government hopes to raise some $2 billion by selling state assets to private firms.

By 1998, Colombia plans to have placed almost all of the country's 7,000 kilometers of highway in private hands. Roadways will be built or maintained by private firms, which will collect tolls. By the year 2000, the country will vastly expand power generation projects. Virtually all of the new investment will come from the private sector.

Three power generation initiatives have already been executed by private consortia with a total investment of $730 million. The government estimates that Colombia's telecommunications sector will require investments totaling $3.3 billion in the 1994-2000 period. Of this, 36 percent is expected to come from the private sector. Privatization of this sector suffered a major setback in 1992 when workers at the state-run telecommunications company, **Telecom,** staged a strike and sabotaged the computer system, cutting off all long-distance telephone service in and out of Colombia for more than a week.

In addition to infrastructure projects, Colombia has begun privatizing banks and several state-run businesses, such as the government's gasoline distribution network. The **Banco de los Trabajadores** was sold for $4.9 million to **Banco Mercantil of Venezuela**; **Banco Tequendama** was purchased for $30.7 million by Venezuela's **Banco Construcción** and the **Intercom Financial Bank of Aruba**; **Banco del Comercio** was sold to Colombia's **Organización Luís Carlos Sarmiento,** and the **Gilinski Group** of Cali purchased 75 percent of the **Banco de Colombia.** Banks slated to be sold include **Corpavi, Banco Popular, Banco del Estado, Bancoldex, Banco Cafetero,** and **Banco Central Hipotecario.**

The privatization drive has been carried out largely through public bidding processes that for the most part have seemed fair. **General Electric,** however, complained about the granting of a contract to a Colombian firm to build a $480 million thermoelectric plant in Barranquilla. The U.S. company said it was not given an equal chance to obtain the contract. "Colombia is still learning how to ... ensure a transparent bidding process," explained Armando Vegalara, the director of **Coinvertir.**

Colombia's geographic location at the northern tip of South America — with ports on both the Atlantic and Pacific Oceans —gives the country a strategic advantage as a center of international trade. A number of multinational companies — including **Hoechst, Siemens, BASF,** and **Cyanamid** — have located their regional headquarters in Colombia because of its impressive economic record and the export opportunities it affords. Because of the free-trade agreements it has signed with other countries, Colombia now has duty-free access to a market of more than 800 million consumers, **Coinvertir** says. It has signed such agreements with Venezuela, Mexico, Chile, Panama, and most Caribbean nations. The United States and the European Community also allow most Colombian products to enter duty free, although there have been threats from the U.S. Congress to cancel Colombia's trade preferences unless the country does more to combat drug trafficking from its territory.

With a minimum wage of only $120 a month, Colombia's qualified and diligent labor force is inexpensive. Employers are required to pay workers an annual service bonus equaling one month's pay for each year worked. In addition, when an employee is terminated, employers must offer severance pay of a month's salary for each year worked. At least 90 percent of ordinary workers and 80 percent of specialists must be Colombian. Although fewer than 10 percent of Colombian workers belong to unions, these groups remain influential in framing Colombia's labor policy. However, a recent law permitting collective dismissals was not met with the vehement opposition expected from Colombia's unions.

President Ernesto Samper has made training the work force a pillar of his economic modernization program. By improving productivity and efficiency, diversifying exports and developing human capital, he hopes to effect what he calls the "great technological leap." The goal is to catapult Colombia into the developed world by the year 2020. Yet if the country fails to curb violence and the immense power of its criminal class, true development may remain a dream. In short, there is no guarantee of success. Yet for foreign investors who have placed their faith — and their fortunes — in Colombia, even the attempts at modernization have provided real opportunities for profit.

Colombia at a Glance

Population: 36.2 million
Labor force size: 18 million

Language: Spanish

Ethnic mix: 58 percent mestizo (Indian and Spanish), 20 percent European (mainly Spanish), 14 percent mulatto (African and Spanish), 8 percent Indian.

Literacy: About 86 percent literacy among the population school age or older.

Climate: There are only two seasons in Colombia, rainy and dry. The climate depends on altitude. Generally, the weather is hot and balmy on the coast and in the flatlands and cooler the higher you go in the Andes, where three-quarters of the population lives. Bogotá, at 8,640 feet (2,633 meters) above sea level, has daytime temperatures averaging 57 F (14 C). There's very little central heating, so you'll need plenty of woolen socks, sweaters, and jackets.

Best times to visit: Weatherwise, almost anytime is acceptable, but avoid the periods from Dec. 15-Jan. 15, June 15-July 15, and the week before and after Easter. Most Colombians take vacations and holidays during those times.

Natural Resources/Chief Agricultural Products: Colombia has oil, coal, natural gas, iron, nickel, copper, emeralds and other gems, silver and gold. Its agricultural production includes coffee, bananas, flowers, cotton, sugar, rice, corn, tobacco, sorghum, plantains, wood, meat, fish, and tropical fruit.

Land area: 1,141,748 square kilometers.

Economic Statistics:

GDP: $64.9 billion (1994).

Per Capita GDP: $1,884 (1994).

GDP Growth Rate: 5.7 percent (1994); 5.2 percent (1993).

Exports: $8.3 billion U.S. (f.o.b., preliminary 1994). Main products: Oil, coffee, coal, nickel, bananas, emeralds, flowers, sugar.

Imports: $10.5 billion U.S. (f.o.b., preliminary 1994). Main products: Motor gasoline, telecommunications equipment, utility vehicles, airplanes, computers, passenger cars, motorcycles.

Import duties: Duties vary in Colombia depending on the product, but the average effective tariff is 11 percent. Some items, such as cars, pay much higher duties (automotive duties range from 50 percent to 70 percent). Goods destined for infrastructure development and production of export products pay no duty at all.

Repatriation of profits: Profits may be repatriated with payment of a remittance tax that is gradually being reduced, from 10 percent in 1994 to 8 percent in 1995 to 7 percent in 1996 and subsequent years.

When You Go to Colombia

Visas: Business people on scouting trips to Colombia usually enter as tourists with just their valid passports; Colombian immigration authorities will grant them an entry permit on landing at the airport allowing them to remain in the country up to 90 days. But anyone definitely planning to conduct business, to set up a business establishment, or even to open a bank account should obtain a three-year multiple-entry business visa from a Colombian consulate abroad prior to coming. That will require, among other things, a request for the visa from a legal entity in Colombia, such as a business connection.

Airlines: From the United States, there is service to Colombia's main cities on American Airlines and the Colombian carriers ACES and Avianca. From Europe, there is service on Avianca, Iberia, British Airways, Air France Lufthansa, and Alitalia. Brazil's Varig and Chile's Ladeco provide good service from other South American countries.

Miscellaneous Tips:
- El Banco Popular has a small office inside the international arrival section of the airport where you can change money to pay for taxis, tips, and the like.
- Keep a sharp eye out for pickpockets in Colombian airports, even at the gates. They seem to be everywhere.
- Don't wear expensive jewelry or carry large amounts of cash while walking around in Colombian cities.
- Because Colombia is a very violent country, ask the United States Embassy (Tel: 320-1300) or another foreign embassy for advice on the safety of any areas to which you plan to travel outside of Bogotá.

- Hotels are often full; make reservations at least 15 days in advance.
- Bogotá is a very formal town; wear suits or dresses to conduct business.

Urban Transportation:

Taxis are cheap and safe. You can rent one by the hour (US$5) or the day (US$33.) Limousine service is available from Limousines of Colombia at Diagonal 127A No. 24A-52 in Bogotá. Tel: (57-1) 274-2439 or 274-2449. Hertz (Tel: 57-1) 284-1445 and 284-2696; fax: 334-7961) leases cars with or without driver. Driving between cities is not recommended because of potential violence.

Hotels

BOGOTÁ

Casa Medina

Many seasoned visitors consider this converted mansion in the business sector of northern Bogotá to be the best of the best, combining modern amenities with elegance and service.

Carrera 7 No. 69a-22.

Tel: (57-1) 212-6657. Fax: 212-6668. $207 and up.

Charleston

Another fine hotel known for modern conveniences, old-world service and elegance.

Carrera 13 No. 85-46.

Tel: (57-1) 257-1100 and 218-0590. Fax: 218-0605. $190 and up.

La Boheme

Located in the Zona Rosa, the night-life district filled with bars, discotheques and restaurants.

Calle 82 No. 12-35.

Tel: (57-1) 236-1840. Fax: 618-0003. $150 and up.

Bogotá Royal

Close to the World Trade Center.

Avenida 100 No. 8a-01.

Tel: (57-1) 218-9911. Fax: 218-3261. $200 and up.

Tequendama

An old, classic downtown favorite and member of the Intercontinental chain. Carrera 10 No. 26-21.

Tel: (57-1) 286-1111. Fax: 282-2860. $190 and up.

MEDELLÍN
Intercontinental Medellín

Located in a plush section of town. Pool, health club, restaurants, discotheque and bar. Calle 16 No. 28-51.

Tel: (57-4) 266-0680. Fax: 266-1548. $208 and up.

CALI
Intercontinental Cali

Elegant hotel with one of Cali's most enticing pools, a casino and luxurious shops. Avenida Colombia No. 2-72.

Tel: (57-2) 882-3225. Fax: 882-2567. $199 and up.

Contacts (all addresses are in Bogotá)

Governmental:

COINVERTIR

The key place to begin to obtain investment information.

Carrera 7 No 71-52, Oficina 702 torre A.

Tel: (57-1) 312-0313. Fax: 312-0318.

Publishes *Business Guide for Foreign Investment in Colombia.*

TRADE POINT-BOGOTÁ

Provides services to people engaged in foreign trade. Has customs officials, representatives of banks, transport companies, and insurance companies, and other professionals offering information on markets, duties and import-export procedures.

Calle 28 No. 13A-59.

Tel: (57-1) 281-8409 and 282-5488. Fax: 283-9967.

INSTITUTE OF INDUSTRIAL DEVELOPMENT (IFI)
Department of Investments
Calle 16 No 6-66, Pisos 7 al 15.
Tel: (57-1) 282-2055, extension 125, or 334-4911. Fax: 286-8116.

Business Organizations:

**COLOMBIAN CONFEDERATION OF
EXPORTERS (ANALDEX)**
Carrera 10 No 27-27, Interior 137, Oficina 902.
Tel: (57-1) 284-3237 and 342-0788. Fax: 284-6911.

NATIONAL ASSOCIATION OF INDUSTRIALISTS (ANDI)
Carrera 13 No 26-45, Piso 6.
Tel: (57-1) 281-0600 or 334-9620. Fax: 281-3188.

BOLSA DE VALORES (Stock Exchange)
Carrera 8 No 13-82, Pisos 7 y 8.
Tel: (57-1) 243-6501. Fax: 281-3170.

SPANISH-COLOMBIAN CHAMBER OF COMMERCE
Transv. 18a No 101-11. Tel: (57-1) 256-1925. Fax: 611-0870.

**COLOMBIAN-FRENCH CHAMBER OF COMMERCE AND
INDUSTRY**
Carrera 18a No 39-31. Tel: (57-1) 232-1135. Fax: 281-1967.

COLOMBIAN-AMERICAN CHAMBER OF COMMERCE
Calle 35 No 6-16. Tel: (57-1) 285-7800. Fax: 288-6434.

COLOMBIAN-SWISS CHAMBER OF COMMERCE
Carrera: 7 No 33-53. Tel: (57-1) 214-2340.

**COLOMBIAN-BELGIAN AND LUXEMBOURG CHAMBER
OF COMMERCE**
Calle 98 No 8-55. Tel: (57-1) 257-9114.

**COLOMBIAN-KOREAN CHAMBER OF COMMERCE AND
INDUSTRY**
Calle 71 No 9-92, Oficina 201. Tel: (571) 235-9880.

COLOMBIAN-JAPANESE CHAMBER OF COMMERCE
Carrera 8 No 62-40. Tel: (57-1) 211-7068. Fax: 235-5869.

COLOMBIAN-CHINESE CHAMBER OF COMMERCE
Carrera 3 No 12-42. Tel: (57-1) 283-7376.

Interpreters/Translators:

Paul Heller. Tel: (57-1) 618-5445.
Mari Eugenia Sanit. Tel: (57-1) 274-6764.
Ana Mallarino de Ospina. Tel: (57-1) 616-4993.
Hanka de Rodes. Tel: (57-1) 253-1251.

Lawyers:

Juan David Chamorro
Specializes in international trade.
Tel: (57-1) 286-9111, Ext. 308.
Juan Manuel Tafut
Affiliated with Coinvertir. Tel: (57-1) 312-0312.
Darío Cárdenas
Tel: (57-1) 312-3600.

In Case of Illness:

Dr. Mario Bernal R. (Cardiology)
Avenida 9 No 117 - 20, Consultorio 429
Tel: (57-1) 215-2300.
Dr. Nathan Eidelman (G.I)
Avenida 9 No 117- 20, Consultorio 624
Tel: (57-1) 214-5473 and 215-2353.

8

ECUADOR

From a Garden Job
To a Flower Empire

By Carlos Cisternas

Kathleen and Hans Peter Hug — she's from the United States, he's Swiss — first came to Ecuador in 1982 with a contract to design and create a garden for the home of a wealthy Ecuadoran at his ranch on the outskirts of Quito. The Hugs, then 28 years old, were amazed at the beauty of the brightly colored flowers and the plants and thought Ecuador was the ideal location to start a plantation to grow flowers for export to the United States.

Deciding to make their home in Ecuador, they continued to work in the design and construction of gardens, and when they had some money saved they began a flower plantation. Today, they are the owners of a vertically integrated flower empire, including 500 hectares (1,250 acres) of growing fields, three retail shops, and a cargo airline that carries their flowers and those of other Ecuadoran growers to the United States for sale. Separately, they have a company for the design and construction of gardens and swimming pools.

In the process, the Hugs have learned to appreciate the qualities of Ecuador's largely Indian working class and have built up deep frustrations with many in the white-collar and professional class, especially government bureaucrats. None of that has diminished their enthusiasm for raising flowers in Ecuador, which they view as an important part of the future of the country.

"Ecuador is a promising land for doing business," believes Hans Peter Hug. "There are many fields in which to invest and make a lot of money. The Ecuadorans, in general, are open, friendly, courteous to foreigners, and tolerant."

But they acknowledge that they had some difficulties in the early years, until they learned about the work habits of Ecuadorans and about the kinds of projects and people to avoid. For example, soon after arriving in the country they received a contract to design the gardens of the House of Ecuadoran Culture. But they found that it was necessary to go to see those in charge of the project many times before anything was decided. The officials of the institution would request papers and plans but then didn't go over them, so when the Hugs went to talk about the proposals they would be told to return later. Later, they would return, and the people they were to see were usually not there.

"After a number of weeks of that I decided to halt the undertaking; we abandoned it completely because of the loss of time and negligence of those in charge," said Hans Peter Hug.

"I once had to fire an architect," he continued, "because he repeatedly failed to see to the building of an embankment for a garden, despite the fact that I told him various times that the work had to be done by a certain time. I showed him the plans and explained what was needed. Finally, I decided to do it myself, explaining to the workers what had to be done. They listened very carefully and diligently built what the architect had failed to do."

Good Workers, Bad Bureaucrats

"The working class, the Indian, is a good worker when you recognize his qualities and offer him the opportunity to learn. They feel pride in their work, even if it is a small task," he said. "On the other hand, the middle class, the white-collar worker, can be slow and lazy.

And the bureaucrat, generally, is an element that delays everything. We have 220 employees, of which about 150 are people of humble origin, and I have seen in them very favorable work qualities."

He says that you have to approach any dealings with the government with a lot of patience in hand. Among the complications that the Hugs encounter are those having to do with export documentation in the customs service. But they say that situation has improved in recent years because the last government, that of President Rodrigo Borja (1988-92), undertook measures to simplify customs clearances.

Before, for example, they had to submit nine copies of any document covering goods for export. One copy for the Central Bank, another for the treasurer's office in the Ministry of Finance, others for various offices of the customs service, the airport, and so on. Now, the number of copies required is only three or four.

The Hugs praise Ecuador's climate and soil, which they say are responsible for the vibrant colors and the quality of flowers grown in the country, aided by the proximity of the sun and the luminosity of the sky. Although the Equator bisects the country almost at the northern edge of Quito, the city sits high in the Andes at more than 9,000 feet (2,850 meters), giving it a dry, cool climate. Their flower plantations are located 10 to 15 kilometers from the center of the city.

Their cargo service, **Trans International Cargo,** hauls about 150 tons of flowers and other goods to the United States every week, making it, they say, the third largest transport company in Ecuador. They sell space on the flights to other flower growers, and also provide them with assistance with documents and selling abroad. They say most flower exports go to the United States because the flower market there is open all year. European countries prohibit flower imports during the months of June, July, and August, when locally grown flowers are available.

The Hugs' other business, the garden and pool service, finds many of its clients in Guayaquil, Ecuador's second city but its most important business center, which sits on the warm and humid Pacific coast.

The Hugs' recommendation to anyone who wants to invest or establish a small business in Ecuador is to bring your own startup capital and quickly obtain an investor's visa once in the country.

"There are big opportunities to do business in Ecuador, many opportunities for small and medium-sized firms, and for those who want to work hard," concluded Kathleen Hug, "with the understanding that there's a good working class here, and some bad elements in the bureaucracy."

Ecuador Overview

Political Atmosphere Sends Mixed Message to Investors

The current government of President Sixto Durán-Ballén has tried to open Ecuador to foreign investment, creating legislation favorable to the entry of private capital. It guarantees the same treatment for national and foreign capital, and foreign investors may freely convert and transfer their profits. Foreign investments do not require prior authorization of government agencies, except those involving national security, radio, television, daily newspapers, commercial banking, and insurance. Import duties have been lowered substantially in line with the norms of the Andean Pact, whose other members are Venezuela, Colombia, Peru, and Bolivia. The goal is to create a totally free trade zone in the future.

Nevertheless, foreign investments have not come in the quantities that were expected, which is usually attributed to the atmosphere of political instability characteristic of Ecuador. *The Economist* and a French trade insurance agency, in separate reports in 1994, both included Ecuador on lists of "high risk" countries for investors because of internal economic difficulties and a history of political volatility.

Ecuador has lived in democracy since 1978, when a decade of dictatorships came to an end. Since then, the country has had five governments of distinct political philosophies: populist, Christian Democratic, rightist, social democratic, and conservative. None of those governments has maintained continuity in economic policy from the previous government, even though all relied on oil exports as their principal means of support. Crude oil exports finance 50 percent of Ecuador's national budget.

Another factor adding uncertainty to Ecuador's economic life is the longstanding border dispute with Peru. The two countries fought a one-month war at the beginning of 1995 in a jungle area 350 kilometers south of Quito and had previously gone to war over the issue in 1941 and 1981. Although the latest fighting was halted with a peace accord and de-militarization of the 78-kilometer stretch of land in dispute, the lack of a definitive settlement raises the prospect of new violence. Because of the war, Ecuador had to lower its economic growth projections for 1995 from 4-5 percent to 3-4 percent.

Privatizations, Mining and Tourism

President Durán-Ballén took office in 1992 proposing to sell off state companies to private investors and reduce the size of the state. To accomplish the privatizations, the government approved a Law of Modernization of the State that permits the sale of state firms considered inefficient. Among the principal firms considered apt for privatization are those in telecommunications and electricity, the Ecuadoran airline, and the social security system, which is to be opened to private pension fund administrators.

The state airline declared bankruptcy and suspended flights in September 1993. The government hopes to revive it with private capital, either foreign or domestic, and convert it into a private corporation. In a number of cases, the government has listed stock in state companies on the Ecuadoran stock exchange, and by this route has sold two cement companies, a sugar refinery, and a fertilizer manufacturer. This program is continuing with offerings of shares in a food processing company, a school construction firm, and others.

Experts say Ecuador has great potential in both metallic and non-metallic minerals, but they are almost entirely unexploited

because of the shortage of mining investments. Since 1992, more than 100 mining companies, both foreign and domestic, have registered for prospecting. The government is considering reforms to the mining law to make it easier to obtain titles to claims and protect private investments in mining. Minerals found in Ecuador are numerous, including gold, copper, mercury, lead, platinum, sulfur, coal, and lime.

Another area in which the government is trying to attract investors, both foreign and domestic, is tourism. Ecuador's natural attractions include jungles, mountains, and coastline, and a variety of climates. Ecuador is also an attractive destination for travelers interested in ecological tourism. Hotels in Quito and Guayaquil need improvements, and a number of smaller cities need hotels, including Cuenca, Loja, and the beach resort towns Salinas, Atacames, and Esmeraldas.

Surplus of Labor and Strikes

Employers will find a surplus of labor in Ecuador at relatively low wages, typically $105 a month for laborers plus various social benefits and extra wage payments three times a year, but the low wages are more than offset by a low skill level and the severe limitation on ever firing workers. Workers may be fired only for cause, including missing at least three days' work without notice, incompetence, and violation of the work contract. A fired employee receives at least one-fourth of a month's wage for each year worked. The government has been considering changes in the labor code, particularly in rules for hiring and firing.

Another characteristic of the labor scene in Ecuador is frequent strikes and national work stoppages called by the leftist-led United Workers Front, or FUT, the largest labor federation in the country. From 1980 to 1994, the FUT carried out 22 national strikes. Generally, they were called to support demands for improvement in minimum wages, but since 1993 they have been called to oppose the government's effort at privatizing state firms.

Businesses in Ecuador, both domestic and foreign, pay corporate taxes of 25 percent of profits, and capital gains are taxed as normal income. A 10 percent value added tax is levied on most sales and commercial transactions, except for food products in their natural state, drugs, and veterinary products. Tax evasion, along with the complicity of officials who are supposed to prevent it, is a common practice.

Imports and Infrastructure Plans

The Ecuadoran consumer goods market is totally open to imports, with virtually no restrictions, and recent reductions in tariffs have helped to expand the potential for imports. For example, until 1992, the tariffs on automobiles were so high that almost no one bought new cars, but the auto tariff has now been lowered to a relatively modest 40 percent.

Ecuadoran consumers favor foreign goods in a number of product lines, including clothing, shoes, radios, tape recorders, and refrigerators. However, any foreign firms or distributors contemplating exporting such items to Ecuador should first take a look at the openly operated contraband markets on the streets of both Quito and Guayaquil to get an idea of what the competition will be in both price and quality. The contraband market in Quito is called Ipiales and that in Guayaquil is La Bahia.

In theory, lower tariffs will reduce this illegal activity, but many retailers in the open-air markets still find it easier to bring in their merchandise without the hassle of dealing with customs officials and other slow-moving bureaucrats. The goods, generally brought across the frontier with Colombia, range from clothes to watches, electronics and almost every kind of household item. They are manufactured in Japan, Taiwan, the United States, Hong Kong, and elsewhere.

The legal importer, whether foreign or Ecuadoran, has to obtain prior approval for bringing in imports in a series of steps that begin in the Central Bank. The government has adopted new regulations that are supposed to make the import process easier and faster, including the establishment of a customs computer system. All merchandise for a value of more than $3,000 has to be examined, and the government has decided to turn over that function to two private firms, to be selected by international bidding. They will examine entering merchandise and calculate the tariff.

Numerous private customs agents have offices around the airports and ports and are more than happy to handle paperwork for importers, but out of this system comes much of the corruption that Ecuadorans complain about so bitterly. Business people with experience with imports say customs agents often propose getting goods out of customs warehouses quickly or more cheaply by paying bribes to officials, but that it is easy to be deceived or cheated in this type of arrangement, or even trapped by customs officials.

Ecuador is planning several major infrastructure projects in the next few years that offer opportunities to foreign firms to bid on contracts for construction, services, or supplies. For instance, plans are being drawn up to build new airports in both Quito and Guayaquil at a cost of $500 million each. A new, 500-kilometer oil pipeline is also planned.

Ecuador at a Glance

Population: 10 million.

Labor force: 2.9 million.

Languages: Spanish and Quechua.

Ethnic mix: Ecuador has 16 indigenous groups, which are thought to constitute slightly more than a third of the population. The remainder of the population is largely of Spanish origin or mixed Spanish and Indian.

Literacy: 90 percent.

Climate and best times to visit: The mainland of Ecuador has two distinct climate zones: the cool, fairly dry temperate zone around Quito with mild temperatures and a mild rainy season from October to April, and the humid, tropical coastal area around Guayaquil, where the hot, rainy season runs from January to May. The most pleasant times to visit Ecuador are the months of June, July, October, November and December.

Natural resources, chief agricultural products: Oil, bananas, coffee, cacao, fish and seafood, and a wide range of minerals that are largely unexploited: gold, copper, mercury, lead, sulfur, magnesium, platinum, coal, lime, clay, and gypsum.

Land area: 262,660 square kilometers, plus the Galápagos Islands, which cover 8,010 square kilometers.

Economic Statistics:

GNP: $17 billion (1994).

Per Capita GNP: $1,475 (1994).

Economic growth rate: 1.7 (1993). 3.9 percent (1994).

Leading exports: Oil, bananas, shrimp, coffee, cacao.

Main imports: Electronics, agricultural machinery, computers, wheat, auto parts, wines and liquors.

Duties on imports: Primary materials 5 percent, semi-finished goods 10-15 percent, finished goods 20 percent, automobiles 40 percent.

Repatriation of profits: In general, foreign investors may freely convert profits to hard currency and transfer them to the exterior. The exception is in mining, which has a special tax structure under which foreign investors may remit profits and dividends annually up to an amount equal to 20 percent of their capital registered in the Central Bank.

When You Go to Ecuador

Visas: Most people do not require an advance visa for visits of no more than 90 days. Business people normally state that they are coming for tourist motives when they land at the airport, then they later request investment visas or special work visas from the Foreign Ministry if they decide to make direct investments or conduct other business affairs.

Airlines: Continental from New York and Los Angeles; SAETA from New York, Miami, and Los Angeles; American from Miami. All have flights to both Quito and Guayaquil.

What to Expect at the Airport: If you fly into Quito, you may feel the effects of the altitude (2,850 meters or 9,300 feet above sea level) right away, or a bit later. Don't get in a hurry to do anything, try to avoid stairs and excessive walking or running. Quito won't make you as breathless as La Paz, the Bolivian capital, but take it easy anyway.

Urban transportation: Taxis are abundant on the streets of both Quito and Guayaquil, but many of the taxis are old and in bad condition. Drivers in Guayaquil don't use meters, so you should ask the fare before taking off. Those in Quito have meters. A trip within either city should run $2.25-$4.50. Auto rental companies have offices in both cities and offer vehicles with or without drivers. Some hotels also offer sedans and limousines for rent.

Telephone woes: Generally, you won't have any problem making calls from your hotel room to the United States and other places outside Ecuador, but domestic service is another matter. There is a great shortage of lines in the interior of the country, so during business hours it is often impossible to call between Quito and Guayaquil.

Hotels

NOTE: Service charges and taxes totaling 20 percent are added to all hotel bills.

QUITO
Hotel Oro Verde
Av. 12 de Octubre y Cordero.

Tels: (593-2) 56-6497 and 56-7128. Fax: (593-2) 56-9189.

Reservations number in United States: (212) 838-3110. Fax: (212) 758-7367. Offers full line of services to business visitors, including secretarial and translation; casino, minibars in rooms.

Individual rates start at $180.

Hotel Colón
Av. Amazonas y Patria.

Tels: (593-2) 56-0666 and 56-1333. Fax: (593-2) 56-3903.

Full business services, including interpretation and translation, auto rental office in shopping mall, computers; also casino, minibars in rooms. Rates begin at $125.

Hotel Akros
Av. 6 de Diciembre 3986 y Checoeslovaquia.

Tels: (593-2) 43-0600 and 43-0610. Fax: (593-2) 43-1727.

Minibars in all rooms, personal computers available. Rates begin at $87.

GUAYAQUIL
Hotel Unihotel
Clemente Ballén 406 y Chile.

Tels: (593-4) 32-7100 and 51-9077. Fax: (593-4) 32-8352.

Rates begin at $90.

Hotel Oro Verde
9 de Octubre y García Moreno.

Tel: (593-4) 32-7999. Fax: (593-4) 32-9350.

Reservations in United States: (212) 838-3110. Fax: (212) 758-7367.

Rates begin at $180.

Hotel Continental
Av. 10 de Agosto y Chile.
Tel: (593-4) 32-9270. Fax: (593-4) 32-3556.
Rates start at $110.

Contacts

Business Organizations:

ECUADORAN-AMERICAN CHAMBER OF COMMERCE
Av. 6 de Diciembre y La Niña, Edificio Multicentro, Oficina 404, Quito.
Tels: (593-2) 50-7450 and 50-7453. Fax: (593-2) 50-4571.
Keeps a list of representatives and distributors for foreign firms.

ECUADORAN-AMERICAN CHAMBER OF COMMERCE IN GUAYAQUIL
Av. General Córdova 812, Guayaquil.
Tels: (593-4) 56-3177 and 56-5761.
Has list of representatives and distributors for foreign firms.

ASSOCIATION OF FLOWER PRODUCERS AND EXPORTERS
Rio Topo 166 y La Prensa, Quito.
Tels: (593-2) 25-1092 and 44-9691. Fax: (593-2) 25-1084.

HOTEL ASSOCIATION OF ECUADOR
Ave. América 5378, Quito.
Tel: (593-2) 45-3942.

NATIONAL ASSOCIATION OF BUSINESSMEN
Av. Amazonas y Colón, Edificio España, Piso 6, Quito.
Tels: (593-2) 23-8507 and 55-0879. Fax: (593-2) 50-9806.

CHAMBER OF COMMERCE OF GUAYAQUIL
Tel: (593-4) 53-4411.

CHAMBER OF COMMERCE OF QUITO
Av. República y Amazonas, Edificio Las Cámaras, Piso 5, Quito.
Tels: (593-2) 44-3787 and 44-3788. Fax: (593-2) 43-5862.

WORLD TRADE CENTER
Av. 12 de Octubre y Cordero, Quito.
Tel: (593-2) 50-8906. Fax: (593-2) 50-8911.

Governmental:
MINISTRY OF INDUSTRY, COMMERCE, TRADE AND FISHING
Av. Amazonas y Eloy Alfaro, Quito.
Tels: (593-2) 52-7988. Fax: (593-2) 54-3562.
Deals with foreign investment and technology transfer.
SUPERINTENDENCY OF CORPORATIONS
Roca 660 y Av. Amazonas, Quito.
Tels: (593-2) 54-1606 and 52-5022 and 52-5262.
Maintains registration of all firms and investments, domestic and foreign.
ECUADORAN CENTER OF INDUSTRIAL DEVELOPMENT
Fosters contacts between Ecuadoran investors and business people and
foreign counterparts.
In Quito: Av. Orellana 1725 y 9 de Octubre.
Tels: (593-2) 52-7100 and 54-3486. Fax: (593-2) 50-1817.
In Guayaquil: Av. García Avilés 217 y 9 de Octubre.
Tels: (593-4) 56-2500 and 56-1292. Fax: (593-4) 30-7628.
**CORPORATION OF DEVELOPMENT AND INVESTIGATION
IN MINING AND METALLURGY**
Av. 10 de Agosto 5844 y Pereira, Quito.
Tels: (593-2) 25-4673 and 43-4579. Fax: (593-2) 25-4674.
Oversees development and promotion of mining.
NATIONAL DIRECTORATE OF MINING
Baquedano 222 y Reina Victoria, Quito.
Tels: (593-2) 55-4110 and 55-4809. Fax: (593-2) 50-9006.
Grants and cancels mining concessions.
U.S. EMBASSY Commercial Section
Av. 12 de Octubre y Patria, Quito.Tel: (593-2) 56-1404.

Lawyers with international clientele (whose listing here does not
constitute a recommendation):

Pérez, Bustamante y Pérez Asociados
Av. Patria 640 y 9 de Octubre, Quito.
Tels: (593-2) 56-1710 and 56-1719 and 56-1722. Fax: (593-2) 56-1798.

Fabián Ponce y Asociados & Cia. Ltda.
Av. 18 de Septiembre 213, Piso 2, Quito.
Tels: (593-2) 23-7320 and 56-3426 and 56-3549. Fax: (593-2) 56-3289.

Translators/Interpreters:

A. Vásconez-Lecaros
Quito.
Tel/Fax: (593-2) 54-4865.
Tecno Master
Miraflores Av. Guayas 401, Guayaquil.
Tel: (593-4) 20-0750. Fax: (593-4) 20-4470.

In case of illness:

Dr. Ney Dolberg (general medicine)
Av. 12 de Octubre 959 y Roca, Quito.
Tel: 23-4324. Beeper for emergencies: 55-0066.
Dr. Angel Fernández (ear, nose and throat)
Ramirez Dávalos 241, Piso 7, Quito.
Tel: 56-3799. Beeper: 50-5856, Receptor 123.

9

MEXICO

Replanting Old Roots
South of the Border

By Lucy Conger

For **General Electric,** Mexico has been revitalized as a land of opportunity in the 1990s. As part of the trend toward globalization, the giant multi-national company has been diversifying its operations and expanding in Mexico. Although the company put down roots in Mexico 100 years ago, in this decade it has been making important changes in its operating style that are creating new successes. A reorganization at **GE**'s Tampico plastics plant has increased productivity and created self-directed work teams. And, after just a few years, a joint venture with a Mexican appliance manufacturer has become a booming business. In partnership, **GE** and the Mexican appliance manufacturer, **Mabe,** say they now produce one third of all kitchen stoves sold in the United States and all of **GE**'s gas ranges produced internationally. It wasn't always this way. As recently as a decade ago, **GE** cut back its Mexico operations sharply, showing that even a giant with annual worldwide sales of $60 billion can get the jitters. Following the oil bust and the international debt crisis of the early 1980s, Mexico, like most other Latin American countries, experienced a deep recession that threw millions out of work, pushed many domestic businesses into bankruptcy and slashed purchasing power by more than 50 percent. That was when **General Electric** made a big mistake, according to Ken Brown, president of **GE de Mexico.**

"In the rush to get out of the devaluation spiral and the lost decade (of the 1980s), we sold interests in some of our business to partners that were not compatible. This hindered our long-term position. Now we are getting back into those businesses, and have to claw back in due to the poor image we allowed to develop or our failure to maintain technology," Brown said. **GE** has now bought back 100 percent of its electrical equipment business, but has only one-third the market share it had before.

The lesson has not been lost on **General Electric.** "There is a corporate commitment to Mexico. It's part of **GE** wanting to be global, and putting up with uncertainty is part of that," says Brown. In fact, **GE**'s commitment to Mexico is so deep that **GE** CEO Jack Welch has selected Mexico, along with China and India, as countries where the appliance giant will remain firmly in place through thick and thin. **GE**'s goal is to develop a market share in those three large countries that is equivalent to one percent of GDP.

GE's hard lesson sets a good example for anyone wanting to do business in Mexico today: be prepared to make a commitment, and in Mexico that means coming in for the long-term.

The **GE** joint venture with **Mabe** is typical of many joint-ventures, Brown explains. Each company had something to offer the other. **Mabe** produced quality products that, in some cases, were better designed than **GE** brands. **GE** manufactured two-door refrigerators in the United States that **Mabe** could not produce. **Mabe** had clear market knowledge and a good product, and **GE** had manufacturing knowledge and marketing expertise. Better yet, the business culture of the two firms was similar, making for a good match. **Mabe** is a family firm that is professionally managed, business-like, cost-conscious, aggressive and ready to go, Brown says. "That corresponds to the **GE** culture: aggressive, fast-moving, team-based, cost-conscious." Once the match was made, the two companies set to work redesigning kitchen ranges and came up with the model that meets U.S. standards and has captured one-third of the market in the United States. The ranges are manufactured at a plant in Mexico City.

The **GE-Mabe** match illustrates criteria that are important to consider in any joint venture. "It comes down to which complementary skills the partners offer so each can see a contribution to growth of the business," says the **GE** executive. The Mexican partner must bring more to the table than contacts south of the border, important as they are. The foreign partner should seek very specific expertise from the Mexican firm, and vice versa: "Do the partners have products or subassemblies useful to export or import? Better, do they make some things more efficiently here in Mexico than we can elsewhere in the world? You should get to a win-win situation, and, if not, come in alone," says Brown.

A specialized manufacturing giant like **GE** brings expertise in production, marketing and finance to any of its business ventures. Like virtually any foreign company entering Mexico, **GE** also brings its own standard management practices — and cultural baggage. This means that in a foreign setting **GE** can teach some skills and must also adapt and learn new practices. In Mexico, a cross-fertilization process is occurring as a result of the intermingling of American and Mexican staff and **GE**'s extensive one-year and two-year study programs that train managers, engineers and marketing specialists from both countries in plants on both sides of the border. The company is developing "best practices" material based on Mexican experience. "Not all good ideas come from the font of wisdom in New York," quips Ken Brown.

Mexican workers and administrators learn the standard **GE** production and management concepts, which are: empowerment, speed, simplicity and integrity. Employees are trained in the **GE** procedures that keep production and sales flowing by managing everything from new product introduction to supplier relations.

Training is key to **GE**'s process of reducing layers and establishing team-work in its staffing, which aims to create organizations with only two levels. This is unconventional for Mexico, where organizations are traditionally multi-layered and extremely hierarchical, with decision-making usually concentrated in a very few people at the top of the pyramid. The **GE** training process prepares workers to make the shift from controlling operations to making decisions within a self-directed team. "We train, train, train and Mexican companies don't" because training breaks down the authoritarianism that predominates in worker-owner relations, says Luis González, human resources director for **GE-Plastics.** This type of management depends on open communication, and overcoming workers' fear of asking questions and speaking their mind is difficult. "To get trust, give trust" is the González formula for developing the communication and responsibility that the **GE** management style strives to achieve. It sounds simple, but it takes time to establish trust and demonstrate trustworthiness to Mexicans. Once again, that's where commitment comes in: be prepared to invest time and caring in Mexico.

For their part, the American managers and executives also learn sometimes painful lessons as they adapt to doing business in another culture. Red tape is one of the early obstacles encountered. "Government relations and regulations are key. They are more important and also more complicated" in Mexico, said Brown. They also take more time to navigate. The same goes for labor relations, which are best left to an experienced Mexican, counsels Luis González, a former labor mediator.

Different cultural values pose even greater challenges for Americans locked into a clockwork mindset and goal-driven behavior. Javier D'Anda, **GE**'s business development director for Mexico, was raised on the Mexican border with Texas, and knows all too well how easily cultural encounters can become cultural collisions. Some assembly plant industries along the border take an aggressive and counter-productive approach to Mexicans' relative concept of time. They may post signs that have a red diagonal line slashing through the word *mañana.* "You must manage differences instead of trying to change them. To create a sense of urgency, create a little crisis," D'Anda says with a smile. Another approach would be to offer incentives. Universally, foreign executives say that Mexican workers will produce more if they are paid a decent wage.

Farmland Industries

When Steve Dees came to Mexico in October 1993 to open a farm products sales and distribution operation, he had no prior international business experience. He brought with him his law degree, corporate experience as general counsel at the home office in Kansas City, some knowledge of Spanish and a strong interest in Mexico, which he had visited as a tourist. He did have behind him one of America's largest agri-businesses and the country's largest cooperative, **Farmland Industries,** a farmer's service and marketing group with annual sales volume of $7 billion.

"We always thought of ourselves as an American company," said Dees, who is general manager and the only American in **Farmland**'s seven-person Mexico City office. Getting past the psychological barriers that kept **Farmland** housebound took time. "We (**Farmland**) had talked about the global market and made diffuse efforts, but we finally got serious and focused on international markets, and Mexico was an important market," he said in an interview in the company's modest Mexico City offices. For **Farmland,** which sells grains, processed pork and beef products and fertilizer and other agricultural supplies, the Mexican market is promising because of the country's growing population, scarcity of arable land and the trade opening that was locked in with the North American Free Trade Agreement (NAFTA), which took effect in 1994.

Once **Farmland** decided to set up operations in Mexico, the company deliberately sent a strong message of the depth of its commitment by naming Dees, a senior executive, to open shop. At the time he was transferred, Dees was serving as executive vice-president in charge of administration and general counsel, and he remains in close contact with headquarters because he continues to be part of senior management of **Farmland.**

The first operations in Mexico were sales and distribution of grains, and **Farmland** got sales rolling by hiring Jesús Guevara, an experienced agent who had been selling grains for a **Farmland** subsidiary. Shortly after entering the Mexican market, Dees also hired the staff that had been working for Guevara in his agent days, a move that gave **Farmland** immediate expertise and avoided the temptation of bringing in an American work force, Dees said. In **Farmland**'s first year of business, sales in Mexico reached nearly 1 million tons of grain.

The company next moved into selling pork products through a Mexican distributor, **SAT-COM.** In less than a year, **Farmland** formed a joint venture with **SAT-COM** called **Farmland Alimentos** to utilize the Mexican firm's refrigerated warehouses and trucks to distribute pork and beef processed food to grocery stores in the three largest cities of Mexico City, Guadalajara and Monterrey. This joint venture provides another example of the benefits of teaming expertise, resources and products across the border. The Mexican partner offered distribution systems, a sales force, delivery trucks, refrigerated and freezer warehouses and knowledge of supermarket chains. **Farmland** offered produce, including fresh pork and beef, pork products, a brand name, capital, and knowledge of U.S. transportation networks, Dees said. Each partner put up half the capital in the joint venture. For Mexican companies to be able to reduce their debt burden even by half is a tremendous advantage because business loans in Mexico are costly. (Business credit averaged upwards of 25 percent nominal annual interest before the December 1994 devaluation, and rates soared far above 50 percent in the months following the economic crisis, even when it was available.)

As the first year of **Farmland**'s international operations drew to a close, Dees embarked on another joint venture. **Farmland** would sell feed grain to one of Mexico's leading egg producers, Guadalajara-based **VITEP,** an investment group made up of 15 companies. Further, **Farmland** made plans to process the paste from "spent hens" that no longer lay eggs to make hot-dogs. "We started with a sales operation, and are now moving in less than one year into a joint venture to produce food. This is a logical move that will allow us to diversify," Dees said.

To hear **Farmland**'s story of near-instant success makes doing business in Mexico sound deceptively simple. Joint ventures simplify business in that they reduce the risk and the investment of each individual partner and create rational divisions of labor. But joint ventures require coordination between two companies, and in this case between two countries. Paperwork often was held up at Kansas City headquarters, for example, when the staff person working on one step of the joint venture left for business travel, Dees said. The novelty of working with Mexico proved intimidating to **Farmland** home-office employees, so paperwork and procedures were centralized in one individual and other employees were unwilling to take over the Mexico portfolio.

As in a marriage, the success of a joint venture depends on the reliability of each partner, Dees cautions. "You can avoid 95 percent of the potential problems if you do business with the right people who have discipline and integrity and are factors in the market." Checking references on the partner is crucial, and the suitor should look into the banking relations and account collections of the partner and the credit information the partner keeps on his customers, he said. In the joint venture, each partner should stick with the business it does well. And, in the Mexican context where so many companies are eagerly seeking access to capital at a lower interest rate, the foreign firm must be careful to not fall into the role of banker for the partner, says Dees.

In its short time in Mexico, **Farmland** has encountered some of the common problems of doing business south of the border, and has also benefited from good luck and common sense. A snarl arose early on when **Farmland** tried to bring in computer equipment from the United States. "Getting the import permits and clearing customs was a red tape nightmare," and Dees soon realized it was cheaper to buy the computers in Mexico, which spared him headaches as well. As is wont to happen in Mexico, attending a fiesta helped Dees clear the initial logistical and communications hurdles. At a reception, he met a businessman who was vacating his offices and offered **Farmland** the furniture and phone lines, which sell for close to $1,000 each. "I didn't realize at the time that phone lines are like gold — buying them was the smartest move I ever made," Dees said. Although the telephone company was privatized in 1990, getting a line installed routinely takes six months or more.

Perhaps because of his long-standing interest in Mexico, Dees has been willing to adapt to the different style of doing business. He came with an open mind, and most executives say that having the right attitude is one of the most important assets for business in Mexico. "I came not having all the answers. My approach is not to try to teach Mexicans how to do business but to learn how to do business in Mexico," he said. One of his first lessons was the importance of face-to-face contact, which is certainly the operating style if not the essence of doing business in Mexico. His agent Guevara advised him that making sales means meeting Mexican clients, who want to know with whom they are dealing. This takes Dees away from his desk and puts him on the road often. "It is pretty easy to get around Mexico but you've gotta keep an open mind," he says, cheerfully describing one 20-hour travel day that ended with a midnight bus ride through the northern desert.

The Appeal of Joint Ventures

It is no accident that companies as different as **GE** and **Farmland** are forming joint ventures in Mexico. Teaming Mexican companies with foreign firms has become the most popular way of starting up operations in recent years as more and more companies enter Mexico. Joint ventures have moved far beyond the more conventional manufacturing operations and now take in sophisticated industries such as discount merchandise clubs and television production. The entertainment giants, **Fox** and **Televisa,** created the "Morning Glory" joint venture to film soap operas and television commercials at **Televisa**'s Mexico City studios and bring in American stars when necessary. Specialized fields such as environmental clean-up and engineering have also spawned joint ventures. For example, a western Canadian company of consulting engineers, the **I.D. Group,** set up a joint venture consulting company in Mexico, called **I.D. Canada-Mexico,** to develop environmental engineering projects in Mexico. The Canadians provide engineering expertise, particularly in environmental clean-up and protection, and the Mexicans "do the footwork, making contacts, establishing relations with government and finding projects (to bid on)," says Eva Kras, a Canadian and long-time resident of Guadalajara who works with the Mexican partners.

Since the trade opening began in 1986, joint ventures have become the option of choice for North American businesses seeking to enter Mexico. Joint ventures are endorsed by business partners, investment advisers, accountants, and consultants alike because they offer the opportunity to maximize the assets of each partner and create a win-win situation all around. Joint ventures can be established by finding a Mexican partner and starting up a new company, but most often the foreign company buys 50 percent or some other portion of an existing Mexican company. The foreign partner should investigate all competitors to detect the weaknesses of each. Then, the foreign firm should take a hard look at itself and decide whether it has the strengths to compensate for the weaknesses in its potential Mexican partner. Typically, the North American partner brings to the table technical expertise, capital, and knowledge of the U.S. or Canadian market. The Mexican partner offers experience in doing business in Mexico, management expertise in the Mexican setting, government relations, and a distribution network. "If you're not a multi-national corporation, you want a Mexican partner," a U.S. businessman with 20 years experience in Mexico, says flatly. The knowledge of Mexican partners is vital and saves time and costly errors in starting up business. In recent years, Mexicans have had a new incentive for participating in joint ventures: gaining access to capital or credit and escaping the exorbitant interest rates charged on business loans in Mexico. The capital provided by the foreign firm can come as a capital contribution, an infusion of capital and access to credit lines, a contribution of machinery, or an inter-company loan to the Mexican partner.

Although joint ventures offer advantages for each partner, the approach taken to these types of business partnerships should look beyond the mercenary. "Whatever the match is, the big problem at the beginning is you have to find a counterpart whom you can trust and have confidence in," says Eva Kras, the Canadian management consultant in Guadalajara. Even if there is trust, Mexican and American or Canadian business partners will look at each other through different prisms. "Anglos judge on what a company can produce and Mexicans judge on how they feel about the person," emphasizes Kras, author of the book, *Management in Two Cultures, Bridging the Gap between U.S. and Mexican Managers.*

Selecting the partner for a joint venture demands serious study, and there are no short-cuts around the detailed homework and background checks that make up what investors call "due diligence." There are various means of getting the facts needed for making an informed choice of a partner. Bank references should be sought, and business associates of the firm in question should be interviewed. International and Mexican business associates alike should be interviewed to determine the customer base of the potential partner and to be sure that payments and deliveries are timely on both sides of the border. It is not uncommon for Mexican businesses to apply a double standard, making international payments on time while falling behind with domestic clients. Standard credit evaluations are difficult because leading rating agencies in Mexico tend to differ only slightly, specialists caution. A proper due diligence investigation requires professional legal and accounting advice because a foreigner lacks the knowledge to understand and interpret Mexican financial statements, valuation of assets and labor agreements. A due diligence team for a joint venture would include an in-house industry expert on machines, a Mexican public accounting firm familiar with U.S. accounting, or an American in a Big Six accounting firm knowledgeable about American and Mexican accounting methods, a Mexican lawyer, and an official from the foreign company, such as a treasurer or operating vice-president, to head the team and lead the negotiations. Cost of this preliminary investigation can total $50,000.

Because joint ventures have proliferated in Mexico in recent years, specific tips and cautions are readily available from business specialists. One formula for success is for the Mexican partner to put up some of the capital in the new enterprise because "there's no other way to make him honest or work to full capacity," says an investment adviser and long-time foreign resident of Mexico. Successful joint ventures combine management from both partners, with Mexicans in basic management positions and foreigners in a few key slots, such as plant manager, says Kathy Newman, international accounting specialist at **Arthur Andersen**'s Mexico City office. "Americans are uneasy doing business without Mexican management, and that's the way it should be. Still, a joint venture is less likely to work if there is not a day-to-day presence of Americans because (if not present) they are less informed and are not taken seriously," she explains.

Many of the pitfalls of joint ventures can be averted through negotiations based on good information. Sensitive points include the arbitration clause, reporting provisions, Mexican labor laws, and valuation of assets, says Newman. Unless stipulated otherwise, joint venture agreements usually imply that disputes will be resolved in Mexican courts, which puts the foreign firm at a disadvantage. Because dispute resolution is key in a joint venture, Newman recommends a clause that provides for disputes to be heard by the American Arbitration Association or the International Arbitration Association with the agreement that their decisions will be binding. Reporting agreements should provide the foreign firm with monthly reporting in an understandable format. Labor treatment is often a sticking point in joint ventures when foreign partners want to reduce the work force. Mexican labor law is protective of unionized workers, and guarantees generous severance payments to fired workers. At some plants the bill for firing workers can reach $2 million to $3 million. Labor liabilities are not recorded in book liabilities, so joint venture partners must decide who will pay these costs. The valuation of machinery and equipment owned by the Mexican partner should be made by a technology specialist who keeps a view to the modernization process that will likely require upgrading machinery, Newman says. Other assets that are part of the joint venture should be assessed with care, because their value is often inflated in Mexico, and "there is always the potential they are operating with two or three sets of books," says Graeme Bromley, a business consultant and long-time resident of Mexico.

With Mexico's recent reductions in tariffs and the elimination of import licenses, the opportunities for import and export business have ballooned. In fact, in the first four years of this decade, U.S. exports to Mexico tripled, and two-way trade between Mexico and Canada doubled between 1985 and 1992. Since NAFTA opened up a huge market in government procurement; U.S. firms have supplied $4 billion of the $8 billion in Mexican government purchases annually. At the same time, as domestic markets in North America slumped, manufacturers looked to Mexico as a new marketplace. U.S. exports to Mexico run the full gamut from manufacturing machinery to passenger buses and computers and include a full range of consumer goods from luxury cars to blue jeans and services that include fast food franchises and insurance.

Finding Sales Reps

For firms or individuals wanting to set up import or export operations in Mexico, initial introductions to Mexican sales representatives, distributors, or manufacturers can often be arranged by contacting their embassy in Mexico or by attending a trade show. Only rarely do these initial contacts blossom into successful, full-fledged business associations, advisers caution. A better strategy for exploring the import-export business begins with marketing research to profile the competition and learn with whom they work, says Graeme Bromley, director-general of **Stratec Consultants International,** a Mexico City-based business consulting firm. Marketing research is tricky and requires specialized knowledge of Mexico, where the market is often not all that it seems. For example, although there are more than 90 million Mexicans, the American Chamber of Commerce claims that no more than 40 million can be considered consumers, and other analysts claim that only 20 million Mexicans have purchasing power to buy imported goods. The foreign producer should visit Mexico at least three times a year to learn the market, some consultants suggest.

Would-be importers must also research the availability of maintenance and repair services for imported goods as well as courier and transportation linkages to Mexico.

This knowledge helps clarify the business strategy, which, in turn, affects the choice of the appropriate Mexican representative. As with joint ventures, a detailed screening process is essential for choosing a business associate or representative. "You need to find out what clients think of him (the sales representative) and what he does for clients," Bromley says. Ideally, a representative should have experience working in a multi-national corporation to have gained familiarity with international business practices and habits, and an engineering and business degree, Bromley says. Representatives who are overextended and work for more than 10 clients, and people lacking multi-nationals among their clients are to be avoided, he adds.

Showing your product is key to opening the Mexican market, and this demands sending the representative traveling to key zones in the country, so a travel budget, that could start at $2,000 per month, should be included in representation expenses. Business will develop gradually after Mexican clients test your representative and the product, and sales may not materialize until the second year. Good maintenance service for your products will win over and hold clients, Bromley says.

Mexico Overview

Rocky Road to
Economic Modernization

Mexico has long remained a mystery to foreign investors and exporters. Endowed with a rich resource base, including oil, a large market based on its population of 90 million people, and a strategic location south of the United States, the potential of Mexico has been abundantly apparent. Until recently, however, Mexican government policy restricted opportunities for foreign business through high tariff barriers and investment restrictions that kept foreign goods and investors away.

Today, Mexico is welcoming foreign investment and expanding its foreign trade rapidly. Former Presidents Miguel de la Madrid and Carlos Salinas de Gortari implemented sweeping economic reforms that improved the business climate. Negotiation of the North American Free Trade Agreement gave rise to a series of measures specifically aimed at attracting investment by removing restrictions on investment and by obligating Mexico to provide guarantees for foreign investment and expand international trade.

Beginning in 1983, the government embarked on an ambitious privatization program that opened important and large industries, including telecommunications, steel, copper mining, airlines and the banking sector, to foreign investment. In 1986, Mexico signed the General Agreement on Tariffs and Trade (GATT), and formalized the trade opening that has eliminated nearly all categories of import licenses and sharply reduced tariffs on imported goods. In 1989, the restrictive foreign investment law was modified, allowing foreign firms to establish wholly owned subsidiaries and opening up 72 percent of economic activities to 100-percent foreign investment, including agribusiness, petrochemicals, construction, financial services, steel, textiles, telecommunications and transportation.

Throughout the 1980s, the shrinking job market and government management of the officially controlled labor unions weakened union clout and paved the way for the introduction of productivity-linked contracts and greater management control over labor. Mexico maximized its strategic location adjacent to the world's largest consumer market by joining NAFTA. New multilateral ties also link Mexico to the Caribbean nations near its Atlantic coastline and the Asian neighbors across the Pacific. By joining sub-regional trading groups in South America, Mexico diversified and expanded its own export markets. These dramatic changes created a dynamic business atmosphere that attracted interest in industries ranging from the automotive giants to retail outlets to franchises and specialized services as varied as real estate agencies and environmental engineering firms.

Mexico's domestic economy also changed radically during the past decade. Following the oil bust and the international debt crisis of the early 1980s, like most other Latin American countries, Mexico experienced a deep recession. Inflation soared to a peak of 167 percent per year in 1987, millions were thrown out of work, and purchasing power fell by more than 50 percent. At enormous cost to wage-earners and salaried workers, the government made drastic reductions in federal spending, maintained a balanced budget and brought inflation down to below 10 percent for 1993. Turbulence in the economy was tamed by eight successive anti-inflation pacts beginning in 1987 that froze wages and prices and averted sharp fluctuations in the Mexican peso exchange rate by setting a fixed, gradual rate of peso slippage. Continuity in economic policy was the hallmark of the 1980s in Mexico. The budget austerity, selling off of government enterprises, wage freezes, and trade opening initiated by President de la Madrid were extended and deepened by President Salinas de Gortari until his term ended Dec. 1, 1994.

Despite these gains, fragility remained in the economy. Major points of vulnerability were the trade deficit, which averaged nearly $20 billion a year from 1989 onward, heavy dependence on foreign portfolio investment, and pressure on the peso. Economic growth was almost nil (0.4 percent) in 1993 and remained sluggish throughout most of 1994 until a strong third quarter pushed the entire year's average above 3 percent. But that could not head off the building nervousness of investors in the Mexican financial markets, both foreign and domestic. Unreassured by government promises not to devalue the currency, some began pulling money out of Mexican securities in the later months of 1994, adding to the pressures already created by the trade imbalance and to the government's difficulties in financing that deficit.

Crisis Tests New President Zedillo

Within days of taking office on Dec. 1, 1994, the new president, Ernesto Zedillo, was confronted by dangerously falling foreign exchange reserves, but his aides continued to rule out a devaluation. Nevertheless, on Dec. 20, the government devalued the peso, which previously had been pegged at 3.5 to the U.S. dollar, by almost 13 percent, causing dismay among investors, including U.S. holders of some $75 billion in Mexican securities. Two days later, the Zedillo administration reversed course again and decided to let the peso float freely against other currencies, setting the currency on a steep decline. That set off panic in Mexican financial markets, which for weeks affected other markets in Latin America and other places as well. Even financial markets as healthy as those in Chile and Argentina suffered what other Latin Americans came to call "The Tequila Effect."

During the ensuing weeks, as officials of the Clinton Administration in Washington and of the International Monetary Fund worked to put together a Mexican rescue package, the peso fell to more than 7 to the U.S. dollar and Mexican interest rates gyrated between 50 percent and 100 percent, with the government fighting an uphill battle to continue rolling over its heavy load of short-term debt. Fears of runaway inflation mounted. In the process, President Zedillo, who was being criticized as indecisive, dumped his first finance minister, Jaime Serra Puche, after just a month in office. The replacement, Guillermo Ortiz Martínez, a former under secretary of finance, had the respect and support of New York investors and many others but could not by himself restore order to the Mexican economy and the confidence of the outside world.

Initially, the government blamed the pressures that led to the devaluation on the resurgence of an Indian revolt in the southern state of Chiapas. It had first erupted at the beginning of 1994 to protest political repression and the government's economic policies. Later, more plausible explanations emerged. Although Mexico had been largely avoiding deficit spending in its domestic budget, it was financing the country's unprecedented import binge — mostly goods from

U.S. exporters, who had swung into action on the heels of the passage of NAFTA — with short-term debt, most of it being purchased by foreigners who could easily withdraw their money. Tightening monetary policy in the United States had also served — through higher interest rates — to draw U.S. capital back home. Shortly after taking over as finance minister, Guillermo Ortiz noted that, had there been no change in Mexican policy, the current account deficit was projected to reach $31 billion in 1995, nearly 8 percent of GDP. At the same time, Mexican manufacturers and other producers, long accustomed to protected domestic markets, had been slow to adapt and market their own output for export to the United States and elsewhere. Further, the direct foreign investment in Mexican manufacturing that many critics of NAFTA in the United States had predicted would cost jobs north of the border had, in fact, been slow to develop. That kind of direct, long-term investment was help that much of Mexican industry had needed in order to become competitive in world markets.

In late February 1995, an international loan package was signed that promised Mexico about $50 billion, of which $20 billion came from the United States. In return, the Zedillo government committed itself to run a budget surplus in 1995 and keep interest rates above the inflation rate. To accomplish these things, Mexico quickly adopted an austerity plan and raised a number of taxes while lifting wage controls. Financial markets in Mexico initially reacted positively, but a lengthy period of economic instability was expected, marked by recession, job losses and high inflation.

Wild West Theory Holds in Mexican Business

The crisis seemed to support the theory held by many executives that doing business in Mexico is similar to operating in the Wild West — meaning a shortage of rules and every opportunity to win, or lose, big. Firms whose success in Mexico was dependent on the country's growing consumer society — such as **Wal-Mart** and **Citicorp**'s retail banking operations — slowed or postponed expansion plans because they expected discretionary spending in Mexico to dry up for a time. Likewise, firms in the United States and Canada and outside the NAFTA region that had been pushing exports to Mexico, including Detroit automakers, saw their sales slide. Many firms also reported collection problems.

However, other foreign business interests saw the crisis, effectively, as a buying opportunity — a chance to jump into a fertile business setting during a temporary setback while costs were lower. They viewed direct investment as being much safer than portfolio investments and potentially very profitable. Direct investment in anything related to telecommunications, infrastructure, and basic housing needs was seen as good business, whatever the general economic picture. Many foreign firms that were manufacturing in Mexico for export elsewhere or considering starting or expanding such operations had the expectation of a good profit picture. **Motorola, Inc.,** for example, announced that it was proceeding with an expansion in Mexico costing $72 million.

Big Mexican firms capable of exporting also were optimistic as their foreign sales of such items as beer, steel, glass, and car batteries soared even before the rescue package was completed. But most Mexican firms, unless they could find a foreign partner, were not in a position to take advantage of the export opening created by the devaluation. Either the quality of their products was not competitive in open markets, or the drying up of domestic credit made it impossible for them to expand or re-tool.

Zedillo Grapples with Political Turbulence

Zedillo came into the presidency at the end of a year of unprecedented political turbulence for Mexico, but the tenacity and independence he showed in dealing with the inherited political crises at the same time he was facing the economic crisis was another of the reasons for cautious optimism in the early months of his term. After opening with the rebellion in the south of the country, the year 1994 had seen the assassination of two leaders of the ruling Institutional Revolutionary Party (PRI). Luis Donaldo Colosio, the PRI's first presidential candidate, was shot to death in the midst of a campaign rally. Zedillo, who had been Colosio's campaign manager, was then thrust into the candidacy and went on to win, as the PRI candidate has done every year since 1929. The other assassination victim, José Francisco Ruiz Massieu, the deputy party leader, was slain by gunmen on Sept. 28, 1994.

Both killings were surrounded by rumors that they were linked to in-fighting in the PRI over how far to go in reducing Mexico's endemic corruption and in negotiating electoral reform with the country's strengthening opposition parties and the rebels in the south. The possibility that major figures in the party may have been linked to one or both killings emerged in the early months of Zedillo's presidency, and he did not seem to flinch when his attorney general arrested the elder brother of former President Salinas de Gortari on charges of having ordered the murder of Ruiz Massieu. President Zedillo had already broken Mexican form by naming as his attorney general Antonio Lozano, a member of the National Action Party (PAN), the first opposition figure to serve in a presidential cabinet in 65 years of PRI rule. Lozano, from the outset, indicated that he intended to aggressively pursue the investigation of the murder cases, as well as corruption and judicial reform, and President Zedillo seemed to stand firmly behind him.

Before he was confronted with the peso crisis President Zedillo had promised an ambitious program of increased federal spending on public works as part of an effort to spread the benefits of a more modern economy to less advantaged Mexicans, but the austerity measures necessitated by the foreign rescue package seemed to make that unlikely. Another part of the Zedillo program that still appeared feasible was to open ports, roads, power and water treatment facilities and segments of the telecommunications industry to private investment, which could help create jobs and improve and expand the vital transport and energy networks that allow business to develop and trade to flow.

Judicial reform was also a central plank of the Zedillo platform, and was heartily endorsed by foreign investors, who continue to seek a more secure investment and business climate in Mexico. Eliminating arbitrary justice in the police forces and the courts will be one of the most difficult tasks of the Zedillo presidency.

Despite the economic modernization steps taken in recent years, Mexico remains a developing nation, and its economy and market differ greatly from the United States. According to government statistics, nearly half the population, or some 43 million people, lives below the poverty line, and a majority of the work force earns less than two minimum wages. Before the peso crisis, that was the equivalent of $9 a day. After the crisis and resulting inflation, two minimum wages equaled only $5.40.

"The Mexican market is somewhere between wild optimism and Ross Perot. If you want to sell Lady Godiva chocolates and you say it's a market of 90 million, it's (really) a very small market," quips **Farmland**'s Mexico City manager Steve Dees, alluding to the divergent bullish and bearish outlooks on Mexico that came to the fore during the debate to approve NAFTA.

A Country With Its Own Business Culture

Despite the rapid modernization and internationalization of the economy, Mexican business culture still differs sharply from North American and western business style. First and foremost, Mexicans are highly sensitive people, a trait that permeates all their relationships, including business dealings. Business is conducted face-to-face, and the main purpose of most meetings is to get to know the other person. From the Mexican point of view, there is no better way to relate to business contacts than over breakfast or lunch, and to talk about family life and personal interests at length before turning to business matters. This is an integral part of the process of becoming comfortable with another person and developing an intuitive sense of whether he or she can be trusted.

"At the outset you build a relation with sincerity," says Charles Griffin, president and director-general of **Grupo Kodak-Mexico** and president of the American Chamber of Commerce. This suggests that things don't happen quickly. Business cannot be done by mail or fax, and it is difficult to close a sale on the first trip, but those personal relations built with care will help the foreigner to separate out the good guys from the bad guys and to create rich relationships that can become lasting friendships as well as productive business associations.

Mexicans look to feel accepted by others, and one of the best ways to demonstrate a genuine interest in Mexicans is by working to learn Spanish. Foreigners will not be expected to understand business contracts in Spanish, but being able to greet people and exchange some small talk will be vastly appreciated and show your commitment to Mexico. Many visitors and business people don't do their homework and learn about Mexico or don't accept the culture. "Those who do their homework find they even have fun," says Jorge Mejia, director of the Arizona state trade office in Mexico City.

"Attitude is everything," says Shauna de Brun, director-general of the **Texel** joint venture textile and thread factory, who went on to explain: "There is a great deal of competence and professionalism here in Mexico, and if foreigners arrive believing they are the only ones who know something about everything they will be greatly mistaken. The style of doing business may be different, but the basic principles of business — profitability, market share and positioning, focus through leadership — are well understood. To approach existing Mexican business with this attitude will gain rapid ground for a business person wanting to do business successfully in Mexico." In other words: If foreigners storm in on the assumption that they are going to teach Mexicans how to do everything, they will find that Mexicans resist by digging in their heels. But a communicative, team approach coupled with sensitive treatment of employees, a fair wage policy and the exercise of authority when absolutely needed will win cooperation and loyalty, says de Brun.

Business Opportunities

While the different business culture makes getting started slower and more difficult than at home, thousands of companies have found that entering Mexico is more than worth the effort. In the years between the 1986 trade opening and the 1994 crash, Mexican consumers indulged many of their whims for U.S. goods, ranging from canned black olives and beauty products to **Domino's** pizzas and Lincoln Towncars, demonstrating a near-insatiable appetite and inflating the trade deficit. Nearly all the major U.S. multi-national corporations have large operations in Mexico. **Ford** and **Chrysler** have made substantial investments in automotive assembly plants in recent years. Since the trade opening began in 1986, fast food franchises, including **McDonald's, Domino's Pizza** and **Pizza Hut,** have proliferated. Specialized service companies, such as **Century 21** real estate and **Blockbuster Video,** are sprouting up all over Mexico. Mexican consumers are probably more familiar with U.S. consumer goods than consumers in any other foreign market. Foreign firms with long experience in Mexico think that kind of demand and taste preference is not likely to disappear with one economic crisis, but will quickly revive once the average Mexican's economic fortunes improve.

The advantages of doing business in Mexico are legion, but most businessmen and women emphasize that the single greatest value is the people themselves. Mexicans are intelligent and warm, and are hard-working when given the proper incentives, which include care along with money. Providing training to workers will win their commitment over the long-term. Except in the assembly plant industry, where too many jobs are clustered along the border, the turnover rate among workers is normally low.

Mexico offers other advantages as a business location. The much-touted low cost of labor is viewed by many in the business community as a passing phenomenon. "Low-cost labor will be short-lived," says **Kodak**'s Charles Griffin. The proximity to the huge U.S. market, which makes for low transportation costs, represents an enormous business opportunity. The domestic market in Mexico is somewhat narrow for the consumer goods typical in many industrialized nations. But, for businesses with a wide vision and a long-term commitment to Mexico, the country offers an enormous market for meeting basic needs, such as education and low-cost housing.

For business people ranging from investors who stay at home and buy Mexican stocks to joint venture partners and manufacturers who set up shop in Mexico, investing in Mexico implies taking risks. These include country risk, business risk, political risk and currency risk. In exchange for taking those risks, Mexico offers a higher premium on financial instruments, such as treasury bills, and historically businesses have enjoyed high profit margins.

During the 1990s, three of the most important sectors that will undergo major expansion calling for foreign lending, technology, and service contracts are telecommunications, energy and infrastructure. Although the economic crisis of early 1995 dampened the prospects for immediate expansion of these key sectors, growth in telecommunications, energy, and infrastructure is inevitable and necessary to support increasing trade and to meet the demands of a growing population. In 1997, the **Teléfonos de Mexico** monopoly concession ends, opening up a growing market hungry for competitive long distance rates, more cellular phone networks and improved telephone service.

The energy sector, and particularly co-generation of electricity and the petrochemical and refining segments of the petroleum industry, are expected to open up to greater participation by foreign engineers, equipment suppliers, investors, and financial deals. Under President Zedillo, infrastructure development will get a boost as part of an effort to improve facilities for trade and to create employment. An ambitious private sector highway construction program is slated for the late 1990s, and the government will issue private concessions to the nation's ports to stimulate upgrading of marine transportation facilities. Environmental industries, including waste water treatment and pollution clean-up, are expected to grow, especially along the U.S.-Mexico border where World Bank and Mexican government funding of $4 billion is earmarked to finance clean-up.

Government procurement offers vast business opportunities for foreign firms. The Mexican government spends some $8 billion annually contracting services and purchasing equipment and supplies, and U.S. companies garner $4 billion of that business. Service contracts in the oil industry will be important in coming years.

Red Tape, Corruption, Other Woes

Mexico lacks the services and infrastructure available in the United States and Canada for supporting and facilitating business and commerce. The shortcomings range from a deficient justice system to faulty phones to inadequate highway systems. Mexican officials are keenly aware of these problems, and have privatized industry and highways and are creating investment incentives to pump money into modernizing infrastructure to improve the conditions for conducting business in the global economy. "The change from the stone age to hi tech will take place in two years here," quips Jorge Mejia, director of the Arizona state trade office in Mexico City, and an optimistic observer of the trade opening.

Finally, getting reliable information useful for management decisions is extremely difficult in Mexico. Many government statistics are subject to question, and serious independent sources of business information are few. The Mexican government touts its economic reforms, including the foreign investment opening and privatization process, as measures that increase "transparency" in the way of doing business in Mexico. This is a polite way of saying that the Mexican government is setting up clear rules of the game for businessmen and investors, eliminating or reducing bureaucratic obstacles, and increasing disclosure. Certainly, positive steps have been taken that are moving Mexico toward greater streamlining of bureaucratic processes and de-regulation, which make it easier for foreign companies to enter and operate in Mexico. At the same time, Mexican businesses tend to become more open about their finances once they are listed on the stock exchange or invite foreign investment through partnerships and joint ventures. This is a process that has begun only recently, and it will take a few more years before full disclosure and bureaucratic efficiency are the norm in Mexico.

Similarly, the two previous governments, of Presidents de la Madrid and Salinas de Gortari, launched several initiatives to combat corruption in government bureaucracies that affect many business-related activities, including customs, large service contracts, and licensing. President Zedillo has pledged to undertake a judicial reform aimed at making the court system work and cleaning up the police forces. If judicial reform succeeds in creating a justice system that works fairly rather than arbitrarily and developing honest police forces that respect human rights, the benefits for business will be great. Most observers of Mexican politics believe that the task is formidable.

Even the savviest businessmen and women have to hone their skills for dealing with bureaucratic delays and corruption, which are far more elaborate and widespread in Mexico than in the United States and Canada. Often, delays in paperwork are a tactic for obtaining a bribe to grease the wheels of the bureaucracy. Corruption persists because of the predominance of the cash economy, which leaves no paper trail, and also because of poor controls that allow a very few staff members to hold keys, and because it is accepted as part of the culture. Setting up a business in Mexico can require scores of forms and numerous visits to government offices, and each step in the process might be expedited with a bribe, but this is not recommended. Paperwork hurdles can be overcome cleanly, with patience and effort. "It takes a long-term commitment to the market to be successful (in Mexico), but not a bribe," says Marco Delgado, director of the Texas state trade office in Mexico City.

Experienced business people suggest that corruption in your own business can be hard to detect. The investor who is buying a company should look carefully at who controls the keys, review closely the financial statements, and look carefully at segments of the production process that could be easily overlooked, such as manufacturing seconds that can be resold. Contracts should be reviewed carefully to check for possible kickback arrangements.

The Vastly Varied States of Mexico

Mexico offers a wide range of business locations. There are as many potential business sites as opportunities for manufacturing and marketing. The ongoing drive to build superhighways is improving transportation to many states in the interior, and the upgrading of ports in coming years will modernize and expand shipping facilities on the Pacific and Atlantic coasts. Mexico has an extensive network of domestic airports, and many provincial airports are being upgraded to accommodate international flights.

Mexico is made up of a number of distinct regions, and those most highly developed for industry and trade remain the Mexico City-central highlands area, the northern border and strategic port cities. **GE**'s business development director, Javier D'Anda, says each of the leading business regions has its own culture. The border region and the northern industrial city of Monterrey is Americanized and industrialized, has few natural resources and takes as its hero the successful entrepreneur, such as Isaac Garza who developed the **Cuauhtemoc** brewery and diversified into steel and cardboard production. The Mexico City-central region is rich in natural resources, Mexican in outlook and worships the old money aristocracy, D'Anda says. Finally, the Gulf and Pacific coast ports have abundant resources, little industry, specialize in service industries, including tourism, relish a slow pace and glorify the regional entrepreneur who developed a local attraction such as the traditional businessman's watering hole, the **Café Parroquia,** at Veracruz harbor.

Manufacturing, financing, and the growing services industry remain clustered in the nation's three largest cities. The sprawling capital, Mexico City, remains the business capital of Mexico, with over half of the nation's industry. With a population of 20 million, it is by far the largest market in the country. The northern city of Monterrey is the leading industrial center and, in the wake of the 1991 bank privatizations, now controls two of the country's three largest banks. Guadalajara, located on a desert plain 676 kilometers northwest of Mexico City, is the third largest city and an important center for the electronics industry. In late 1994, a new superhighway linking Guadalajara to Mexico City was completed, sharply reducing the travel time between the country's two largest markets.

Manufacturing and financing also cluster at other strategically located areas in Mexico. The U.S.-Mexico border is the natural home to the assembly plant industry, which in 1993 was the country's largest source of export earnings. With more than 2,000 plants that employ more than 500,000 Mexicans, the *maquiladoras* assemble clothing, car parts, electronic circuitry, television sets, and other products that are shipped across the border for packaging and distribution in the U.S. market. The leading cities in the assembly plant industry are Tijuana, near San Diego, California, and Ciudad Juárez, across from El Paso, Texas. Other sites are becoming popular for assembly plants or manufacturing. These include the port of Progreso, near Mérida, on the Yucatán peninsula, which is within easy shipping distance of New Orleans and Miami, and the northern state capital of Aguascalientes, which has developed industrial parks and offers incentives to investors, and San Luis Potosí.

The natural habitats for the oil and gas industries are the Gulf Coast states of Tamaulipas, Veracruz, Tabasco, Campeche, and Chiapas, where Mexico's largest on-shore and marine oil and gas fields are located. Production of winter vegetables and fresh produce for export is most highly developed in the states of Guanajuato, Sonora, and Sinaloa, but avocado production is centered in Michoacán state, and extensive cultivation of bananas and other tropical fruits is located primarily in Tabasco and Chiapas.

For historical reasons, other industries grew up in particular sites and have remained there. The textile industry, which is experiencing major dislocations as part of the global modernization process, is centered in Mexico City and Puebla, although recently established plants are clustering in the state of Hidalgo. The shoe industry has bases in Guadalajara and in León, Guanajuato.

In particular circumstances, some industries are finding that relatively unconventional locations can offer important advantages. The towns of San Juan del Río, 200 kilometers north of Mexico City in Queretaro state, and Celaya, about 300 kilometers northwest of the capital in Guanajuato state, are among the small towns where the transmission cable manufacturer, **Condumex,** a subsidiary of **Teléfonos de Mexico,** has set up plants. The advantage of such locations are that the work force is stable, so there is less turnover.

Two important factors in site location must be kept in mind in Mexico: water and the labor pool. Water is relatively scarce throughout most of Mexico because most of the country is a desert. Many provincial capitals are already suffering from a shortage of water, and in the near future industrial development may be constrained by the lack of water or the high cost of piping water in from long distances. More than half of Mexico's hydraulic resources are located in southeastern Tabasco and Chiapas states, some 1,000 kilometers from the densely populated, industrialized, and desert center of the country.

The availability of a stable work force may be an important factor in site location. In the past decade, *maquiladora* managers have complained bitterly of turnover rates as high as 25 percent a year in the border cities, where changing jobs is made easy by the concentration of assembly plants and the ready access to alternative employment.

Mexico at a Glance

Population: 90 million.

Population growth rate: 2.1 percent a year.

Labor force: 26 million plus; 1 million reach working age annually. Employment in the informal economy is high, totaling more than 5 million people, accounting for an estimated 25-33 percent of Mexico's GDP.

Language: Spanish is the official language; some 60 Indian languages are spoken by more than 10 million indigenous peoples.

Ethnic Mix: Majority of population is mestizo, a mixture of Indian with descendants of Spaniards.

Literacy and Educational levels: Literacy, according to government statistics, is 90 percent. Education is highly variable. Mexican elites are as well or better educated than top-ranking American and European CEOs, professionals and Cabinet officials. There is a relatively large pool of university educated professionals. The vast majority of the population has less than a sixth-grade education.

Climate: Varies with altitude and region. Mexico City and the central plateau, where the majority of the population lives, is situated more than 5,000 feet above sea level, which provides a temperate, spring-like climate. Northern Mexico has a dry, desert climate. The south is tropical.

To consider in deciding when to visit: Dry season is from November-May. Least pollution in Mexico City between May and October. Worst pollution in Mexico City from December to March. During rainy season, from May to November, storms usually occur only during several hours of the afternoon.

Religions: Roman Catholics, 85 percent; evangelical Protestants, more than 10 percent.

Natural resources: Petroleum, large reserves of natural gas, silver, copper, gold, zinc, lead, barite, manganese.

Natural resource scarcity: Water is relatively scarce in many parts of Mexico because most of the country is a desert. The notable exception is the southeastern Gulf Coast region comprising Tabasco, Campeche and Chiapas states, which concentrate about 30 percent of the nation's water resources. Investors planning to set up industrial plants or irrigated agriculture should make a careful study of the availability of water in their region. Planning should consider recycling of industrial water.

Chief agricultural products: Coffee, maize, wheat, rice and beans, sugar; a wide range of tropical and temperate fruits, tomatoes, winter vegetables, forestry products.

Land area: 1.97 million square kilometers.

Economic statistics:

GDP: $379.6 billion (1994)

Per Capita GDP: $4,328

Economic growth rate: 3.5 percent (1994)

Main exports: Automobiles, petroleum, automobile engines, trucks, vegetables, tomatoes, coffee, electric cables, iron.

Main imports: Auto parts for assembly, auto chassis and parts for repair, computers, electronic equipment and parts, paper and cardboard, cellulose pulp, automobiles, synthetic resin products, soybeans, gasoline, animal and vegetable oils, butane and propane.

Duties on imports: Generally speaking, duties are 15-20 percent for computer and electronic equipment and consumer goods; 10 percent on some machinery and equipment made in Mexico; 5 percent on intermediate goods that Mexico does not produce in sufficient quantity, and zero on industrial parts and intermediate goods that Mexico does not produce at all. These rates all fit within NAFTA regulations. Mexico generally applies the same rates to non-NAFTA countries, but after the December 1994 currency crisis it began to consider raising to 35 percent the duties on textiles, leather, and shoes, a step that would be targeted at China and other Asian export nations.

Repatriation of profits: Under NAFTA rules, there are no restrictions on repatriation of profits to the United States and Canada. There are, likewise, no restrictions on repatriation to GATT-member nations, although that treaty allows Mexico to seek authorization for limited restrictions if its hard currency reserves become dangerously low.

When You Go to Mexico

Visas/Documents: For business visits, a business visa is required. This can be obtained from Mexican consulates abroad. Many business visitors travel to Mexico on tourists visas, which is not legally correct.

Airlines: Direct international flights arrive at Mexico City, Guadalajara, Monterrey, Cancun and all other beach resort cities.

● International carriers serving Mexico City include AeroCalifornia, Aeroflot-Russian International, Aerolineas Argentinas, Aeromexico, Aeroperu, Air France, American, America West, Avensa, Avianca, Aviateca, British Airways, Canadian Airlines International, Continental, COPA, Cubana, Delta, Iberia, Japan Airlines, KLM, LACSA, Ladeco, Lan Chile, Lloyd Aero Boliviano, Lufthansa, Malaysia Airlines, Mexicana, TACA, TAESA, United, Varig.

● International carriers serving Guadalajara include AeroCalifornia, Aeromexico, Alaska Airlines, American, Continental, Delta, Mexicana, SARO, TAESA, United.

● International carriers serving Monterrey include Aeromexico, American, Continental, Delta, Mexicana, SARO, TAESA.

● Domestic flights are available on the national airlines, AeroMexico, Mexicana and Taesa, and the growing number of regional carriers.

Arrival at airport: Mexico encourages tourism and business visitors, so passing through migration and customs is simple, expeditious and standard. A customs declaration form is provided in flight to incoming international travelers, and luggage inspection is made on a random basis of about 10 percent of passengers.

Airport transportation: At Mexico City and most other international airports in the country, two types of taxi service are available: the airport taxis which have controlled fees (the customer buys a ticket and pays a flat fee set by zones), and the taxis hovering at the terminal, which often charge tourists whatever the traffic will bear. At beach resorts, hotels often send buses to the airport. Ask your travel agent about special airport pick-up services.

Hotels

NOTE: Mexico City's top hotels and many of those elsewhere in the country set their prices in dollars and convert them to pesos on a daily basis. Thus, you may find the peso prices quoted to you fluctuating, but not the dollar equivalents. Even though a bill is paid with a credit card, it is converted to pesos at the daily exchange rate. All rates include 15 percent tax. Many of the hotels are eager to quote lower corporate rates.

MEXICO CITY
Top of the line hotels offering the best service; very expensive. (Quoted rates of $180-$270 a night):
Four Seasons
Paseo de la Reforma 500
Tel: (525) 230-1818. Reservations fax: (525) 230-1817; Guest fax: (525) 230-1808.
A gracious, elegant newly built hotel with a large interior courtyard. Business center (translation, interpreting, typing, copying, fax), meeting center, boardroom, meeting/banquet rooms.
Camino Real
Mariano Escobedo 300.
Tel: (525) 203-2121. Fax: (525) 250-6897.

Across from Chapultepec Park, the Camino Real is a gem of the best modern Mexican architecture with spacious lobbies and rooms.

Maria Isabel-Sheraton Hotel

Paseo de la Reforma 325 (between U.S. Embassy and Angel de la Independencia).

Tel: (525) 207-3933. Fax: (525) 207-0684.

Standard Sheraton comfort, some rooms have lovely view of Paseo de la Reforma and the Angel statue, excellent desks in rooms for working.

Hotel Marquis

Paseo de la Reforma 465.

Tel: (525) 211-3600. Fax: (525) 211-5561.

New, flashy all-marble lobby area, bilingual secretarial services.

Hotel Nikko

Campos Eliseos 204.

Tel: (525) 203-4020. Fax: (525) 280-9191.

Luxurious high-rise.

Casa Vieja (not a hotel; 20 exclusive apartment-suites)

Eugenio Sue 45, Colonia Polanco, 11560 Mexico, D.F., Mexico

Tel: (525) 282-0067. Fax: (525) 281-3780.

Luxury atmosphere; serves breakfast only; excellent security. Its rates, which vastly exceed those of other top hotels in Mexico City, are $374 for a small room, $483 for a medium room, and $748 for a large room.

Good hotels, all services. ($150-220):

Hotel Galeria Plaza

Hamburgo 195, (1 block off Reforma near Angel de la Independencia)

Tel: (525) 211-0014. Fax: (525) 207-5867.

Hotel Imperial

Paseo de la Reforma 64

Tel: (525) 705-4911. Fax: (525) 703-3122.

Recently renovated hotel with charming art deco details, large conference rooms, business center.

Moderate (Quoted prices of $50-$120):

Hotel Bristol

Plaza Necaxa 17 (Calles Sena and Panuco), (3 blocks off Reforma near American Embassy)

Tel: (525) 208-1717. Fax: (525) 533-6060.

In a quiet residential area near the Pink Zone.

Hotel Maria Cristina

Rio Lerma 31

Tel: (525) 566-9688 and 703-1787. Fax: (525) 566-9194.

Lovely, quiet garden in well located hotel one block off Paseo de la Reforma near the Pink Zone.

Hotel Calinda Geneve

Londres 130 (2 blocks off Reforma)

Tel: (525) 211-0071. Fax: (525) 208-7422

Located in the Pink Zone, has traditional European style, functional rooms, lovely breakfast room under a large skylight.

Best Western Hotel De Cortes

Ave. Hidalgo 85 & Paseo de la Reforma (across from Alameda Park)

Tel: (525) 518-2181. Fax: (525) 512-1863

Intimate, 27-unit hotel in an 18th century mansion with lush patio-dining area.

Best Western Hotel Majestic

Madero 73 (Faces Zócalo).

Tel: (525) 521-8600. Fax: (525) 512-6262.

Colonial style hotel with beautiful tiles, and pleasant rooms, rooftop terrace overlooking Zócalo boasts spectacular view and mediocre food.

GUADALAJARA

> NOTE: Hotels listed in Guadalajara are located in two clusters: the downtown area near the Plaza de Armas and Plaza Tapatio where most government buildings and many businesses are located; and the area around Ave. Lopez Mateos and Ave. Vallarta, a developed commercial area about 25 minutes by car from downtown, where many businesses and major shopping centers are located.

Top of the line hotels, expensive ($100-$200):

Camino Real

Ave. Vallarta 5005

Tel: (523) 647-8000. Fax: (523) 647-6781.

Five heated pools, wading pool, putting green, tennis court.

Guadalajara Carlton

Av. Ninos Heroes and Ave. 16 de Sept.

Tel: (523) 614-7272. Fax: (523) 613-5539.

In downtown area, 12 blocks south of Plaza de Armas.

Exelaris Hyatt Regency Guadalajara

Ave. Lopez Mateos and Moctesuma

Tel: (523) 678-1234. Fax: (523) 622-9877.

Standard Hyatt comfort. Refrigerators; sauna and whirlpool at additional cost.

Holiday Inn Crowne Plaza Guadalajara

Ave. Lopez Mateos 2500.

Tel: (523) 634-1034. Fax: (523) 631-9393. Reservations from North America: Call 1-800-HOLIDAY.

Nicely landscaped, putting green, tennis courts, exercise room, rooftop restaurant.

More moderate ($30-$65):

Best Western Hotel Fenix

Ave. Corona 160 (2 blocks from Plaza de Armas)

Tel: (523) 614-5714. Fax: (523) 613-4005.

Centrally located, functional rooms, some balconies, servi-bars.

Hotel Frances

Maestranza 35

Tel: (523) 613-1190.

Colonial-style hotel with charm, a few blocks from Plaza Tapatio in downtown.

Hotel Calinda Roma

Ave. Juarez 170 (downtown)

Tel: (523) 614-8650. Fax: (523) 613-0557.

Small pool and rooftop garden.

Hotel del Bosque

Av. Lopez Mateos Sur 265

Tel: (523) 121-4700. Fax: (523) 622-1955.

Features gardens and large pool, terrace bar.

MONTERREY

NOTE: Businesses and corporate headquarters of Monterrey firms are located in Monterrey or the suburban community of San Pedro Garza Garcia, about a 25-minute drive from Monterrey. Business travelers may want to choose their hotel accordingly to reduce commuting time.

Top-of-the-line business hotels, expensive ($100-$250):

Gran Hotel Ancira Monterrey

Radisson Plaza, Ave. Hidalgo 498 Oriente

Tel: (528) 345-1060. Fax: (528) 344-5226.

A very comfortable downtown hotel with convention facilities.

Holiday Inn Crowne Plaza

Ave. Constitucion 300 Oriente

Tel: (528) 319-6000. Fax: (528) 344-3007.

Reservations from North America: 1-800-HOLIDAY.

In downtown, rooms are of standard Holiday Inn quality, has eight board rooms and business center.

Fiesta Americana Monterrey

Jose Vasconcelos 300 Oriente, San Pedro Garza Garcia, Colonia del Valle.

Tel: (528) 363-3030. Fax: (528) 363-4207.

Convention facilities.

Ambassador-Camino Real Monterrey

Ave. Hidalgo 498 Oriente

Tel: (528) 340-6390. Fax: (528) 363-4207.
Convention facilities, gym and tennis courts.

Urban transportation: There are four types of taxis in most Mexican cities:

● Hotel-based, "tourism" taxis which are the most commodious vehicles and charge the highest rates;

  "Sitio" taxis, or taxis with a home base;

● Roving taxis which can be flagged down and charge the lowest rates, normally set by meter (though meters are often broken, and the rate should be negotiated before boarding);

● Radio taxis, which can be telephoned to pick you up at your door.

● Taxi service by the hour can be negotiated with any of these types of taxis except the radio taxi.

● To arrange for a limousine, call the Four Seasons Hotel. Cost to pick up at airport is $150; plus 4-hour minimum at $100 an hour.

Telephones: Telephone service is likely to be the biggest headache for visiting businesspeople from the beginning to the end of their stay. The phones do not work well. Further, Mexico charges the highest rates in the world for international long distance, so calling home is expensive. Hotels typically add a service charge of 35 percent to 100 percent to calls made from the room (even when direct-dialed). Business calls should be made from the place of business, and not from the hotel, whenever possible. Hotels may charge a fee for handling your fax. Leading hotels rent out cellular telephones for a reasonable daily fee plus use.

Courier services: An expanding number of courier services are available in all major Mexican cities, including Federal Express, DHL, and Mexican counterparts to U.S. firms called Estafeta and AeroFlash, among others. Be sure to ask how long delivery of your package will take, especially if one-day service is a must. Many of the couriers, including at least one U.S. company, take two to three days to deliver to the United States although they charge the standard full courier fee.

BUSINESS HOURS: Formally, working hours are from about 9 a.m. to 8 or 9 p.m., broken by an extended lunch hour, which in Mexico City runs from 2:30 or 3 p.m. to 5:30 or 6 p.m., and in the provinces is 2-4 p.m. Business is conducted over breakfast (from 8:30 or 9 a.m. onward) and lunch, so executives and senior government officials often do not arrive at their offices until 10:30 or 11 a.m. Banking hours are normally from 9 a.m. to 1:30 p.m.; money exchange houses are usually open from 9 a.m. to 6 p.m.

Contacts

Business Organizations:

AMERICAN BUSINESS INFORMATION CENTER
U.S. Trade Center, Liverpool 31, Colonia Juarez, 06500 Mexico, D.F., Mexico.
Tel: (525) 211-0042, ext. 3735; or 591-0155. Fax: (525) 566-1115.
Open on a walk-in basis from 10 a.m. to 5 p.m.

AMERICAN CHAMBER OF COMMERCE OF MEXICO
Lucerna 78, Colonia Juarez, 06500 Mexico, D.F., Mexico
Tel: (525) 724-3800.
Also has offices in Guadalajara and Monterrey.

CANADIAN COUNCIL FOR THE AMERICAS
Executive Offices, Third Floor, 145 Richmond Street West, Toronto, ON M5H 2L2, Canada
Tel: (416) 367-4313. Fax: (416) 367-5460.

CANADIAN EXPORTERS ASSOCIATION
99 Bank Street, Suite 250, Ottawa, ON K1P 6B9, Canada
Tel: (613) 238-8888. Fax: (613) 563-9218.

CANADIAN MANUFACTURERS ASSOCIATION
75 International Blvd., Fourth floor, Etobicoke, ON M9W 6L9, Canada
Tel: 416-798-8000. Fax: 416-798-8050.

FORUM FOR INTERNATIONAL TRADE TRAINING
155 Queen St., 6th Floor, Ottawa, ON K1P 6L1, Canada
Tel: (613) 230-3553. Fax: (613) 230-6808.

The Canadian law firm **BAKER & MCKENSIE** maintains offices in four Mexican cities, which can be located through headquarters:
Baker & McKenzie
112 Adelaide St. East, Toronto, ON M5C 1K9, Canada
Tel: (416) 865-6910 or 865-6903. Fax: (416) 863-6275.
CANADIAN CHAMBER OF COMMERCE IN MEXICO
c/o Royal Bank, Hamburgo 172, Piso 5, 06600 Mexico, D.F., Mexico
Tel: (525) 207-2400. Fax: (525) 208-1591.

Governmental:

OFFICE OF MEXICO, U.S. DEPARTMENT OF COMMERCE
Room 3026, 14th and Constitution Avenue, N.W., Washington, D.C. 20230
Flash Fax Tel: (202) 482-4464. Service Tel: (202) 482-0300.
U.S. EMBASSY Commercial Section
Paseo de la Reforma 305, Colonia Cuauhtemoc, 06500 Mexico, D.F.,
Mexico. Mail: P.O. Box 3087, Laredo Texas 78044-3087
Tel: (525) 211-0042. Fax: (525) 207-8938.
U.S. CONSULATE Commercial Section
Progreso 175, 44100 Guadalajara, Jalisco, Mexico
Mail: P.O. Box 3088, Laredo, Texas 78044-3088
Tel: (523) 625-0321. Fax: (523) 626-3576.
U.S. CONSULATE Commercial Section
Avenida Constitucion 422 Pte., 64000 Monterrey, N.L., Mexico
Mail: P.O. Box 3098, Laredo, Texas 78044-3098
Tel: (528) 345-2120. Fax: (528) 342-5172.
EMBASSY OF CANADA Commercial Section
Schiller no. 529, Colonia Polanco, 11560 Mexico, D.F., Mexico
Tel: (525) 724-7900. Fax: (525) 724-7982.
CANADIAN CONSULATE
Edificio Kalos, Piso C-1, Local 108A, Zaragoza y Constitucion 6400
Monterrey, Mexico
Tel: (528) 344-3200. Fax: (528) 344-3048.

OFFICE OF THE PRESIDENT OF MEXICO

Residencia Oficial de Los Pinos, Col. San Miguel Chapultepec, 11850 Mexico, D.F.

Tel: (525) 515-7994. Fax: (525) 516-5762.

AGRICULTURE AND WATER RESOURCES MINISTRY (SARH)

Av. Insurgentes Sur 476, 5o Piso, Colonia Roma Sur, 06760 Mexico, D.F.

Tel: (525) 584-0808; 584-0010. Fax: (525) 284-1177.

COMMERCE AND INDUSTRIAL PROMOTION MINISTRY (SECOFI)

Av. Alfonso Reyes 30, 2o Piso, Col. Condesa, 06140 Mexico, D.F.

Tel: (525) 286-1543; 286-1757. Fax: (525) 553-9266.

COMMUNICATIONS AND TRANSPORTATION MINISTRY (SCT)

Xola y Av. Universidad, Cuerpo C, P.B., Colonia Narvarte, 03028 Mexico, D.F.

Tel: (525) 538-5148; 538-0450. Fax: (525) 519-9748.

ENERGY, MINES AND PARASTATE INDUSTRY MINISTRY (SEMIP)

Av. Insurgentes Sur 552, 1er Piso, Colonia Roma Sur, 06769 Mexico, D.F.

Tel: (525) 584-4304; 584-2962. Fax: (525) 574-3396.

FINANCE AND PUBLIC CREDIT MINISTRY (Treasury-SHCP)

Republica de El Salvador 47, P.A., Centro, 06080 Mexico, D.F.

Tel: (525) 709-6675; 709-6532. Fax: (525) 709-3272.

COMPTROLLER GENERAL'S OFFICE (Secogef)

Av. Insurgentes Sur 1735, P.B., Ala Norte, oficina 22, Col. Guadalupe Inn, 01028 Mexico, D.F.

Tel: (525) 662-2762; 662-3263. Fax: (525) 662-0386.

FISHERIES MINISTRY (SEPESCA)

Periferico Sur 4209, 3er Piso, Jardines d ela Montana, 14210 Mexico, D.F.

Tel: (525) 628-0891. Fax: (525) 628-0780.

Lawyers:

NOTE: These are some of the law firms that specialize in corporate finance, international trade law and business law. Their listing here does not constitute a recommendation or a guarantee of professional ability or integrity.

DeOvando y Martinez del Campo, S.C.
Bosque de Alisos 47-A, Despacho 101, Bosques de las Lomas, Mexico, D.F., 05210, Mexico
Tel: (525) 259-5353. Fax: (525) 259-5259.

Jauregui, Navarrete, Nader y Rojas
Paseo de la Reforma 199, Pisos 15, 16 y 17, 06500 Mexico, D.F., Mexico
Tel: (525) 291-1655. Fax: (525) 535-8062.

Ritch, Heather y Meuller, S.C.
Amberes No. 5, Colonia Juarez, 06600 Mexico, D.F., Mexico
Tel: (525) 207-6533 or 533-6820. Fax: (525) 207-5599 or 207-3561.

Rubio Villegas y Asociados, S.C.
Rio Duero 31, Colonia Cuauhtemoc, 06500 Mexico, D.F., Mexico
Tel: (525) 533-5676 or 208-1700. Fax: (525) 208-2046 or 207-4410.

Santamarina y Steta
Campos Eliseos 345 - Piso 2, Colonia Polanco, 11560 Mexico, D.F., Mexico, Tel: (525) 728-0300. Fax: (525) 280-7866 or 280-3214.

Sepúlveda y Ruiz de Velasco
Torre Optima, Ave. de Las Palmas 405 - 6o Piso, Colonia Lomas de Chapultepec, 11000 Mexico, D.F., Mexico.
Tel: (525) 540-9600. Fax: (525) 540-9698 or 540-9699.

Interpreters/Translators:

Heather Drake
Horacio 522-402, Col. Polanco, Mexico, D.F. 11570.
Tel: (525) 545-6560. Works in English, Spanish, French.

Gustavo Pelcastre
Cerrada de Pedregal 37-C, Jiutepec, Morelos 62550.
Tels: (525) 651-4302 (in Mexico City) and 73-206990 (in Jiutepec near Cuernavaca). English, Spanish, Swedish.

Martha Elena Cruz Soto
Oriente 168, Nro 30, Col. Moctezuma, Segunda Sección, Mexico, D.F. 15500. Tel: (525) 571-2769. English, Spanish, French.

David Valdespino Secarado
Francisco Villa 122, Edificio I, Dept. 201, Col. El Triunfo, Mexico, D.F. 09430. Tel: (525) 633-8673. English, Spanish.

Accountants/Auditors:

Ruiz Urquiza Y Cia. SC/Arthur Andersen & Co., S.A.
Bosque de Duraznos 127, 11700 Mexico, D.F.Tel: (525) 326-6400 or 326-6401. Fax: (525) 326-8969 or 596-4692.

Price Waterhouse
Rio de la Plata 48, 06500 Mexico, D.F.
Tel: (525) 273-3340.

Peat Marwick
Bosque de Duraznos 55, Bosques de las Lomas, 11700 Mexico, D.F.
Tel: (525) 596-7797. Fax: (525) 596-8060.

Deloitte Touche
Jaime Balmes 11, Edificio B, Piso 9, Plaza Polanco, 11510 Mexico, D.F.
Tel: (525) 395-0455.

Francisca (Paquita) Beans, Tax preparer
Rio Duero 24, Colonia Cuauhtemoc, 06500 Mexico, D.F., Mexico
Tel/Fax: (525) 208-7169.

Useful Business Publications:

Guide to Mexico for Business, Published by the American Chamber of Commerce of Mexico. American Chamber also publishes many specialized directories and a monthly magazine on doing business in Mexico. Available through: American Chamber, Lucerna 78, Colonia Juarez, 06500 Mexico, D.F. Tel: (525) 724-3800.

Directory and Practical Guide, 1994. Available from: Canadian Chamber of Commerce, Hamburgo 172, 5° piso, Colonia Juarez, 06600 Mexico, D.F. Tel: (525) 525-0741. Fax: (525) 525-0438.

Canada-Mexico: Partnering for Success, A Prospectus Handbook, 1994. Write: Prospectus Inc. 346 Waverley St., Ottawa, Ontario K2P 0W5. Tel: (613) 231-2727. Fax: (613) 237-7666.

Doing Business in Mexico, The Mexican Tax System, and other publications are available from: Price Waterhouse, Rio de la Plata 48, 2°piso, 06500 Mexico, D.F. Tel: (525) 211-7833. Fax: (525) 286-6248.

Tax and Financial Aspects of Doing Business in Mexico and *NAFTA Survey Report* are available from Arthur Andersen. Contact: Kathy Newman, Arthur Andersen, Bosque de Duraznos 127, 11700 Mexico, D.F. Tel: (525) 326-8800. Fax: (525) 326-6468.

Face to Face: Doing Business the Mexican Way, by Kathryn Leger. Available through Royal Bank of Canada International Trade Centers. In Mexico City: Tel: (525) 207-2322. Fax: (525) 208-1592.

Global Survey, 1994: Regulatory and Market Developments. Write: Institute of International Bankers 299 Park Avenue, 17th Flr. New York, N.Y. 10171. Tel: (212) 421-1611. Fax: (212) 421-1119.

Foreign Investment Laws 1994, a supplement of *LatinFinance.* Order from: *LatinFinance,* 2121 Ponce de Leon Blvd., Suite 1020, Coral Gables, Florida, 33134. Tel: (305) 448-6593. Fax: (305) 448-0718.

The Mexican Investment Board publishes a series of brochures on such topics as the Mexican tax system, intellectual property, and starting operations in Mexico. Available from: MIB, Paseo de la Reforma 915, Lomas de Chapultepec, 11000 Mexico, D.F. Tel: (525) 202-7804. Fax: (525) 202-7925.

Mexico Business, a bi-monthly magazine. Published at: 3300 Chimney Rock, Suite 300, Houston, Texas 77056. Tel: (713) 266-0861. Fax: (713) 266-0980.

In case of illness:

Good medical care can be got in Mexico's leading cities, but care should be taken to be referred to a doctor by a knowledgeable Mexican or long-time resident. Hospitals and medical laboratories must be selected with care; quality varies greatly. The best medical care is available in the leading cities of Mexico City, Guadalajara and Monterrey; in general, the quality of care falls off sharply in the smaller cities.

Some Mexico City hospitals where English is spoken:

American British Cowdray Hospital (ABC Hospital)
Calle Sur 136, on corner of Ave. Observatorio, Colonia Tacubaya
Tel: (525) 272-8500. (525) 515-8359 Emergency.

Hospital Angeles Del Pedregal
Camino a Santa Teresa No. 1055, Colonia Heroes de Padierna
Tels: (525) 652-2011, 652-0422, 652-3011.

Hospital Español
Av. Ejercito Nacional No. 613, Colonia Granada
Tel: (525) 531-3300 or 545-6580.

Medica Sur
Puente de Piedra 150, Colonia Tlalpan
Tel: (525) 606-2277 or 606-6222.

10

PARAGUAY

Personal Trust Crucial
To Doing Business

By Esteban Caballero Carrizosa

Moving to Paraguay after college, Kathy Uliani discovered, did not save her from one of the inconveniences common to her Baby Boom contemporaries back home: losing one's job in a corporate downsizing. So, when the American bank for which she was working closed its branch in Asunción, the Paraguayan capital, she followed the same path often chosen in the United States and went into business for herself.

For that, she had some advantages not usually enjoyed by foreigners doing business in Paraguay because she was able to surround herself with some of her husband's relatives as partners and advisers.

Whether or not you've got cousins or in-laws you can lean on, her experience illustrates a norm of Paraguayan economic life: People try to surround themselves with those they can trust, and in Paraguay that often means relatives. Most businesses in Paraguay are still family businesses. Even those that present themselves as corporate entities are usually, in fact, family affairs.

This importance of families is part of the transition that

Paraguayan society is going through. It is a society with striking contrasts, half modern, half traditional, and the importance of family and personal relations is part of the legacy being bequeathed to modern Paraguay.

Who's who is also a key element, because Paraguay is such a small country. It has only 4.7 million people. It often seems that everybody knows each other and that the key factor in doing business successfully is being part of a network of friends, relatives, and partners. Once you are part of a network you feel safer, Kathy Uliani says.

That's probably not the kind of business concept she learned as a business administration major at California State University in Chico, from which she graduated in 1977. She married Roland Bendlin, a Paraguayan she met as a student, they moved to Asunción, and she found the bank job.

Those were boom years in Paraguay as the result of the investments pouring in for construction of the world's largest hydroelectric dam, the Itaipú dam, on the border of Paraguay and Brazil. As the result of the easy money, businesses in Paraguay allowed themselves to become trapped in debts, many of them denominated in dollars. Suddenly, in 1982, the boom ended, the currency was devalued, dollar debts sky rocketed in value, and business closed.

Later, when the bank closed its branch, Uliani decided she was ready to start something of her own. Her husband told her two of his cousins were opening an import business and were looking for a third partner, so she had the "safe" structure she felt she needed.

Safety in a Crowd

Business safety in Paraguay, she says, means having a network that helps you to know what the competition is doing. Despite the familial nature of business in Paraguay, she says cutthroat competition is the norm, that there's no consensus on correct behavior or a business ethic. She said, for example, that her firm might acquire the right to represent a particular foreign product in Paraguay and set about trying to get it into the market, only to discover that, meanwhile, another import firm had gone to the manufacturer and tried to take away the representation rights by offering to import larger quantities. (Some countries in Latin American try to avoid this with laws requiring that manufacturers extend exclusive distribution rights to one importer, though this may not be useful to the manufacturer if the importer isn't a hustler.)

Uliani says that for larger foreign firms setting up their own distribution branches in Paraguay this problem can be overcome because such firms are strong enough to impose their own standards and requirements.

Uliani's firm, **Paraguay Trading,** has been operating for more than three years and is now importing various products of mass consumption: chocolates, cookies, pasta, and pantyhose from Chile; dishwashing detergents from Argentina, and baby food and small batteries from the United States. She pointed out that what constitutes mass consumption products in Paraguay is very limited because it is not an urban, industrial society with a large middle class. Rather, Paraguay has a relatively small upper middle class and the rich, plus a mass of poor people whose consumption is limited to basic necessities.

She says that sophisticated import products — particularly video players, stereos, designer clothing, and whisky — are also a good business in Paraguay, but that they are sold to the thousands of so-called "commercial tourists" who come every year from Brazil and Argentina to buy items that are cheaper than in their own countries. Most of this business is done at Ciudad del Este on the eastern border, where Argentina, Brazil, and Paraguay meet. However, much of this merchandise is smuggled into Paraguay or brought in with the assistance of corrupt customs officials, making it difficult for honest retailers to get a piece of the business.

Uliani says that despite the limited nature of the market in Paraguay, would-be investors or importers ought not to rule out everything before studying and testing the market. She pointed out that for years business people had dismissed the idea of setting up pizza franchises in Paraguay because of the small size of the market. But in 1994 three **Pizza Hut** locations opened in Paraguay, and people love them, she says, proving that "It's just a question of being creative."

To limit customs problems, Uliani says **Paraguay Trading** uses the services of three customs agents and keeps them more or less in competition with each other in order to compare prices for their services. Occasionally, she says, customs officials ask manufacturers and suppliers for copies of their price lists to be certain that the prices being declared by the importers are correct.

She said goods arriving by truck from Brazil, Argentina, and Chile tended to be inspected and released very quickly by customs, while products coming by air or sea from the United States and other countries outside the immediate region tended to be tied up for a lengthy period in customs. She said her firm, for example, has to take baby food orders six months ahead of expected delivery time to the customer.

Paraguay Overview

Strong Arm Politics and Economic Modernization

Paraguay's recent history can be summed up as a combination of authoritarian politics and economic modernization. From 1954 to 1989, the country was ruled by Gen. Alfredo Stroessner, who every five years was reelected in staged elections and made sure no significant opposition could arise. Nevertheless, during his reign, important infrastructure and public services were developed. Construction or improvements in telephone services, water supply, airports, electrical networks, hydroelectric dams (Itaipú and Yacyretá), and roads are usually associated with his regime.

In February 1989, General Stroessner was overthrown in a military coup led by Gen. Andrés Rodriguez, who stepped into the presidency and initiated a period of transition to democracy. In the next five years Paraguay experienced quick and profound political changes. A new Constitution was written in 1992, and today the political opposition has a majority in Congress while the Executive is still in the hands of the Colorado Party, the same party that supported the now-exiled Stroessner.

The transition to political democracy has improved Paraguay's international status and helped reduce its isolation. The country has improved relations with the international financial community and with governments all over the world. One sign of that is its membership in the Common Market of the South, or Mercosur, which also includes Brazil, Argentina, and Uruguay.

Paraguay is facing major economic challenges. It wants to move beyond its traditional economic model of exporting two major raw materials (cotton and soybeans), begin to diversify exports and add value to them. This could be accomplished by going into labor intensive manufacturing, energy intensive industries, agroindustrial activities, or developing new economic niches that will give Paraguay competitive advantages against the two regional economic powers, Brazil and Argentina.

Overall, the country seems to be stable both politically and economically. Macroeconomic indicators, such as inflation and exchange rates, have remained relatively stable for the last five years. The government keeps strictly to a balanced budget. Politically, the transition period has been peaceful. The national elections of May 1993 were judged to be free and fair by the Organization of American States, although an international delegation of observers led by former U.S. President Jimmy Carter thought there were still signs the military was trying to influence the outcome. So far, elections have not produced a change in executive power from one party to another, although the opposition has increased its political leverage through its control of Congress.

Receptivity to foreign business is good in Paraguay, and there are few restrictions on foreign investments. But, as Kathy Uliani's advice indicates, the outsider needs careful guidance through the labyrinth of Paraguayan tradition. Corruption is endemic, and the judicial system is just beginning to restructure itself to guarantee equal terms and conditions for all.

Low-Skilled Labor But Good Tax Breaks

Paraguay has cheaper unskilled labor than its immediate neighbors, Argentina and Uruguay, and low absenteeism for the region. The average monthly cost of labor, without including training costs, was put at $219 in 1994. The minimum wage by itself is $197 a month, to which must be added 16.5 percent of gross wages for social security and other employer taxes. Employers are permitted to pay a training wage of at least 60 percent of minimum for up to one year.

However, the productivity level of unskilled Paraguayan labor is also low, and businesses feel the need to invest in training in a significant way. At the same time, skilled and educated workers are scarce. Middle- and top-level managers and professionals often have to be imported.

The Labor Code guarantees job security to anyone who has worked for a single employer at least 10 years. Such a person may be fired only under three conditions: 1) evidence of malfeasance submitted to, and approved by a court; 2) bankruptcy or major reduction of business size, and 3) the employee voluntarily accepts dismissal.

Corporate taxes in Paraguay are generally 30 percent of profits, although they are reduced to 10 percent when reinvested. There are no restrictions on the repatriation of profits. There is a withholding tax of 5 percent on dividends remitted abroad and 17.5 percent on interest and royalty payments abroad. A 10 percent value added tax is applied to transactions involving goods and services within Paraguay, including imports. The VAT paid on equipment and inputs can be credited against the firm's liability on the sale of its output. There are no export duties, nor is the VAT applied to exports. Import duties range from zero for raw materials to 10 percent for finished consumer goods. Equipment is levied duty at a rate of 5 percent.

For new investors, Law 60/90 grants a 95 percent reduction in corporate income taxes for a five-year period, plus a complete exemption on withholding taxes and import duties on equipment, raw materials, and parts, and a 50 percent reduction in the corporate tax rate for the reinvested profits. Only investment projects approved by the Ministry of Industry and Commerce are eligible for these benefits.

One of the roadblocks that investors face in Paraguay is a complicated and time-consuming process for the creation and registering of stock companies. The President of the Republic must sign the incorporation documents, and they must be reviewed by judges, the Attorney General, the Minister of the Interior, and the Ministry of Finance. In addition, a cash deposit must be made in the Central Bank and any foreign director must have residency status in Paraguay. However, the Congress has been considering revision of the law to make incorporation less bureaucratic.

Problems of Infrastructure, Quality and Credit

Nonetheless, business analysts tend to think that the major difficulties facing foreign investors in Paraguay do not necessarily pertain to the domain of legal and procedural constraints. There are more serious matters that have to do with infrastructure and transport. For example, less than 10 percent of the roads are paved. There are no suitable investment sites where you can set up manufacturing or processing businesses close to labor and raw-material sources. As a landlocked country, Paraguay also presents the challenge for exporters of getting their products to ports in Brazil, Uruguay, or Argentina.

The local capital market is minuscule, with very high rates when credit can be obtained. Real interest for large companies has recently been nearly 12 percent, but the consumer rate was almost 19 percent, and that is the rate that small and medium-sized businesses must pay. Dollar-denominated loans have recently carried an interest rate of nearly 13 percent.

Another thing for investors to take into consideration in Paraguay is quality. Agricultural products in Paraguay do not have quality controls and standards. In one example, an Argentine investor, attracted by Paraguay's cheap labor and tax breaks, set up a leather manufacturing plant, but he was forced to import the raw material from Argentina because he found that cattle in Paraguay were not cared for adequately to assure good hides.

Comparative Advantages

Despite these handicaps, Paraguay offers a number of attractions for investors. If you are interested in exporting from Paraguay, comparative advantages lie in the processing of foodstuffs and other agricultural products, including oils, veneer, plywood, tea, nuts, spices, citrus juice, meat, fruits and vegetables, fresh dairy products, furniture, parquet, and pulp.

Paraguay has abundant supplies of hydroelectric power, so energy-intensive industries will find comparative advantages in the country.

In the area of infrastructure plans, on which foreign firms may bid, there is a project to develop a canal system — called a *hidrovia* in Spanish — for the River Plate basin, which includes the Paraguay, Paraná, and Plata rivers. It has received credit guarantees from a regional agency called FONPLATA and the Inter-American Development Bank. The project, to be completed in the year 2015, is now in the phase of environmental impact studies. Several public institutions are involved. The best channels to information are the Department "Cuenca del Plata" of the Ministry of Foreign Affairs, whose director is Engineer Ramón Cabrera (Tel: 49-3873, Ext. 520), and the Inter-American Development Bank representative, Agustín Riveros (Tel: 49-2061 or 49-2062 or 49-2063).

Projects are also underway to pave additional roads with financial support from the World Bank and the Inter-American Development Bank. The Department of Bidding and Special Projects of the Ministry of Communications and Public Works is the best source of bidding information (Tel: 44-3473, Ext. 838). Further, the Municipality of Asunción and the Government have received credit commitments from the Inter-American Development Bank to build controls to prevent river flooding in the low-level neighborhoods of Asunción. The source of bidding information is the director of Urban Development, Gonzalo Garay, an architect (Tel: 61-0563).

Finally, there is the privatization process, which may offer opportunities for foreign investors. **Paraguay Airlines** was recently sold to an Ecuadoran consortium. Six other state entities can be privatized, including a distillery and gasohol producer, the merchant fleet, the railroad that runs from Asunción to Encarnación, a fertilizer producer, and the silos of the Ministry of Agriculture.

The Government has yet to decide whether to privatize the more modern state enterprises, including the telephone, electricity, and water companies, the river ports, the refineries, and social security. This issue is very much caught up in politics and Paraguay's battle with itself over how much to modernize the economy. President Juan Carlos Wasmosy says he favors widespread privatization of these firms, but many of his fellow party leaders oppose such steps because it would cost them votes from public servants. To that is added strong labor opposition to privatization, creating uncertainty about how far the privatization effort will go.

Paraguay at a Glance

Population: 4.7 million.

Labor force: 1.4 million.

Languages: Spanish and Guaraní.

Ethnic mix: Overwhelmingly mestizo, a mix of European and Indian; about 5 percent European.

Literacy: 81 percent. Compulsory education through seventh grade; about 83 percent of school-age children enrolled.

Climate and best times to visit: Paraguay is very hot during the South American summer, December through March, with temperatures in January and February that can exceed 40° C (104F). The best time to visit is during winter, June-August, when temperatures average 14° C (58F).

Natural resources, chief agricultural products: Cotton, soybeans, forest products.

Land area: 406,752 square kilometers.

Economic Statistics:

GDP: $7.4 billion (1993)

Per Capita GDP: $1,575

Economic Growth: 5 percent (1994 preliminary)

Main exports: Cotton, soybeans, wood products.

Main imports: Machinery, motors, transport equipment and parts, fuel and lubricants, beverages and tobacco, pharmaceutical and chemical products.

Duties on imports: 0-10 percent.

Repatriation of profits: There are no restrictions.

When You Go to Paraguay

Visas: No visas are required for U.S. citizens or visitors from neighboring countries; those from most other countries will need a visa, and you should apply to a Paraguayan consulate well before beginning the trip.

Airlines: American provides daily service to Asunción from Miami via São Paulo; Varig from Rio de Janeiro and São Paulo; Aerolineas Argentinas from Buenos Aires, and Ladeco from Santiago.

What to Expect at the Airport: Coming out of customs, you'll see a currency exchange window on the right, where you can obtain the local currency, guaranís; there is no black market for currency. Baggage handlers receive the equivalent of about $1 per bag. Also on your right is a taxi cooperative counter, where you can request a taxi to your hotel. The ride usually costs $15-$20.

Urban Transportation: Aside from the plentiful street taxis, the following auto rental services are available: Hertz (Tel: 60-5708); Only Rent a Car (Tel: 49-2732); Touring Cars (Tel: 44-7945); Tape Ruvicha (Tel: 49-8847); Dinamica (Tel: 49-2731).

Hotels

> NOTE: The following hotels, all in Asunción, have connections for computer modems, fax services, and minibars in rooms. A 10 percent value added tax is added to room charges.

Excelsior

Chile 980. Tel: (595-21) 49-5632.

Highly rated hotel near downtown. Prices begin at $120.

Guaraní

Oliva e Independencia Nacional. Tel: (595-21) 49-1131.

Well regarded hotel in the central plaza. Room rates begin at $100.

Presidente

Azara 255. Tel: (595-21) 49-4931.

More economical, but very central and with good service.

Rates begin at $75.

Contacts

Governmental:

PRO-PARAGUAY

Padre Cardozo 469.

Tel: (595-21) 20-4880 and 20-0425. Fax: (595-21) 49-1250.

Public agency dedicated to promoting Paraguayan exports and attracting foreign investors. Offers the following services and information: trade opportunities and market data, contacts between exporters and importers, participation in fairs and expositions, information for investors, organization of export groups, promotion of joint ventures, profiles of investment projects, marketing courses.

MINISTRY OF INDUSTRY AND COMMERCE

España con Estados Unidos. Tels: (595-21) 20-4693, 21-0261, 20-4693, 20-4638. Fax: (595-21) 21-0570.

MINISTRY OF AGRICULTURE AND LIVESTOCK

Pte. Franco c/ 14 de Mayo.

Tels: (595-21) 44-7017, 44-5201. Fax: (595-21) 44-5420.

MINISTRY OF FINANCE

Palma y Chile. Tels: (595-21) 44-7995 and 44 010 through 17.

MINISTRY OF PUBLIC WORKS AND COMMUNICATIONS

Oliva y Alberdi. Tels: (595-21) 44-5410 and 44-4458.

Business Organizations:

FEDERATION OF PRODUCTION, INDUSTRY AND COMMERCE
Palma 751. Tels: (595-21) 44-6638 and 44-4963.
PARAGUAYAN-AMERICAN CHAMBER OF COMMERCE
Tels: (595-21) 44-2136. Fax: (595-21) 44-2135.
Does not provide services to visitors, but will allow you to make contact with its members. President: Hugo Aranda.

Lawyers who have worked with international clients (inclusion in this list does not constitute a recommendation):

Fiorio & Alvarado
Tels: (595-21) 61-0228 and 61-0231. Fax: (595-21) 61-0240.
Dr. Hugo Corrales
Tel: (595-21) 49-6281.
Dr. Julio Ernesto Giménez Balbiani
Tels: (595-21) 44-9084 and 49-1660.
Dr. Carlos Mersan, Estudio Mersan
Tels: (595-21) 49-2573, 49-6403, 44-7739, 44-9052. Fax: (595-21) 49-6039.
Peroni, Sosa y Altamirano
Tels: (595-21) 20-8791 through 5.

Interpreters:

Erna Hill, Tel/Fax: (595-21) 60-3854.
Esteban Caballero, Tel/Fax: (595-21) 49-2158. Home: (595-21) 20-3401.

Translator (written documents):

Victoria Brown, Tel/Fax: (595-21) 21-0388.

In case of illness:

Dr. Juan Felix Bogado Gondra, Tel: (595-21) 2-3345.

11

PERU

Stress-Free Buyout
For Owens-Illinois

By Peter Hudson

Bringing **Owens-Illinois Inc.** to Peru proved a remarkably stress-free experience for Michael Bail, now manager of **Vidrios Industriales S.A., Vinsa,** of Lima. The U.S. company, the world's largest glass container manufacturer, bought a controlling stake in its smaller Peruvian cousin in March 1993 and Bail just walked straight in.

"We had no major bureaucratic problems to deal with," he says. "In many ways it was easier than moving into a new state in the U.S."

Bail's experience bears witness to the new open-arms approach that the government of Alberto Fujimori has adopted toward foreign business since taking office in 1990. It is also in sharp contrast to the years of economic chaos, administrative hassle and often outright hostility that foreigners faced when trying to do business in Peru during the Seventies and Eighties.

Little wonder then that the government has won the support of a large majority of the foreign business community. "Fujimori may be saying it to get publicity, but I still think that he's right that

Peru has the least regulations in the world for new investment," Bail says.

Owens decided to come to Peru in 1991, when the Fujimori administration was still struggling and the country was still suffering a major recession. Bail, however, had had his eye on the country from Colombia, where he had been vice-president of **Cristalería Peldar S.A.,** another majority-owned **Owens** operation, since 1982.

"The company has had a good experience in Latin America and was interested in expanding," he says. "Peru's glass industry was untouched by foreigners and was potentially a growth market."

First stop in Lima was the National Industrial Society, SNI, an excellent source of information, according to Bail. There the company was put in touch with the glass committee, which explained that there were two major local players in the market, **Vinsa** and principal rival **Manufacturera de Vidrio S.A.**

"Our original strategy was to try to unite the two, with **Owens** as a third partner," Bail says, "but it was not to be, **Manufacturera** didn't want to let go of majority control."

The next visit was to a local legal office, Studio Oleachea, before sitting down to negotiations, a process that was to last more than two years. There was nothing complicated about it, however. "We could probably have done it without any experience," he says. "It couldn't possibly have taken any longer."

The talks with **Vinsa**'s then owners, **Compañía Nacional de Cerveza S.A.** were more formal than the relatively direct North American approach, Bail adds, but not markedly different from how things are done in Bogotá.

Negotiations were conducted in Spanish, even if English is widely known at a corporate level and good translations of legal documents are available at a price. Bail still rates a good command of Spanish as a priority. "It is frustrating to have to rely on translators to know what is going on," he says.

The only other must, according to Bail, is to do the back-up work thoroughly. In **Owens**' case that meant the due diligence was done by the law firm, in conjunction with **Ernst & Young,** one of the big six international auditing firms, all of which have offices in Lima.

Once the deal was finally signed, the takeover was a breeze. "We've had more or less zero contact with the government," Bail says, "although I did talk to some people from the foreign investment committee by phone."

The hard work started when **Owens** moved in, taking control of a plant that, in common with much of Peru's industry, had gone to seed during the economic chaos of the Eighties. "Our major problem has been taking a company that had been working in a vacuum and trying to get it up to speed," he says.

Tax on Business Assets a Burden

The tax system, although relatively easy to manage, has not helped. For instance, a two-percent tax is levied on a company's assets, whether or not it is making a profit, an added burden for companies like **Vinsa** that are revamping their plant.

The government also levies an 18 percent sales tax on all purchases, including capital expenditure. Companies recover the money by retaining the tax that they invoice on their own sales, but that process can take time, and the rebate is not adjusted for inflation.

"We've got a huge credit," Bail says, "and the government won't even let us use it to pay our taxes or import duties." Local industry is lobbying for abolition of the tax on fixed assets and a relaxation of the rules on sales tax to at least allow them to pay tax on capital expenditure gradually over the lifetime of the investment.

The other main obstacles to the company's growth are the slowness of economic recovery and the size of the informal sector. Peru actually grew by a respectable 6.8 percent in 1993 and a world-beating 12.7 percent in 1994, but the increases were largely centered in the mining and fishing sectors, which do little to help employment or boost consumer spending.

"The process has been slower than we expected," Bail says. "When I was back in Toledo, Ohio, recently, telling head office how the economic turnaround was just around the corner, I found I was making pretty much the same speech as the year before."

He remains optimistic, however. Construction also boomed in 1994, although that had much to do with the informal sector, which is still at least as powerful as the formal economy. Peru's cement manufacturers, for instance, reckon that as much as two-thirds of their output goes to what they term "do-it-yourself construction."

Arising as a response to years of red-tape and bureaucracy, the do-it-yourself mentality can still be seen all over Peru, especially in Lima, notorious for its street-traders, offering virtually any product, no questions asked and no tax paid. The market is rife with cheap imitations and contraband from Bolivia, Ecuador, and Chile, much to the annoyance of the more conventional producers. In addition, the majority of the population still works in the informal sector, completely outside the framework of the State. To the frustration of **Vinsa,** they also tend to buy in bulk, which means that even sauces and olives are sold in bags rather bottles.

"Peru may have a population of 24 million, but the formal economy is only a third that size, even if you stretch it," Bail says. "Annual Peruvian glass consumption is running at six containers a person, amongst the lowest in the world. That represents a tremendous opportunity for us by offering a top-quality, lower-cost packaging alternative."

A Roller Coaster Ride in Plastics

If Michael Bail's Peruvian experience has been a foreign investor's dream, Hans Traver has been along on the hairy roller coaster rides of Peru's last three decades. Traver's experience began in 1962, when he established **Peruplast,** today the country's largest plastic packaging manufacturer, in a business environment that was as stress-free as the one the government is now trying to recreate.

Traver had been working as the international product manager for what was then known as **Union Carbide International Co.** Tiring of life in New York, he accepted an offer to go into business in Peru with **Union Carbide**'s local chemicals representative. "He knew nothing about plastics, and I knew nothing about Peru," Traver says, "so we made a good pair."

With minimal capital, the two men bought plastic extruders from the United States on credit, took the equipment out of customs, also on credit, laid down a concrete floor at their new business premises and set up the extruders in a day, working by the light of a Volkswagen delivery van as evening wore on.

The electricity company, which was then Swiss-owned and Swiss-run, turned up as promised on the next day to connect the factory to the grid and they had their first roll of plastic by noon.

"Peru wasn't complicated in 1962," Traver says, "but then Velasco fixed that."

Gen. Juan Velasco Alvarado took over the country in a military coup in 1968. In a broadly socialist program, his government tried to force the pace of industrialization by nationalizing entire swaths of Peruvian industry. In an attempt to improve the conditions of the millions of impoverished and neglected peasants, it also launched a land reform, turning over ownership of the massive estates to state-controlled peasant cooperatives or parceling out the land in small holdings. Although well-intentioned, the reform was a disaster and agricultural production dropped off throughout the Seventies and Eighties as the peasants struggled to produce crops with neither capital nor know-how.

Velasco Brought 20 Years of Hassle

Even more alarming for foreign businessmen like Traver, the Velasco government ushered in more than 20 years of unremitting hassle for foreign business. Denied local credit and facing a barrage of official hostility, companies such as **General Motors** and **Ford** were just part of a mass exodus of foreign firms during the period.

Traver took his family back to Texas in 1975 after xenophobia had reached such heights that his daughters were pelted with stones in the streets. For seven years, he largely ran his business from abroad, returning to Peru every other week to check on operations.

Velasco was ushered aside shortly after Traver's departure, as the economy ground to a halt. His replacement, Gen. Francisco Morales Bermúdez, reversed many of Velasco's policies and held democratic elections in 1980, which saw Fernando Belaunde Terry, a centrist and populist politician, elected by a landslide.

The political changes encouraged Traver to return to Peru permanently in 1982, and he began to buy back the 41 percent of **Peruplast**'s shares that had been parceled out to its employees under the Velasco government's workers' share project.

Belaunde did little to halt Peru's decline, however. "During that time, we started to clean things up and make the company manageable again," Traver says, "but there was no foreign credit, no foreign currency and therefore no growth."

During the Belaunde government, economic growth averaged only 0.5 percent a year, annual inflation reached 158 percent and the *Sendero Luminoso,* a Maoist guerrilla movement whose name means Shining Path in English, began to take control of large areas of the countryside, disrupting the economy and forcing widespread migration to the cities.

His successor, Alan Garcia Pérez, at the head of the leftist APRA party, added the final touches to the economic disaster started by his predecessors. "Garcia repeated every one of Velasco's mistakes," Traver says, "and added graft and corruption."

During the Garcia government, total inflation reached a mind-boggling 700,000 percent. After a brief initial surge, GDP dropped by over a quarter. Foreign credit dried up, as the government refused to service its debt and, amidst the economic crisis, the Peruvian population began to believe that *Sendero Luminoso* was on the verge of taking power.

Survival was Traver's only goal during that period. "The government had a monopoly on powdered milk, rice, and fertilizer and needed to package them," he explains. "We had the most modern plant, so we won the majority of the bids and managed to get import licenses. Price controls meant that our margins were very thin, and since our books were kept in official dollars, we were making negligible profits in a fictional currency. But we managed to stay alive."

Peru Overview

Enter Fujimori,
Bringing Economic Shock

Alberto Fujimori, the Japanese-Peruvian who won the 1990 presidential elections is widely credited with having halted the slide. Although elected on a platform that called for a non-recessionary economic program and continued state involvement in industry, his policies in office bore much more resemblance to the neoliberal package of shocks and deregulation prescribed by his main opponent in the elections, Mário Vargas Llosa, one of Peru's leading novelists.

His government dealt *Sendero Luminoso* a number of crippling blows, most notably the capture of its leader, Abimáel Guzmán, together with other principal leaders on Sept. 12, 1992.

But the watershed event in the government was the army-backed *autogolpe,* or do-it-yourself coup, on April 5 of the same year. Freed from the restraints of a troublesome Congress, Fujimori churned out 57 decrees, that, along with the laws passed before the coup, threw the economy open to both foreign and local business.

These changes were incorporated into the new constitution, approved by a small majority in a 1993 referendum. The new constitution allowed Fujimori to stand for reelection in mid-1995, but more importantly from the point of view of business, it left legislators free to pass laws only if compatible with the free-market model.

Under the constitution, the State is basically forbidden from using funds for economic activities and foreign and local companies are guaranteed equal treatment. Article 64 also guarantees the right to hold foreign currency, blocking any return to the days of the Velasco government, when possession of dollars carried a jail sentence of six months for every twenty dollars held. The exchange market became completely free, with no foreign exchange controls.

Peru signed agreements with a wide range of countries guaranteeing against expropriation and guaranteeing the right to repatriate capital and profits. Investors also have access to insurance through the Overseas Private Investment Corporation, OPIC, and the World Bank's Multilateral Investment Guarantee Agency, MIGA, to which Peru subscribed in 1991.

Setting up a company is easy, according to Luis Fuentes, legal representative of the American Chamber of Commerce of Peru and member of its executive committee. "Foreigners can be shareholders and on the board of directors of a company," he explains, "and they don't even have to have been to Peru, if they don't want to."

The law limits the number of foreign employees in a firm to 20 percent, with no more than 30 percent of wages to be paid to them, although foreigners who are married to a Peruvian or have a Peruvian child are counted as nationals. "Apart from that about the only ways in which foreigners are discriminated against is that they can't run for President and they can't own land on the country's borders," Fuentes says.

Red Tape and Corruption Both Declining

As for Peru's fabled red tape and corruption, "That's all changing," Fuentes says. "Before, you had to negotiate all sorts of quotas and licenses, and often pay bribes if you wanted the thing done properly. Now you can visit the Ministries and entire floors are deserted, where there used to be rows of paper-pushers. The idea is to reduce government intervention to a minimum."

As is natural, some problems persist. The national land registry is universally acknowledged to be a mess and Fujimori's judicial reforms seem to have done little to remedy the slowness and petty corruption that exists in the nation's courts.

Peruplast's Hans Traver also sounds a cautionary note. "Fujimori has stamped out theft at the docks and there's a lot less red tape," he says, "but officials still tend to follow the rules blindly." Recently, he said, his company unwittingly contravened a customs authority rule that he hadn't even known existed. The officials agreed that no harm had been done or intended, but rules are rules and the company had to pay a $45,000 fine.

One way that the government has helped business is by making labor laws more flexible. "Overall, Peruvian labor laws are now no more of a problem for us here than in the U.S.," Traver says.

The workers themselves are "all hard-working, cheerful and willing," he says, "but they don't work with the same efficiency or knowledge." **Vinsa**'s Michael Bail agrees that at least part of the workforce is undereducated, but adds that there is also a pool of labor, especially of younger workers, who have good technical training and adapt well to new technology. Both companies are bridging the gap with strong employee training programs.

Professional staff are "roughly at U.S. levels, in all senses" Traver says. "Our engineers might not win a competition, but we'd have no need to be ashamed. But then top managers in Lima are expensive. We pay ours around $100,000 a year and a good salesman picks up $50,000. Manual workers receive considerably less, but nobody should think that they're going to start a business here on cheap labor."

Neither company has had problems with labor relations. **Peruplast** had a union but it petered out, while workers at **Vinsa** were realistic about the company's chances of survival if **Owens** didn't invest. "The union leaders made better speeches than I did about the need for modernization," Bail says.

While making private industry feel comfortable, the government has been vigorously selling off state enterprises, to strong foreign interest. The star sale was the **CPT** and **Entel** telecommunications companies, which were sold to **Telefónica de España** for $2.02 billion in February 1994. In addition to the sale price, **Telefónica** has agreed to invest $1.9 billion to upgrade the system and more than double the country's telephone lines by 1999.

Foreigners Returning to Key Mining Sector

Nowhere has the return of the foreigners been more keenly felt than in mining, however, which already generates about $1.6 billion in exports, around three-fifths of Peru's total.

The sector has long been dominated by **Southern Peru Copper Corp SPCC,** a subsidiary of **Asarco, Inc.,** a New York-based copper mining company. **SPCC** has been a feature on the Peruvian corporate map since 1954 and is today the largest private company in Peru with income of $460 million and profits of $45 million in 1993.

It is rapidly being joined by other foreign mining giants as the privatization process continues. Among those that have picked up second-hand state mining properties are the **Shougang Corporation,** Beijing; **Anglo-American Corp.,** Johannesburg; **Cyprus Minerals,** Englewood, Colorado, and **Lac Minerals,** Toronto.

Meanwhile, **Newmont Mining Corp.,** Denver, is already planning expansion at its Yanacocha gold mine, which started up in mid-1993 and is set to quickly double Peru's gold output. **Placer Dome Inc.,** Vancouver, is hoping that it can repeat the process, after buying a three-year option on the Jehuamarca gold deposit from the government in January 1994.

The enthusiasm is promising to turn into a Peruvian gold-rush, with Britain's **RTZ** leading the claim-stakers, closely followed by Canadians such as **Barrick Gold, Cambior,** and a host of smaller companies.

The picture is much the same in oil. With the government's new green light to foreign investment, companies such as **Mobil, Great Western** and **Arco Oil and Gas** have been looking at Peru with renewed interest, particularly as **PetroPeru,** the state oil company, is readied for privatization. Sale of the oil firm has been politically contentious, and initial sale plans were delayed in 1994, but the government said it was going ahead in 1995, with the only uncertainties having to do with the mechanics of the sale. But the biggest oil producer is an old hand, **Occidental Petroleum Corp.,** Los Angeles. **Oxy** drilled its first Peruvian well in 1972 and today produces 60,000 bpd of oil, half of Peru's total.

The sell-off of the electricity system began in July 1994, with the sale of Lima's two distribution companies. A local consortium took control of one of the companies, the other was won by a consortium led by Canada's **Ontario Hydro Inc.** The sale of the power plants took longer, with the 40mw Cahua hydroelectric plant sold just after the April 1995 elections. The buyer was **Sindicato Pesquero S.A.**, the biggest fishmeal producer in Peru and part of the Galsky group. The same company bought three of the first five **Pescaperu** fishmeal plants sold by the beginning of 1995, with more sales to come later in the year. Fishing is Peru's number two export earner, behind mining.

The public water system and the railways were also due on the block before the end of 1995, but the sale or lease of the nation's ports was bogged down by political pressures, particularly after a border conflict with Ecuador put national security back at the top of the Peruvian agenda.

One of the few areas where the government has been taking a leading role is in road construction and maintenance. It recently undertook two programs for a total of $463 million, largely funded by the World Bank and the Inter-American Development Bank. As the elections approached, the government also poured money into schools and a variety of social projects through the Ministry of the Presidency.

The government has encouraged private companies to bid for concessions for the construction and running of major projects, and here as elsewhere in the economy foreigners and Peruvians enjoy equal treatment.

The hands-off approach has its drawbacks, however. Unhindered by any exchange controls, the flood of foreign money has buoyed the sol, which has revalued by an estimated 8 percent against the dollar since August 1990. That and the economic shocks at the beginning of the Fujimori government have made Peru one of the most expensive Latin American countries.

The private sector has also been clamoring for State intervention to resuscitate the stricken agricultural sector. Agriculture is traditionally one of the country's main exporters, and the Peruvian climate is particularly auspicious. But years of neglect, poor marketing and distribution, and confused property rights, together with an under-priced dollar, have made it cheaper to import many products than to buy from local suppliers.

Middle Class Growing; Poor Still Suffer

Meanwhile, although the economy may be doing well, the good news has yet to percolate to a large proportion of the population. The National Institute of Statistics and Information estimates that a quarter of the population is living in extreme poverty. Almost half of the country's children suffer from chronic malnutrition, according to Foncodes, the government welfare agency. Both problems are particularly acute in the countryside, with the main cities, such as Lima, Callao, and Arequipa, recording better figures.

Nevertheless, with economic growth, the middle class, which had all but disappeared, is starting to grow again, offering opportunities for investors. Supermarkets, for instance, are starting to do well again, after the bankruptcies of the Eighties and early Nineties. The Chilean chain, Santa Isabel, has been expanding aggressively since its arrival in 1993.

—Peru's macro-economy has been booming, as these charts for fishing, mining, and commerce demonstrate, but many Peruvians are still on the outside looking in.

Manufacturing is also taking off, with the country's lag in social conditions meaning that basic products like foodstuffs and building materials are the major growth areas. Foreign companies that are benefiting from the upturn include **Goodyear, Nestlé, Volvo, Toyota, Procter & Gamble** and **RJR Nabisco,** which bought local manufacturer **Field & Royal** in 1993.

Goodyear has been manufacturing in Peru for more than 50 years. "We've got a niche market," says William Massey, president of the company and also of the American Chamber of Commerce. "We bring in some of our tires and manufacture about three-quarters locally. We make a very robust product, which would be overdesigned for the U.S. or European markets."

The company is not thinking of exporting in the short-term. "The infrastructure is still rather expensive," Massey says, "so we can't get our costs down to Chilean or Colombian levels. We could compete in Ecuador, but there we're up against a 14 percent import duty."

Massey sounds some other warnings for potential investors. "This is still a very small market for consumer products. I wouldn't come in here to start from scratch when import duties are coming down to zero. The only way in would be to buy an existing company." The best areas for investment in Peru are mining, fishing and specialized agriculture, products like asparagus and mangos that are highly labor-intensive, he says.

"The future is in added value," he adds, "exporting tinned fish rather than fishmeal and copper billets rather than concentrates. And tourism has got to make a comeback."

U.S. companies in Peru are mainly importing, rather than manufacturing locally, says Dean Anderson, commercial officer at the U.S. Embassy. "Companies like **Abbot** are bringing in pharmaceuticals, for instance, while **Warner Lambert** closed down their factory here and are importing sweets for sale under their local brand name."

Economic Boom Requires Imports

The embassy is recommending that companies wanting to export to Peru concentrate on products that service the economic boom. Its list includes: industrial chemicals, construction machinery, security and safety equipment, computers and peripherals, telecommunications equipment, oil and gas equipment, electrical supplies, mining equipment, medical products, and food processing and packaging equipment.

"We are getting a lot of calls from companies interested in selling here," Anderson says. "Last year we were getting two calls a month, now it's up to eight or nine a day. They are mainly looking for agents and distributors and want to know about their prospects." There are a lot of textile companies looking to farm out garment manufacturing to Peruvian companies, he adds, with locals such as **Nettalco S.A** working overtime to produce for U.S. labels such as **Jantzen** and **Liz Claiborne.**

Meanwhile, Peru is also being welcomed back into the financial fold. Fujimori made his peace with the international banking system, although the two sides have yet to thrash out a plan for dealing with the national debt. Peruvian companies are again raising foreign debt, after years in the financial wilderness, and a rash of them are also planning to have their shares traded in the United States, via American Depository Receipts.

The previous 30 years have taken their toll, however. Most Peruvian companies are struggling to re-equip and are having to adapt rapidly to the free market after years of working in an environment of tariffs, quotas, and government regulations.

The Fujimori government's economic shock tactics ushered in a period of painful adjustment. Real interest rates, which were negative during the hyperinflation of the Garcia period, suddenly rose to 30 percent and more, crippling large numbers of companies that had taken on more debt than they could handle. The economy went into recession at the same time as companies were suddenly hit by foreign competition.

"When imports were freed, we were pretty well-equipped," **Peruplast**'s Hans Traver says. "But a lot of our customers went belly-up. Those two years were terrible, we suffered a disastrous loss of sales."

Since then the economy has begun to pick up. Economic growth was a spectacular 12.7 percent for 1994. Traver said 1993 and 1994 were the best years in the history of his company.

The speed of the changes has been dizzying. When **Owens** started work at **Vinsa,** for instance, the government was levying 40 percent import duties on glass containers. Within a month it was 20 percent and by mid-1993 it was 15 percent. "That still gives us a reasonable margin of protection, though," Bail says, "and we are making major strides in improving our quality and efficiency."

Paradoxically, the possibility of continuity is proving attractive for **Owens.** For one thing, foreign investors can guarantee themselves tax stability by signing contracts with the government. The contracts are open to companies that invest more than $2 million or over $500,000 if they create more than 20 jobs or export more than $2 million a year.

Even more importantly for business, there is also the promise of political stability. "Peru has experienced every sort of political and economic experiment possible," Bail says, "but we're seeing the prospect of continuity for the first time."

"Of course, when we were planning to enter Peru we didn't know that Fujimori was going to be able to run again," he says.

But in the April 1995 elections, none of the leading candidates even questioned the free-market model. Even so, voters had no doubt about returning Fujimori to office, giving him a landslide 64 percent of valid votes and an unexpected majority in Congress. Although the opposition tried to focus on poverty, Fujimori's support was highest among the poorest voters, who were impressed by new-found economic and social stability and the President's non-stop tour of the shanty towns to inaugurate new schools and public works. They were also apparently convinced by his arguments that after an initial term dedicated to putting the economy and the country in order he would make his second term of office a campaign to improve the lot of the poor.

Peru at a Glance

Population: 22.6 million.

Labor force: 7.1 million.

Languages: Spanish and Quechua, the latter the sole language of some two million indigenous people who live largely in the countryside, outside the formal economy.

Ethnic mix: Indigenous 45 percent, mestizo (mixed indigenous/European) 37 percent, European 15 percent, African, Japanese, Chinese, other 3 percent. Almost half the Peruvian population is of Quechua or Aymara origin, originally from the sierra. On the coast mestizos are dominant, while in the Amazonian jungle there are a number of smaller populations of indigenous peoples.

Literacy and Educational levels: 87 percent literacy; 12.6 percent of population over the age of 15 has completed no formal education at all, 56 percent finished primary school and at least one year of secondary education, 3.1 percent studied in a university.

Climate and best times to visit: Lima and much of the coast is grey, humid and depressing for most of the six months from April to September, but business is possible without much difficulty all year-round. Little rain falls on the coast, which is mainly arid desert, and temperatures rarely drop below 13C (56F), although high humidity in the cooler months makes it seem colder. Maximum summer temperatures are usually around 30C (86F). The period between November and March, when the climate is most pleasant on the coast, largely coincides with the rainy season in the sierra and jungle, when travel can become difficult.

Natural resources, chief agricultural products: Copper, gold, silver, lead, zinc, fish, petroleum, coffee, cotton and wool (Also, coca leaves are grown to produce base cocaine, one of Peru's chief exports, though illegal.)

Land area: 1,285,217 square kilometers.

Economic Figures:

GDP: $29.76 billion (1994)

Per Capita GDP: $1,312 (1994)

Economic growth rate: 12.7 percent (1994)

Main exports: Fishmeal, copper, textiles and garments, zinc, gold, non-traditional agricultural products (such as asparagus and mangos), lead, iron ore, refined silver.

Main imports: Foodstuffs, machinery, transport equipment, iron and steel semi-manufactures, chemicals, pharmaceuticals, fuels and lubricants.

Duties on imports: Tariffs have been consolidated in two levels: 15 percent and 25 percent. More than 90 percent of imports are in the first category.

Repatriation of profits: There are no restrictions. Foreign currency is freely available at market rates. All companies, whether Peruvian or foreign-owned, are taxed at 30 percent of profits.

When You Go to Peru

Visas: For most visitors, a visa is not required unless they plan to stay for more than 30 days.

Airlines: American Airlines and Faucett from the United States, Air France, Alitalia, Ibéria, KLM, and Lufthansa from Europe, Aerolineas Argentinas, Aeroperu, Avianca, Lan Chile, Lacsa, Lloyd Boliviano, Servivensa, Varig, and Viasa from other points in Latin America.

What to Expect at the Airport: Visitors are often required to leave a deposit of between 10 percent and 100 percent of the value of electrical items brought into the country. This applies, for instance, to CD's (both the machines and the disks) and laptop computers. The customs officials are very adept at telling the difference between a 386 and a 486, or whether the computer has a hard disk, and are therefore usually pretty good at telling how much it is worth. The deposit is returned when you leave the country with the equipment. It may be possible to avoid payment if you fax a Peruvian company before your arrival telling them what you are bringing with you. They then have to contact a customs agent to complete the formalities.

Urban Transportation:

The principal auto rental firms have stands at the airport (Avis, Budget, Hertz, National) and offices in the business district. Taxis do not have meters and you may have to bargain. However, they are generally cheap and many taxi drivers are more reasonable and honest than their reputation may suggest. It helps to know roughly how much you should be paying, but at time of writing it should not cost much more than the equivalent of $10-15 for even the longest journeys in Lima, and as little as $1 for short rides. Taxis may be hailed in the street with ease day and night although many are in poor condition (20-year-old crash-hardened VW beetles are common).

There are also many radio taxi services, which cost up to twice as much but are correspondingly more comfortable. They may also give receipts (*boleta* or *factura* in Spanish) if you ask when scheduling the pickup. Taxi Seguro (Tel: 448-7226) and Taxi Miraflores (Tels: 446-4336 and 446-3953) are among the best known of a multitude of companies. Lady's Car (Tels: 470-8528 and 470-1371. Fax: 470-8476) offers a 24-hour taxi service with only women drivers, all of whom are bilingual (mainly English and Spanish, but also some Italian, French, German and Japanese speakers) and can arrange to meet travelers at the airport.

Limousine services are also available, including Real Limousine (Tel: 441-8245 and 442-3665) and Limousine Service S.A. (Tels: 445-5716 and 447-9440. Fax: 447-9200).

Hotels

NOTE: All hotels add 18 percent tax and 10 percent service charge to the bill. There is a chronic shortage of business-class hotels in Lima, so book early. All the hotels listed have national and international direct dial telephones, color TV, air conditioning and minibar. Apart from the Sheraton they have cable TV and modem and fax connections.

Sheraton
Paseo de la Republica 170, Lima 1.
Tel: (511) 433-3320. Fax: (511) 433-6344.
Message taking is sporadic and fax and modem connections are diffi-

cult. It is in the middle of run-down central Lima, and if you are coming on business, you are likely to prefer being in the close-in suburbs, San Isidro or Miraflores. Rooms start at $110.

El Olivar de San Isidro

Pancho Fierro 194, San Isidro, Lima 27.

Tel: (511) 441-1454. Fax: (511) 441-1388.

Pleasant and quiet location, convenient for shops and bars, attentive service. Rooms start at $135.

Cesar's

Corner of La Paz and Diez Canseco, Miraflores, Lima 18.

Tel: (511) 444-1212. Fax: (511) 444-4440

Secretarial service available 16 hours a day. Very popular, well-placed, traditional style. Rooms start at $155.

Las Americas

Av. Benavides 415, Miraflores, Lima 18.

Tel: (511) 445-9494. Fax: (511) 444-1137.

Modern hotel with non-smoking floors.

Rooms start at $150.

Contacts

Business Organizations:

AMERICAN CHAMBER OF COMMERCE

Michael Donovan, Director

Av. Ricardo Palma 836, Miraflores, Lima 18.

Tel: (511) 447-9349. Fax: (511) 447-9352

NATIONAL INDUSTRIAL SOCIETY (SNI)

Dr. Luis Abugatas, Executive Director

Los Laureles 365, San Isidro, Lima 27.

Tel: (511) 440-8700. Fax: (511) 441-5877

Governmental:

COMMISSION FOR THE PROMOTION OF PERU
Ministerio de Industria, piso 13, Calle 1 Oeste s/n, Urb. Corpac, Lima 27.
Tels: (511) 440-6178, 440-3255, 440-6071. Fax: (511) 411-5844 or 441-4461.
New agency to promote foreign investment opportunities. Beatriz Boza, Executive Secretary

COMMISSION FOR PROMOTION OF PRIVATE INVEST-MENT (Copri)
Av. Las Artes 260, San Borja, Lima 41.
Tel: (511) 430-0660. Fax: (511) 475-0078.
Government agency supervising the privatization and liquidation of Peru's state-owned companies. Carlos Montoya, Director

NATIONAL COMMISSION OF INVESTMENT AND FOREIGN TECHNOLOGY (Conite)
Jr. Miroquesada 320, piso 4, Lima 1.
Tels: (511) 428-9358, 427-7696. Fax: (511) 427-7696
Government agency that oversees foreign investment. Jorge Muñiz, President

MINISTRY OF ENERGY AND MINES
Av. Las Artes 260, San Borja, Lima 41.
Tel: (511) 475-0065. Fax: (511) 475-0689
Daniel Hokama, Minister

U.S. EMBASSY Commercial Section
Tel: (511) 433-3200, exts. 252/251. Fax (511) 433-4687

Potentially Useful:

The Andean Air Mail & Peruvian Times S.A. publishes the *Lima Times,* a monthly English-language magazine, and the *Andean Report,* a weekly Peruvian business newsletter. Members of the staff offer translation/interpretation services and may be able to help visitors with business and other inquiries. Contact: Eleanor Griffis, Pasaje Los Pinos 156, Oficina B6, Miraflores, Lima 18. Tels: (511) 446-9120, 45-3761. Fax: (511) 446-7888.

Lawyers (no recommendation is intended by listing here):

Barrios, Fuentes, Urquiaga y Dañino
This law firm works for, and is a member of, the American Chamber of Commerce. It handles a large number of leading corporate and multinational clients. Contact: Luis Fuentes
J. Arias Araguez
250 Miraflores, Lima 18.
Tel: (511) 445-4000. Fax: (511) 445-1015.

Accountants/Auditors:

Hansen-Holm, Alonso & Co. (the local affiliate of Coopers & Lybrand)
Contact: Antonio Alonso or Werner Hansen-Holm
Juan de Arona 830, San Isidro, Lima 27.
Tel: (511) 442-6910. Fax: (511) 442-2073.
Price Waterhouse
Contact: Carlos Querol or Ernesto Leyva
Las Begoñas 441, piso 14, San Isidro, Lima 27.
Tel: (511) 442-0567. Fax: (511) 442-6522

Interpretation/Translations:

Spence & Lithgoe Traducciones S.A.
Jr. Berlin 832, Miraflores, Lima 18.
Tel: (511) 445-9461
ESIT, Av. Manuel Olguín
215, Monterrico, Lima 33.
Tels: (511) 435-5970, 435-0601.
Traducciones Profesionales
Av. Pardo 1350, of. 701, Miraflores, Lima 18.
Tel: (511) 444-3632.

In case of illness:

Dr. Miguel Campos

A fellow of the American College of Physicians.

Av. Tuleda y Varela 138, of. 304, San Isidro, Lima 27.

Tels: 442-8156, 442-7627.

12

URUGUAY

Selling on the Backroads
Far from Indiana

By Danilo Arbilla

In three years in Uruguay, Charley Piatt has been delighted with the beaches of the South Atlantic coastline and impressed by the meticulous habits of many of his workers. He's also experienced the frustration of trying to keep to delivery schedules on country roads and to balance the expectations of his bosses in Indiana with the operating methods of Latin American suppliers and distributors.

Piatt manages the manufacturing and distribution operation in Montevideo of **Chore-Time/Brock International,** a firm with headquarters in Milford, Indiana, that makes feeders for poultry, cattle, and hogs, and grain silos.

At the beginning of the Nineties, the firm decided to set up operations in one of Uruguay's tax-free manufacturing zones. Piatt moved to Montevideo on Oct. 3, 1992, to take charge.

"Our idea was to set up operations in Uruguay and offer our products and services to customers in Brazil, taking advantage of the tax breaks," he said, referring to lower tariffs in force among the four nations that make up the Common Market of the South, known as Mercosur or Mercosul. Members are Brazil, Argentina, Uruguay, and Paraguay. Some components used by **Chore-Time** are manufactured in Uruguay and others brought from the United States, he said.

Piatt has been so pleasantly surprised by the quality of work being done in his firm's warehouses that he sent a letter to the firm that provided warehouse workers praising their work.

"One of the most frequent problems encountered by our distributors in the United States and the Netherlands," he wrote in his letter to the firm, **Hamling, S.A.,** "is that the wrong parts get shipped. In our line of products there are many pieces that are similar but which have distinct functions and if the shipments don't contain the exact pieces then we have to send them by a different means, such as air freight, which is much more costly."

"In Montevideo," he added, "we have an inventory of more than 1,000 parts, many of which are similar in appearance" and despite "the problem of loading trucks in the middle of the night," the "percentage of errors is considerably less" than those registered in the United States and Holland.

But in some other aspects of his operation he encountered frustrating national customs that caused him difficulty getting bids and estimates from potential local suppliers within his deadline schedule and in the required form. He attributed this, at least partly, to the fact that when he began operations in Uruguay the country still had a protected economy with a very low level of competition.

"I understand the problems that can come up regarding quality, delivery time, and pricing in general, and we were never bothered by any obstacle within the expected," he said, "but neither I nor the company could understand the Uruguayan custom of delaying for so long in giving the customer a cost estimate."

This led Piatt to conclude that the Uruguayan style of doing business is "to delay so long in giving an estimate — at times months — that the buyer is so frustrated by the wait that he ends up paying whatever price."

"Another big problem was the shortage of trucks for shipments to our customers in Brazil. We had big problems over trucks that reached their destination days or weeks later than the scheduled day." Piatt said he realized that his company "doesn't ship to ordinary places," but to "farmers, who are, of course, in the country, possibly far from the principal cities.

He said he could understand that the state of the roads often caused delays but that it was difficult to explain such delays to the home office "because they look at the maps, see the routes, and don't know — for example — that the routes here are not four-lane highways."

His Uruguayan experience has helped Piatt to see how doing business in a different country can shape one's perspective. For instance, when cost-saving production measures in the United States allowed the firm to reduce prices on goods already sold and to pass those lower prices along to buyers in South America as well, distributors in the region were less than enthusiastic.

"None of them could understand the price reductions," he said, "and some were very angry when we did it. They said the buyers had already paid for the products at the higher price."

He also learned about inflation, Brazilian-style. In May 1994, before Brazil's new currency plan sharply reduced inflation that was running 40 percent a month, Piatt made a swing through Brazil to visit distributors.

"Look, one of them said to me, I am one of your best distributors, but I don't have a current price list, so I always have to request the price on whatever small part and that wastes my time and money in telephone calls. Why don't you give me a new price list?"

"I looked at the price list in my briefcase," Piatt recalled, "and saw that it was also for 1991. Look, I said, mine is the same as yours; it's the current list. The Brazilian could not believe that a price book would last longer than a month, let alone last for years."

Assimilation Works Both Ways

With time, Piatt found himself understanding and assimilating the methods of Latin American businessmen, but that earned him some problems with his superiors in Indiana.

"My boss would ask, 'How much tax will we have to pay on such and such?' and 'When is something going to be shipped?' I found myself replying in the Latin manner, saying, for instance, 'If it goes to such and such state (of Brazil) we'll have to pay a certain amount, if it goes to another state we'll pay another amount; if we do it this month we'll get it done in such and such time, if we do it later there'll be more delays.'"

"At one point, my boss said, 'If we wanted a Latin American manager for this business we would have hired one, but we wanted a North American manager, and you're it. Please, don't give us Latin replies.'"

"But with time we both learned that it was more or less impossible to get definite answers to many things, that the only way was to go ahead and try it. Now, our home office doesn't ask for exact figures."

Piatt thinks the most important lesson he has learned in Uruguay is realizing how quickly the rules of the game can change. He recalled that his firm spent a year and a half doing a study about certificates of origin in the Mercosur trading region, and when it was finished the rules had already changed. "Once we learned the answers they changed the questions on us," he said.

Piatt says that through its customs broker his firm maintains good contacts with "mid-level government bureaucrats" and that "as a small firm we don't need contacts with high-level government people. Uruguay is a country where such contacts are not necessary, although it's possible that things may be different for a bigger company."

He says that when **Chore-Time** first came to Uruguay it hired lawyers and accountants from prestigious Uruguayan firms to handle paperwork, which made the home office rest easier, but he found that such firms were not much help in getting mundane things and minor paperwork done quickly. For that, he says he now uses more ordinary mortals.

Uruguay Overview

Reluctantly Embracing
A Market Economy

By coming to Uruguay, **Chore-Time** is testing the waters in a country that was traditionally one of the most statist in Latin America but which is now slowly converting to a market economy under the influence of its much larger neighbors and main trading partners — Argentina and Brazil. Many people and organizations in Uruguay, particularly trade unions, still hold socialist sentiments today, and these are regularly vented within the framework of the country's healthy political democracy. For 160 years, Uruguayan politics has been dominated by two centrist political parties, the Colorado Party and the National Party. However, since the early 1970s a new player on the scene, the *Frente Amplio* or Broad Front, a coalition of socialist, communist, and other generally leftist parties, has been the fastest growing political force in the country. That there is still considerable sympathy for statist ideas is also apparent in the fact that there are 275,000 public employees in a population of fewer than 3.2 million, their tenure virtually guaranteed in the constitution. There are 580,000 retirees, some of whom start drawing pensions as young as age 35.

But Uruguay today has the welcome mat out for foreign investors, who for the most part are promised the same treatment as local investors in Uruguay. No special authorization is necessary to set up business in the country, to import or export, to make bank deposits and carry out other banking business, to obtain credit, or receive the benefits of government business promotions.

The exceptions apply to investments in electricity, hydrocarbons, basic petrochemicals, atomic energy, exploitation of minerals considered strategic, banking and finance, railroads, radio and television. Local investors receive some preferences in those fields, but foreign investors may get into them through joint ventures with local investors.

The currency exchange market is free and open, in both the purchase and sale of any currency. Exchange operations may be conducted in whatever amount, without tax, in banks, other financial institutions, and exchange houses. The country also permits unrestricted transfer of capital and remittance of profits.

Among the country's efforts to attract foreign investment are the duty-free zones, where firms may operate factories and warehouses for goods intended for export without paying any taxes, except the social security payroll taxes.

A Politicized Labor Movement

While Uruguay offers one of Latin America's best educated labor forces, the highly politicized labor movement can present some problems in doing business. The right to organize and strike, guaranteed in the Uruguayan constitution, has never been regulated, and as a result many unions use strikes as a political platform. Even firms that do not have internal labor problems may encounter delays and other obstructions caused by strikes and protests by employees of state firms and agencies.

The Inter-Syndicate Plenary of Workers-National Convention of Workers, known at the PIT-CNT, controls all trade union activity in Uruguay and has its greatest strength among state employees, bank personnel, workers in construction and certain industries. Although the PIT-CNT has experienced declining popularity in recent years, it still has the clout to summon ample support when it calls general strikes.

Employers are also faced with labor legislation that sometimes seems onerous, particularly because the judicial system has a strong tendency to favor the worker in any legal action. The World Bank, in a 1993 study, criticized the training and educational level of Uruguayan judges, while praising their reputation for being free of corruption. The World Bank report said the judges "lack familiarity with modern technology and the value of intangible goods." It added that Uruguayan labor legislation "causes confusion for the foreign investor" and "damages the image that Uruguay tries to project abroad as a country with a broad, liberal investment framework."

Paying for Uruguay's generous retirement system is a heavy weight for both employer and employee. Employers pay into the social security system 20.5 percent of their payroll, and workers add 18 percent. But with only 900,000 workers paying in and 580,000 drawing out, the social security system runs a deficit of $300 million a year.

There is no personal income tax in Uruguay, but businesses pay 30 percent on net profits and two percent on the assessed value of their firms. Individuals pay from seven-tenths of a percent to 3 percent on the value of their property. A 22 percent value added tax is applied to most goods and services, and is higher for some products.

Politics Divided in Thirds

In elections on Nov. 27, 1994, Uruguayan voters returned to the presidency Julio María Sanguinetti, a member of the Colorado Party who had previously served in the office between 1985 and 1990. But he won by the narrowest of margins, his party receiving just 32 percent of the vote, against 31 percent for the National Party and 31 percent for the Broad Front. A fourth party, the New Space, obtained 5 percent.

The outcome not only left President Sanguinetti with a narrow base of support but also divided the parliament in thirds, meaning the new president must seek opposition support in order to pass legislation. The biggest issues confronting him are the need to reform the retirement system and reduce government expenditures.

He must attempt these changes in a country that, since the beginning of the 20th Century, has had an economy with strong state involvement, not only in a regulatory role but a directly interventionist one as well and, in many cases, as a monopoly producer of goods. This tradition of state protectionism and the development of social benefits greater than those enjoyed in other Latin American countries impressed on Uruguayans a sort of "culture of the state" that would later serve as a brake on efforts to open the economy and put more of it in private hands.

The 1990-95 government of Luis Alberto Lacalle began a campaign intended to bring Uruguay in line with global trends toward greater economic freedom. Lacalle undertook privatizations and some deregulation but encountered many hurdles. Political fragmentation in the parliament led to impasses, which were resolved only after many of the proposals were submitted to a plebiscite and lost. Nevertheless, the Lacalle government did accomplish some of its goals, including closing down the state fishing company, the beginning of efforts to sell the state-owned airline, the return of the natural gas company to private ownership, and the elimination of the insurance monopoly.

Gradual Trade Opening

In trade matters, Uruguay has been undergoing a gradual opening since about 1974. Tariffs on imported consumer goods have been falling since the Seventies, when top rates hit 116 percent, to a maximum of 20 percent today. Capital goods are free of customs duties today, and imported primary materials face a tariff of just 10 percent. In addition, since 1991, Uruguay has been part of the Mercosur trading bloc and as such is committed to eliminate all tariffs on goods from the other member countries — Brazil, Argentina, and Paraguay — by the year 2000.

The Uruguayan economy has shown steady economic growth for the past decade, including a 5 percent growth rate in 1994. Its primary macro-economic problems are chronic inflation and a budget deficit that runs about 3 percent of gross national product. The deficit is largely attributed to the immense bureaucracy and the costly retirement system.

Studies by the U.S. Embassy in Montevideo find that the best prospects for exports to Uruguay fall into the areas of agricultural chemicals, manufactured goods and machinery, transport equipment, food processing equipment, computer hardware and software, other office equipment, machinery for alternative energy sources, medical and laboratory equipment.

Among areas for investment, Uruguay's large population of people older than 65 seems to offer a possible market for geriatric equipment and services. Also, the government has designated tourism and forestation as development priorities, and those areas are seen as having good potential for foreign investors.

Three infrastructure projects that are planned or underway also need investment capital and construction expertise. They are:

● A maritime canal being developed by Uruguay and four of its neighbors — Bolivia, Brazil, Paraguay, and Argentina — to provide access to the Atlantic Ocean from the Paraná, Paraguay, and Uruguay rivers.

● A bridge connecting the Uruguayan city of Colonia with Buenos Aires, the Argentine capital. Private firms will be selected to build and operate the bridge, collecting tolls from users.

● Studies are underway to decide whether to build a natural gas pipeline between Montevideo and Buenos Aires, which would be done by concession to private firms at an estimated cost of $70 million to $80 million.

Uruguay at a Glance

Population: 3.167 million.

Labor force: 1.26 million.

Language: Spanish.

Ethnic mix: Almost totally European; the ancestry of Uruguay's population is roughly half Spanish and half Italian.

Literacy and Educational levels: 96 percent literacy. More than half of the population has completed secondary school or beyond.

Climate and best times to visit: Uruguay is entirely situated in the temperate zone of the Southern Hemisphere and has weather that compares to many places in the Northern Hemisphere. Its summers, which occur from December to March, are hot. Winters, from June to September, are chilly and windy. Fall and spring are probably the best times for business trips. You still need warm clothes, but layered so that you can shed them on warm days.

Natural resources, chief agricultural products: Sheep, wool, cattle, beef, leather hides, fish and seafood.

Land area: 176,214 square kilometers.

Economic Statistics:

        GDP: $15.5 billion (1994)

        Per Capita GDP: $4,894

        GDP Growth: 1.5 percent (1993), 5 percent (1994

Main exports: Textiles, frozen meat, leather and other tannery goods, flour, transport material.

Main imports: Food items, mineral products, chemical products, electronics and electric machinery, and transportation equipment.

Duties on imports: In general, they range from zero to 20 percent. Among the four nations of the Mercosur trading bloc, including Uruguay, tariffs are gradually being reduced to zero.

Repatriation of profits: There are no limitations.

When You Go to Uruguay

Visas: Most visitors may enter Uruguay for up to 90 days for tourism or business without a visa; only a valid passport is required.

Airlines: Service to and from Europe, the United States, or Asia generally means a connection in Buenos Aires, São Paulo, or Rio de Janeiro. Airlines providing service include United, Ladeco, Varig, and Lan Chile to New York or Miami; Iberia and Varig to Spain, Air France and Varig to France, KLM to the Netherlands, and Varig to Asia. In addition, there is a shuttle service, referred to as an "air bridge," between Montevideo and Buenos Aires with flights almost hourly on Uruguayan and Argentine airlines. Air service to the interior of Uruguay was recently privatized, but there are few flights.

Urban Transportation: Comfortable Mercedes Benz taxis provide service from the airport to the city with metered rates, though the taxis you'll find on the streets once you're in town are far less elegant. There are occasionally taxi shortages at the airport.

      The major auto rental firms have services in Uruguay, some at the airport itself, others downtown. They include Avis (Tel: 598 2-92-

7579); Hertz (Tel: 598-2-61-2857 or 92-3920); Budget (Tel: 598-2-92-5353; Fax: 598-2-92-1339); National (Tel: 598-2-61-5267; Fax: 598-2-61-5152), and Class (Tel: 598-2-92-0237; Fax 598-2-91-4055).

If you want a vehicle with a driver, try Remises del Turista, with bi-lingual drivers (Tel: 598-2-91-4348; Fax: 598-2-91-4668); Limousinas del Uruguay in the Victoria Plaza Hotel, offering limousines with bar and television; Remises Obelisco (Tel: 598-2-41-9421), or Central de Remises (Tel: 598-2-92-1812; Fax: 598-2-92-1813).

Hotels

NOTE: Uruguay has long been short on good hotels, but that should be remedied soon. Three five-star hotels are under construction and expected to be completed by the end of 1995, and a fourth, the Victoria Plaza, is completing a major addition. All of the new ones promise good quality telephone service and connections for computer modems.

MONTEVIDEO
Victoria Plaza
Plaza Independencia 759.
Tels: (598-2) 92-0237, 90-5742, and 90-1588.
The genteel, but frayed principal hotel of Montevideo is undergoing a major renovation and expansion that should be finished in 1995.
Rates begin at $128.
Lafayette
Soriano 1170.
Tel: (598-2) 92-4646; Fax: (598-2) 92-7367.
Rates begin at $113.
Balmoral
Plaza Libertad 1126.
Tel: (598-2) 92-2393; Fax: (598-2) 92-2288.
Rates beginning at $95.
Internacional (Holiday Inn)
Colonia 823.

Tel: (598-2) 92-0001; Fax: (598-2) 92-1242.
Rates begin at $73.

PUNTA DEL ESTE
Hotel Casino San Rafael
Rambla L. Batlle Pacheco.
Tels: (598-042) 8-2161 and 8-2166.
Rates begin at $245.

Hotel L'Auberge
Barrio Parque Golf.
Tel: (598-042) 8-3357.
Rates begin at $325.

La Capilla
Viña del Mar y Bulevard Artigas.
Tel: (598-042) 8-4059.
Rates begin at $180.

Contacts

Business Organizations:

UNION OF EXPORTERS
Rincón 454, piso 2.
Tel: (598-2) 95-6050; Fax: (598-2) 96-1117.

CHAMBER OF INDUSTRY
Av. Libertado Lavalleja 1672.
Tel: (598-2) 91-5000.

CHAMBER OF COMMERCE
Rincón 454. Tel: (598-2) 96-1277; Fax: (598-2) 96-1243.

AMERICAN CHAMBER OF COMMERCE
Bartolomé Mitre 1337, esc. 108.
Tel: (598-2) 95-9048; Fax: (598-2) 95-9059.

ASSOCIATION FOR U.S.-URUGUAYAN TRADE
Rincón 454 esc. 520.
Tel: (598-2) 95-1807.

Governmental:

COMMISSION FOR THE PROMOTION OF INVESTMENT
Edificio Libertad - Government House
Av. L.A. de Herrera 3350, piso 2.
Tel: (598-2) 47-2110, ext. 1233; Fax: (598-2) 80-9397.

OFFICE OF PLANNING AND BUDGET
Edificio Libertad, Av. L. A. de Herrera 3350, piso 3.
Tel: (598-2) 81-9525; Fax: (598-2) 29-9770.

CENTRAL BANK
Paysandú y Florida.
Tel: (598-2) 98-5008.

MINISTRY OF ECONOMY AND FINANCE
Colonia 1089, piso 3.
Tel: (598-2) 92-1017.

MINISTRY OF INDUSTRY, ENERGY AND MINING
Rincón 747.
Tel: (598-2) 90-0231; Fax: (598-2) 92-1245.

MINISTRY OF LIVESTOCK, AGRICULTURE AND FISHING
Constituyente 1476.
Tel: (598-2) 48-2256.

MINISTRY OF TRANSPORT AND PUBLIC WORKS
Rincón 561.
Tel: (598-2) 95-7386; Fax: (598-2) 96-2893.

COMMISSION FOR THE COMMON MARKET OF THE SOUTH (Mercosur)
Paysandú 919.
Tel: (598-2) 92-1000; Fax: (598-2) 92-3655.

URUGUAYAN GOVERNMENT FINANCIAL OFFICE IN THE UNITED STATES
2021 L Street N.W., Suite 201, Washington, D. C. 20036.
Tel: (202) 223-9833; Fax: (202) 223-2119.

Lawyers who have worked with foreign clients, but whose listing here does not constitute an endorsement:

Guyer y Regules
Plaza Independencia 811, planta baja.
Tel: (598-2) 92-1515; Fax: (598-2) 92-5454.
Hughes & Hughes
25 de Mayo 455, 4° piso.
Tel: (598-2) 96-1142; Fax: (598-2) 96-1003.
Olivera y Peirano
Misiones 1424, piso 2.
Tel: (598-2) 96-5859; Fax: (598-2) 96-5863.
Ferrere Lamaison
Acevedo Díaz 9966.
Tel: (598-2) 43-4242; Fax: (598-2) 42-4241.
Bado, Kuster, Zerbino & Rachetti
Paysandú 935, piso 3.Tel: (598-2) 92-0395.

Interpreters/ Translators:

Sara Ceres de Crespi
Guayaqui 3425 esq. Juan Benito Blanco.
Tel: (598-2) 79-2528.
Evelyn Tavarelli
Av. 18 de Julio 1296 esc. 603.
Tel/Fax: (598-2) 98-1128.
Estudio de Traductores de Montevideo
Juncal 1355 esc. 404.
Tel: (598-2) 96-4853; Fax: (598-2) 96-4854.

In Case of Illness:
Dr. Jorge Stanham
Ramble M. Gandhi 519. Tel: (598-2) 70-1051.
Hospital Británico
Av. Italia 2420. Tel: (598-2) 47-5465, 47-5467, and 47-5468.

13

VENEZUELA

A Day in Jail for Executive Didn't Lessen GTE Enthusiasm

By Jane Knight

L ife's scriptwriters pulled a dirty stunt on Bruce Haddad when he moved to Venezuela. Instead of a role lying on tropical Caribbean beaches, he found himself in a different production altogether, one that involved his arrest, two coup attempts, and his being regularly mimicked on a local television comedy program.

Not that it was a part the 40-year old **GTE** executive found he couldn't perform, but experience in 10 cities of the United States plus the Dominican Republic wasn't even a dress rehearsal for the role he took on when a **GTE**-led consortium won the bid for part-ownership of Venezuela's state-run telecommunications company **CANTV**. The mild-mannered North American moved out of the tranquil haven of Fairfield County, Connecticut, and into the mayhem of Venezuela's capital, Caracas, in 1991 as **CANTV** president.

The unexpected arrest two years later that put him at the mercy of a judicial system well known for its corruption and sub-standard jails stands out among a list of bizarre episodes that will not leave Haddad short of a dinner-table conversation or two on his Venezuelan adventure. While showing the health minister around a **CANTV** facility on Oct. 29, 1993 — Haddad has the date forever imprinted on his mind — a phone call detailed the arrest warrant issued by an over-zealous judge for alleged complicity in the murder of 50 people, killed in a highway explosion that occurred when a **CANTV** sub-contractor hit a natural gas pipeline.

Haddad did not go home that night. In a swift but effective disappearing act organized with the efficiency for which **CANTV** has become noted, the executive and his wife vanished for several days as they played musical houses, moving without trace from friend to friend. The hours dragged by slowly as Haddad spent his time running up the phone bill, negotiating terms for giving himself up in an effort to avoid the nightmare prospects of a long and unpleasant prison term. But after a nationwide outcry at the stupidity of his arrest, including several verbose editorials attacking the judge, the **CANTV** president spent only one day in jail before his release, followed some time later by vindication. "I never anticipated being personally drawn in with the arrest warrant," he recounted. "The judicial system in Venezuela is one of those things. It was a unique experience and one I will never forget but in no way did it deter my enthusiasm for Venezuela."

That enthusiasm has been evident ever since Haddad, as **GTE**'s vice president-controller, reviewed business operations in a consortium including Spain's **Telefónica** and **AT&T** for the audacious plan to go into partnership with the Venezuelan government in the telecommunications field. The auction of a 40 percent controlling stake in **CANTV** presented the opportunity **GTE** had long been seeking, allowing it to take advantage of a wave of privatization that had swept Latin America in the 1990s, and to create a stronger presence in the area by adding to its Dominican Republic operations. Having already lost the auction for the Mexican telephone company, **GTE** was determined not to let **CANTV** slip through its fingers when it came to the auction block in 1991, making an irresistible offer of $1.885 billion — $600 million more than the government's minimum for the 35-year contract. While the bid was more than adequate to get **CANTV**'s name placed on the contract's dotted line, it was far from sufficient to quiet the strong anti-privatization noises murmuring steadily through the plush seats of Venezuela's Congress.

Nationalist Opposition Lingers

When Haddad flew into Venezuela that December to take part in a public ceremony and transfer process, the theatrical performance laid on barely masked the mood of opposition among a number of strong nationalists, who complained that Venezuela's heritage was being eroded. The complaints and public discussion went on, making the whole nation take an interest in the foreign investment team, which consequently found it had no problem in gaining access to important government ministries or in making other key contacts.

Such contacts were a vital part of doing business in Venezuela, something Haddad was later to capitalize on by joining the prominent boards of the Venezuelan American Chamber of Commerce and Industry and Conapri, the council for investment and promotion. "This is a society where personal relationships and associations mean very much and go a long way to be able to get things done where the bureaucratic system would block them," he explained, adding that it was not just important to have the contacts, but to conform with Latin American idiosyncrasies. "Venezuela is very much based on touching and feeling and understanding everyone's personal situation. Even in a business situation there is time spent asking about family matters before jumping into business." After a two-year stint in the Dominican Republic, he had garnered a good sense of Latin culture and temperament, but also had more than the standard phrase-book grasp of the Spanish language, a point he describes as absolutely essential.

Armed with pre-knowledge, at least on language and cultural matters, Haddad quickly discovered that although Venezuela is a Third World country, Caracas gives every impression of being a business and financial center that could match that of any developed capital city in the world. From a downtown office looking out onto the marble-fronted office blocks and commercial centers built when the country's oil gusher reached new peaks during the Seventies and Eighties, he said, "I had never been to Venezuela and I was very impressed by the size of Caracas, its modernness, the infrastructure that already existed such as the Metro, the modern buildings."

Unfortunately, beneath the foundations of Caracas' modern façade of glitz and glamour, the roots of decay had spread to such an extent that they were threatening the lifeblood of the telecommunications industry, a fact that soon became painfully obvious to the foreign investment team. "It quickly became clear why the government chose to pursue privatization," recalled Haddad. "This was a company very close to collapsing. From the standpoint of the infrastructure and management, the technical facilities of the network, the cooperation of the people and so forth, privatization was the quickest way to turn that around."

The Crackle of Silence from the Receiver

CANTV was famous for all the wrong reasons. They included the sound of silence from the telephone receiver, conversations interrupted by crackling lines, and an average of five cutouts per call. There were also unexpected conference calls created by crossed lines and waits of months and years rather than weeks for connection and repair work. In the wet season, the ordinary dial tone was replaced by an ominous squelchy sound. The public, which delighted in recounting individual grievances, did so with glee in a **CANTV** poll shortly after privatization but was adamant that the company's name should be retained because it represented part of the nation's cultural heritage. "It's the company the country loved to hate but loves," joked Haddad.

The **CANTV** president, also **GTE**'s executive vice president for international operations since late 1994,* still shows amazement when he reels off the statistics that first shocked him: almost 60 percent of pay phones were out of order; 20 percent of the already scarce international long-distance circuits were down, and infrastructure was

---

*Haddad moved back to the United States in mid-1995, though continuing as GTE's executive vice president for international operations.

up to half a century old. The budget to maintain this crumbling system was a mere $50 million annually before privatization — barely enough to keep blood going through the veins, let alone calls through the decaying network, according to Haddad, who plowed some $650 million into the company in 1993.

"We are slowly untangling a spaghetti network, particularly in Caracas. The network was very poorly designed and we are untangling the design and replacing miles and miles of old cable that is rotting away," he added, comparing the job to building a highway while vehicles are passing over it.

Addressing what was judged to be the most pressing issue, the foreign investment team decided that customers should be able to complete their phone calls without having to press the redial button mid sentence. But in carrying out this alteration behind-the-scenes, **CANTV** laid itself open to more criticism, including that of then-presidential candidate Rafael Caldera, who complained in the middle of a lunch-time conference that nothing had changed since privatization except the cost of making a telephone call. Blessed with hindsight, Haddad would have made some more immediate visible changes, such as improving the network of public phones and remodeling consumer outlets. "Those things we did later on as opposed to earlier," he said. "But some things need to be done quickly that are visible even though they do not have as much substance as other areas, to give the public a sense of change."

Despite the criticism and the poor state of the company, there were some positive points, but these beacons were spaced out: A program to convert the lines into digital technology was one fifth of the way completed; some steps had been taken to introduce modern services, albeit without planning; and, unexpectedly, many employees were found to be experts in their field. "We found a great wealth of technological expertise and knowledge within **CANTV.** The employees had just not had the tools and resources in the past to use their knowledge and there wasn't a good planning process," said Haddad. Although modern-day sales techniques using customer-service ethics and quality-control programs had not reached the **CANTV** switch-board, there was no across-the-board dislike of hard work that some foreign investors come to fear in Third World countries. "Some of the hardest-working employees I have ever seen are here in **CANTV**. They are dedicated and show a willingness to put in overtime. At the same time, there is the other extreme that we are having to work so hard to turn around — apathy, laziness, and less than ethical behavior."

However, the close governmental connection of the past had left a dangerously high level of political patronage simmering in the upper echelons of a company already suffering from small-scale cor-ruption by a rank and file open to accepting a few thousand bolívars to repair phone lines. Moreover, the 22,000-strong labor force was divid-ed into no fewer than 29 unions, many of them anti-privatization mon-sters, making the prospect of labor disputes far from appealing.

With his work already cut out for him, Haddad little expected the history-making political events lying in wait. The liberal mood of 1991 that had proved so welcoming to foreign investors, with a new investment code and a range of free-market reforms, rapidly turned sour the following year. The country's fragile political stability was broken into dangerous shards as groups of military opportunists orga-nized two coup attempts — one in February, the other in November.

Working by the Light of Bombs

Haddad spent both occasions working in the office as rebels roamed the streets in tanks and peppered the Caracas skyline with bombs. When one of those bombs, together with machine-gun fire, hit a major international telephone link during the second coup attempt, Haddad found himself out in the field checking the extent of the dam-age rather than overseeing the company's finances in his comfortable office. "We have been working through a very difficult period in Venezuelan history. It just happened that the privatization of **CANTV** coincided with major challenges for Venezuela," commented Haddad.

The coup attempt's physical damage to the company was noth-ing compared to the long-drawn-out verbal battle it is still fighting, taking a defensive position against a barrage of verbal attacks waged from all fronts. The government's telecommunications watchdog, Conatel, has continuously hounded **CANTV** since privatization, recently succeeding in getting a $120,000 fine slapped on it for breach of contract. Moreover, the ever-present murmur of complaints among the public erupted into a stream of fury when customers thought they were being charged twice for their telephone bills, a problem that led to another criminal investigation. "The judge announced that there would be no arrests associated with that incident," said Haddad with a wry smile that recalled his earlier experience with the justice system. He acknowledges that the company made a mistake by not adequately informing its customers that new billing procedures were being introduced to incorporate unpaid amounts from previous statements, a fact capitalized upon by **CANTV**'s ever-watchful political enemies.

Several years down the privatization road, **CANTV** still faces considerable opposition, despite the obvious benefits to the economy of such a large investment program. The government that pushed privatization has long since been replaced, and three more administrations have breezed in and out, each with its own philosophy on carving up the nation's heritage. All together, these government administrations have marched Haddad through a total of 20 grillings before Congressional committees, always winding up on the age-old topic of whether **CANTV** should have been privatized in the first place. In addition to the high levels of Congressional rancor, Haddad has to face angry shareholders who have been known to shout, boo, and fling their annual reports at him, something he claimed did not bother him at all because "it is very much part of the territory."

If the verbal abuse was not sufficient to give the **CANTV** president sleepless nights, the deteriorating economic situation certainly was, especially after exchange controls were imposed in July 1994. With no dollars on the horizon to meet its $125 million monthly needs, **CANTV** failed to make several debt payments and was forced to change its expansion plans, shaving almost $100 million from the $705 million originally planned for investment in 1994. It announced that

$461 million will be pumped into the company during 1995, the lowest figure in its investment history.

Ironically, although the government is still a major shareholder in the company, Haddad found himself facing a brick wall when government ministries were asked to pay unpaid telephone bills dating back to 1988 for some 14.9 billion bolívars (more than $87 million). Having tried cajoling, threats, and discussions, the **CANTV** president decided to treat the government in the same way the firm treated any other bill defaulter — he started cutting off telephone service.

With a seemingly endless selection of nightmares to choose from at bedtime, it was difficult to see the attraction of Venezuela for Haddad and **GTE.** But as a result of his efforts, Haddad became the ambassador for all investors in Venezuela, and **CANTV** his flagship, with the company's development one of the major success stories of investment in Venezuela. There is no need to read a **CANTV** report detailing increases in customer satisfaction levels from 30 percent to 70 percent to see the difference — that is evident every time someone picks up a phone in Venezuela. While Haddad was fending off arrest warrants and trying to wipe away some of the dirt from the company name, **CANTV** still managed to install 450,000 new lines in 1993, add 250,000 new customers, and most importantly, clear a profit of 30.72 billion bolívars ($307 million at the rate of exchange at that time).

"This has been an opportunity to be part of something that will be important to the development of the entire country. It is something that is rare in one's career," said Haddad. Added to which, it was an opportunity to be spoofed in a popular Venezuelan comedy television show, where Haddad's double uttered corporate double-speak in heavily accented Spanish. "I'm in the news a lot. I'm fair game," said Haddad. "It is so well done, I have to say I enjoy it."

Venezuela Overview

A Country Lurching from Crisis to Crisis

Throughout 1994, it looked as if Venezuela had constructed a permanent roadblock along the badly laid out, but defined investment road, with plentiful signs posted along the way: "Danger," "Warning," "Keep Away." The collapse of 14 financial institutions, the imposition of strict exchange regulations, price controls, and the removal of constitutional guarantees in a contracting economy seemed to give one warning after another to the foreign investor: Don't do it. The government's statistics put the 1994 economic contraction at 3.4 percent, but many private economists thought the actual contraction was greater than that. Further, in the first months of 1995, three more financial institutions failed.

Coming on the heels of two coup attempts in 1992 followed by the removal of President Carlos Andrés Pérez for alleged corruption in May 1993, the significant deterioration in Venezuela's economic climate made many investors scurry back to their maps to scout out better-marked routes to profits. As Venezuela's credit risk rating dropped to the levels of Algeria and Nigeria, investment was predicted to reach a record low in 1994, having fallen from $556.85 million in 1992 to $243.09 million in 1993.

But the roadblock, expected by economic analysts to be in place for most of 1995 as the economic recession continued, could begin to ease by the beginning of 1996. Meanwhile, the government began patching up its investment infrastructure and developing a system, albeit piecemeal, to ensure the smooth running of existing and future investment. A macro-economic plan put on the road at the end of August 1994, although failing in its aim to dramatically slash inflation, which totaled 70.8 percent in 1994, at least gave the government a direction to follow. The administration of President Rafael Caldera, which spent its first seven months of office reacting to the string of crises, finally heard the pleas of foreign investors and began smoothing out the potholes caused by the harsh new regulations. Not only was the repatriation of profits guaranteed, but maximum lending rates were forced down from more than 70 percent in early 1994 to between 30 and 40 percent in May 1995.

Caldera's government was in a predicament even before he took office in February 1994. Shortly before his inauguration, the collapse of **Banco Latino** triggered the domino-like disintegration of a badly managed and poorly supervised financial system. By the year end, 13 other financial institutions had failed, to be followed in the first few months of 1995 by three more. By pumping about $5 billion into the ailing banks, the government unleashed already high inflation levels, which had hit 45.9 percent in 1993. Meanwhile, a drop in the country's operating reserves as depositors scrambled to remit funds to safer banks abroad caused the bolívar to slide out of control from its original crawling peg devaluation of 15 centimos a day. The controlled devaluation had already been upset in April 1994 with the resignation of Central Bank President Ruth de Krivoy, but the bank failures saw the exchange rate plummet to 200 bolívars to the dollar, almost double the rate at the beginning of the year.

When temporary exchange controls were introduced at the fixed rate of 170 bolívars to the dollar at the beginning of July 1994, all industry sectors were forced onto a strictly controlled dollar diet, with only $70 million released in the first six weeks. But just as sectors heavily reliant on imports started warning of impending shortages because of the dollar drought, the regulations became more flexible, administrative procedures eased up and the repatriation of profits was guaranteed under the auspices of a new exchange control administration president. However, the bureaucratic process was still not ideal for companies that had to queue up for a slice of the dollar ration, estimated at $30 million per day instead of the more healthy daily diet of $50 million. The addition of one more piece of red tape to a country bogged down by bureaucracy also unplugged another area for the plentiful corruption by creating a thriving black market in dollars.

Price controls on hundreds of items proved a further deterrent to the manufacturing sector, which faced the threat of anti-hoarding raids and property seizures without compensation after constitutional guarantees were removed. These guarantees were to be restored as soon as mechanisms to apply exchange restrictions and price controls could be written into the law, although this in itself will cause further wariness among foreign investors.

Foreign Investment Regulations Eased

On the plus side, a good framework of business regulations is in place, at the heart of which lies the fundamental precept that foreign firms are treated in exactly the same way as Venezuelan companies. They need no prior authorization for investment, which can be made in the form of trademarks, patents, and technical knowledge, but must register with the Superintendency of Foreign Investment, known as SIEX. The companies are not bound by any capital repatriation limits or profit transfer limits and may obtain external credit without either prior authorization or registration..

Taxes and tariffs have been slashed to reasonable levels: import duties are now a standard 15 percent compared with up to 932 percent on some items in 1989; and corporate tax rates of 34 percent are levied in a simplified system that allows for the indexation of profits for inflation and the bolívar's devaluation. The implementation of a 10 percent wholesale tax in May 1994 (increased to 12.5 percent in 1995), the start of a luxury tax of between 10 and 30 percent, and a bank debits tax of 0.75 percent will help create a viable tax system and economic support in a country well known for tax evasion.

Equally as important, a package of legislation designed to instill market principles into the domestic economy, including a consumer protection bill and anti-monopoly and anti-dumping bills, was adopted following Venezuela's entry into the General Agreement on Tariffs and Trade in 1989. The previously weak link in the business regulations chain, that of intellectual property rights, was considerably strengthened with the passage of an August 1993 law designed to stop copyright violations against U.S. films, records, music and computer programs. Such violations were valued at $82 million in 1992. However, like industrial property regulations, which improved with the adoption of Andean Pact Decisions 344 and 345 in October 1993, these were still deemed insufficient by the U.S. government in its National Trade Estimate Report on Foreign Trade Barriers.

Labor Law Still a Thorn

One of the only issues not tackled was labor law, an enormous legislative thorn in the side of the foreign investor, draconian at best, and designed for a closed, protectionist economy. Although the minimum monthly wage of 15,000 bolívars in urban areas means salaries are competitive, this has to be balanced against a range of employee benefits estimated to raise their cost fourfold. A governmental decision in Spring 1994 ordered employers to bear the onus of the maxi-devaluation and pay a 6,000-bolívar monthly bonus to workers earning less than 45,000 bolívars. One year later, employers were ordered to pay a 500-bolívar daily bonus to workers earning less than 150,000 bolívars a month as a means of compensating for rapidly rising prices. Most distasteful to employers among the legal benefits, which include vacation, transportation and food bonuses, day-care provisions, and Christmas profit sharing of up to four months' salary, is the issue of severance pay. Awarded on the basis of one month's salary for every year worked when the employee resigns and double indemnities when the employee is fired without just cause, employers are often faced with huge lump sum payouts, a policy they can only avoid by a high staff turnover.

Not surprisingly, there is a shortage of skilled workers, with fewer than two out of every 100 Venezuelans having technical training, and only 150 engineering graduates from an annual total of 300,000 university graduates, according to a 1993 study performed by the Industrial Education Foundation (Fundei). Nor can this gap be plugged by foreign hires, as only 10 percent of the work force can legally be foreigners, their salaries not to exceed 20 percent of a company's payroll.

—*Political and economic choices have been tough on Venezuelan President Rafael Caldera.*

Failing to deal with the labor issue was one gap in an overall program of reforms with their roots in Pérez' second presidential period. Starting in 1989, he proceeded to shake up the closed-market economy of decades through a gamut of free-market reforms. They included slashing import tariffs and corporate taxes, all but eliminating price controls, freeing interest rates, and initiating a privatization program.

Its economy totally reliant on oil, the Venezuela that had thrived on the black liquid ooze in the 1970s and had guzzled down billions of petrodollars to build up a strong infrastructure, started to choke in the 1980s when tumbling oil prices couldn't keep up with a government whose motto was spend, spend, spend. With all its cash squandered, and without even being able to count the vast sums of money owed, Venezuela went into the ensuing 1983 debt crisis by beginning the slow but controlled devaluation of the bolívar from a fixed rate of 4.3 to the dollar.

Pérez' subsequent moves to introduce a free-floating exchange rate, starting at 40.50 bolívars to the dollar, coupled with his ambitious economic liberalization program, were reactionary enough to bring the people from the slum dwellings out onto the streets as bloody riots rocked a country already heading into a sharp recession. It was only later that the justification for the measures became apparent, with several years of sustained growth, as GDP climbed 5.3 percent in 1990, 10.4 percent in 1991 and 7.3 percent in 1992.

Amid Turbulence, Democratic Traditions Held On

Despite his economic success, the removal of Pérez from office for alleged corruption in May 1993 told its own story of his political popularity. The turbulence of his last two years found Venezuela perched on the edge of a new dictatorship. Somehow, the country retained its balance, and democracy came through when Caldera was elected to his second five-year period as president in December 1993, the most recent in a line of peaceful transitions of power since the toppling of the oppressive Pérez Jiménez dictatorship in 1958. Walking a political tightrope because his 19-party Convergencia movement controlled only 12.5 percent of Congress, Caldera showed his political muscle when he won a face-off in July 1994 over the reimposition of constitutional guarantees. Although the country's political stability seemed fragile in the hands of a man who was 78 years old and ailing, the democratic tradition of the past holds considerable sway among the population.

That long history of political stability, coupled with the liberalization of the economy, has resulted in foreign investment in all sectors, ranging from the **Compañia Inglesa,** which raises cattle in Venezuela's plains, to Canada's **Placer Dome** seeking gold in the Guayana heartlands, and to **Citibank** in the streets of Venezuela's capital, Caracas. But the bulk of foreign interest is in the manufacturing sector, which commanded 64.5 percent of all investment in 1993, according to the SIEX. **Heinz, SmithKline Beecham, Owens-Illinois, Avon, Seagram, Gillette, Philips, Johnson & Johnson** and **Nestlé** are just a smattering of the numerous multi-nationals that have decided to make Venezuela more than a port of call. There are as many names in the automobile sector itself, where **Fiat, Toyota, Ford** and **Chrysler** all had multi-million-dollar product expansions and plant modifications planned before the imposition of exchange controls.

Among the strongest votes of confidence in the country are those shown by **Procter & Gamble,** which is going ahead with a 1993 decision to make Venezuela its Latin American headquarters, and Brazil's **Brahma Beer,** which bought Venezuela's **Cerveceria Nacional** in 1994. Even **McDonald's** is branching out, with a $23 million expansion.

Venezuelans' "foreign is good — United States is king" attitude makes them easy prey to all imported goods, but especially beauty products, foodstuffs, and clothing. Winner of 20 percent of international beauty contests in the last 14 years, the country is one huge beauty parlor, claiming the highest per capita expenditure of any country on beauty products. Even the poorest people in the slum areas are willing to scrape together their last pennies to buy the latest lipstick rage. Recent advances in the agricultural and agro-industrial sectors have not been sufficient to prevent 70 percent of all foodstuffs' being imported, with Venezuelans wolfing down huge quantities of imported chips, pancake mix, and even muffins. Records, sound equipment, clothing, sports and outdoor equipment, good-quality furniture, kitchen appliances, and cookware — Venezuela swallows them all hungrily.

The machinery and equipment fields are among the most promising, a need heightened by the government's ambitious plans to increase production of its mineral reserves. Aims to hike oil production to 4 million barrels a day by the year 2000 from the current 2.3 million will create an opening for oilfield service and supply equipment of all kinds, while tractors, trucks and metal-processing equipment will be required to tap other mineral reserves. More affected by cutbacks but just as necessary are farm machinery and spare parts, and sophisticated medical equipment plus general hospital instruments.

In a country whose streets are polluted by both cars and crime, imports of car parts are climbing in spite of a tightening up of the regulations, while car security systems, in addition to closed-circuit television systems and burglar alarms, are coming into their own.

Yet imports are just the tip of the iceberg when it comes to the country's opportunities, and government officials are not slow to tick off Venezuela's advantages: a cheap power supply (2.6 cents per kilowatt hour), reliable and cheap labor supply, and a physical infrastructure that includes more than 86,000 kilometers of roads and more than 60 airports, seven of them international. Venezuela also offers investors tariff-free trade among its fellow Andean Pact members — Colombia, Peru, Bolivia, and Ecuador.

Few Limitations on Foreign Investments

Almost the only restrictions against 100 percent foreign ownership lie in the television, broadcasting, and Spanish-language press sectors. The door was flung open to full foreign participation in the banking sector with a January 1994 bank law, and the government is already looking overseas for buyers of some of the ailing banks, something analysts claim will make it more willing to create an investment-friendly environment. The reform of the banking sector was duplicated in the insurance sector, heavily burdened by losses as shown by the near collapse and takeover of the largest participant, **Seguros La Seguridad,** and foreign participation is no longer limited to 20 percent.

One of the biggest lures for investors is the petroleum sector, closely guarded after the oil nationalization in 1976, and still guaranteed to raise heated debate among congressmen who want to retain Venezuelan control over oil rights and production. However, the government's need for finance and ambitious expansion plans by **Petroleos de Venezuela S.A.** have coupled to provide a need for external participation, although that need still requires congressional consent. After joining forces with foreign companies to reactivate marginal oilfields and planning a $5.6 billion natural gas investment in the Cristobal Colón project, **Petroleos de Venezuela** is anticipating a large response for its profit-sharing agreements in high-risk areas despite tax levels in the order of 85 percent.

Equally controversial is the potential sale of the **Corporación Venezolana de Guayana (CVG),** a huge white elephant that oversees Venezuela's basic industries in the Guayana region, with outstanding debts of $6 billion. A study commissioned by the Caldera government recommended that the corporation's 56 affiliates, including iron ore mines, aluminum and steel mills, and hydroelectric complexes, be sold, creating an estimated $3.5 billion in investment opportunities. The report was subsequently buried after widespread criticism, but the government may be forced to go to the auction block because its financial purse strings will not stretch enough to pay off the enormous debt.

Sale of the **CVG** could form part of a revived privatization program for 1995 after 1994's economic situation forced Caldera's government, already cautious of selling off the state's assets, to abandon 19 intended sales valued at $465 million. That 1994 wasn't the right time to sell off anything was brought home in May of that year, when the $60 million auction of state-run airline **Aeropostal** failed when interested parties withdrew, complaining that the price was too high and labor clauses too burdensome.

Initiated in 1991 with the proposed sale of more than 400 state concerns, the privatization program yielded $2.1 billion in its first year of operation. But it hit a stumbling block in the form of the February 1992 coup attempt, so that only $500 million flowed into the state coffers that year, while political unrest continued, and just $350 million was yielded in 1993. The only hope of raising any privatization booty in 1994 through the sale of three electricity companies was effectively scuppered when the government in August announced it was enforcing cuts in what it considered to be inflated energy rates. However, a considerable number of the 400 companies with price tags around their necks are waiting for the revival of privatization, including hotels, sugar mills, shipbuilding concerns, cement companies, metallurgy and textile companies, and of course, **Aeropostal.**

More immediate opportunities are offered in the concessions law of May 1994, which allows private contractors to reconstruct and add to the country's crumbling infrastructure in return for being able to charge tolls. As these projects require only presidential and not congressional approval, they are expected to be authorized quickly and efficiently, with the added precedent-setting bonus that disputes will be heard in international tribunals rather than in local courts.

Venezuela at a Glance

Population: 21.2 million (1994 estimated).

Labor force: 7.5 million (1993).

Language: Spanish is the national language.

Ethnic mix: Diversified, with about 65 percent of the population of mixed European, African and Native American descent. Some 20 percent are white, 8 percent black and 7 percent Native American, according to independent estimates.

Literacy and Educational levels: 94.5 percent literacy among the work force, of whom nearly 40 percent have completed secondary school. An overseas training program started in 1964 helped more than 40,000 Venezuelans take courses in foreign universities.

Climate and best times to visit: Climate is tropical but temperatures vary considerably with altitude, ranging from 16° to 33° C (61° to 91° F) in Caracas, and from 20° to 40° C (68°to 104° F) in Maracaibo. The dry season from December to May is the best time to visit, although the rainy season (May to November) is not unpleasant.

Natural resources: Oil, with proven reserves of 64.45 billion barrels at year end 1993, excluding the heavy oils in the Orinoco Oil Belt ; natural gas reserves of 3.91 trillion cubic meters at year end 1993; coal, with proven reserves of 1.7 billion metric tons; also gold, bauxite, iron ore, diamonds, and hydroelectric power.

Chief agricultural products: Rice, corn, sorghum, tomatoes, sugar cane, beef cattle. Main export crops: Coffee, tropical fruit, and cacao.

Land area: 912,050 square kilometers, excluding a large border zone being disputed with neighboring Guyana.

Economic Statistics:

> GDP: $59 billion (1994) (Central Bank figure)
>
> Per Capita GDP: $2,629
>
> Economic growth rate: Negative 3.4 percent (1994)

Main exports (1993): Oil, $10 billion; iron and steel, $630 million; aluminum, $605 million.

Main imports (1993): Machinery and equipment, $2.3 billion; automobiles and parts, $1.8 billion; industrial chemicals, $1.1 billion.

Duties on imports: The Andean Pact's 15 percent tariff applies.

Repatriation of profits: The government has guaranteed unlimited free profit repatriation in spite of temporary exchange controls implemented in July 1994.

When You Go to Venezuela

Documents: Tourist cards valid for 60 days (renewable) are issued by the airline if the visitor has a return ticket or proof of funds and does not intend to carry out commercial transactions. For those visiting Venezuela for commercial reasons, transient business visas valid for 120 days or one year may be obtained at Venezuelan consulates abroad. For those planning to live and work in Venezuela, a regular transient visa, valid for one year, must be applied for in Venezuela by a third party, normally the company seeking an overseas employee. Delays in obtaining this type of documentation mean that many executives travel to Venezuela on a tourist card, converting to transient visas by leaving and re-entering the country once their papers are ready.

Airlines: American and United fly from Miami, and United also flies from New York. Of the Venezuelan airlines, which generally have cheaper fares than U.S. airlines, Viasa has direct flights from Miami, New York and Houston; Avensa flies from New York and Miami, and Servivensa and Zuliana cover the Miami route. From Europe, British Airways has well regarded service, while TAP (Air Portugal) and Alitalia tend to have the most economical fares. Iberia, KLM and Lufthansa also fly to Venezuela.

What to Expect at the Airport:

● After the imposition of temporary exchange controls in July 1994, there were reports of visitors being stopped at the airport and forced to give up their dollars, often without being given a receipt. This practice is totally illegal and should be reported to a senior official.

● Samples can be brought into the country without any problems as long as they do not have any commercial value, although if they are used in exhibitions or congresses, the event must have first been approved by the Foreign Trade Institute. Samples with commercial value can only be imported with the payment of import tariffs, which will later be refunded when the samples leave the country.

Hotels

Unless otherwise stated, the hotels we list all have mini-bars and computer sockets in rooms, with reliable message-taking services and good health club facilities. Business centers are equipped with fax, photocopying machines, translation and secretarial services.

Caracas Hilton
Avenida Libertador y Sur 25, El Conde

Tel: (582) 503-5000.

Located in Caracas' downtown area, the Hilton offers special executive floors with complimentary breakfast and drinks, fast check-in and staff available to confirm air reservations. Efficient business center, conference facilities, a limousine service and a popular health club and pool. Room prices start at $198; suites at $329.

Hotel Eurobuilding
Calle La Guarita, Chuao
Tel: (582) 907-1111.

Modern conveniences such as microwaves in the kitchen. In addition to its business center, the hotel also rents cellular phones and has a limousine service.

Room prices start at $195; Eurosuites at $220.

Hotel Tamanaco Inter-Continental
Final Avenida Principal de Las Mercedes
Tel: (582) 208-7111.

Less central than the Hilton, the Inter-Continental is set in 38 acres of grounds. In addition to the business center, laptops, cellular telephones and fax machines are available for hire. A limousine service is available for $50 an hour, minimum three hours. The Inter-Continental chain also has hotels in Maracaibo and Valencia, Venezuela's other two main cities, which can be booked through the Caracas number.

Rooms in Caracas start at $200; suites at $400.

Altamira Suites
Primero Avenida y Primero Transversal de Los Palos Grandes
Tel: (582) 209-3111.

For longer visits, the Altamira Suites is a popular option, although with limited services. All suites have a kitchenette and dining area, but there is no mini-bar in the room. Only fax and photocopying services are offered and there is no limousine service.

Room rates range from $78 to $133.

Urban Transportation: All major auto-rental companies operate in Caracas and can be booked either at the airport, through hotels, or directly, with rates averaging about $70 a day. (Hertz 952-5511, Avis 261-5556, Budget 283-4333, and National 239-3645). Taxis are cheap but have no meters, so foreign visitors often end up paying large fares. The main hotels have their own, smarter but more expensive taxi lines, and offer limousine services. An efficient Metro system runs east to west through Caracas.

Contacts

Governmental:

U.S. EMBASSY Commercial Section
Avenida Principal, La Floresta
Tel: (582) 285-3111 and 3222.
Commercial Consul: Edgar Fulton

FOREIGN TRADE INSTITUTE
Centro Comercial Los Cedros, Mezzanine 3 and ground floor, Avenida Libertador.
Tel: (582) 531-0009.
Promotes non-traditional exports and collates all trade figures.
Dr. Alberto Poletto, president.

FINANCE MINISTRY
Edificio Norte, 3rd floor, Oficina 312, Centro Simon Bolivar.
Tel: (582) 41-3444.
Customs section of ministry provides information to companies wishing to import into Venezuela.

SUPERINTENDENCY OF FOREIGN INVESTMENT (SIEX)
Edificio La Perla, 3rd floor, Bolsa a Mercaderes.
Tel: (582) 483-6666.
Registers all foreign businesses, but can also provide statistics and information.
Dulce Maria Torres, director of registration and control.

Business Organizations:

VENEZUELAN-AMERICAN CHAMBER OF COMMERCE AND INDUSTRY (VenAmCham)
Torre Credival, 10th floor, 2nd Avenida de Campo Alegre
Tel: (582) 263-0833.
Advice and contacts for investors and has a useful business library.
Antonio Herrera, vice president.

VENEZUELAN INDUSTRIAL COUNCIL (Conindustria)
Esquina Puente Anauco, Edificio Cámara de Industriales, Mezzanine, la Candelaria Tel: (582) 573-0222.
Offers limited advice and statistics to investors.
José Redmond, president.

VENEZUELAN FEDERATION OF CHAMBERS OF COMMERCE AND INDUSTRY (Fedecameras)
Avenida El Empalme, Edificio Fedecamaras, 5th floor, El Bosque
Tel: (582) 731-1711.
An umbrella group for all industry-sector chambers, Fedecameras gives information only about its members.
Edgard Romero Navas, president.

ASSOCIATION OF VENEZUELAN EXPORTERS (Avex)
Centro Comercial Concresa, 2nd. floor, Oficina 435, Redoma de Prados del Este Tel: (582) 979-7242.
Information on its 600 members for importers around the world.
Carlos Púlido Salvatierra, president.

PROMEXPORT
Edificio Fedecamaras, Avenida El Empalme, El Bosque
Tel: (582) 731 1089.
Database offers in-depth market analyses for exports and imports, product trends and forecasts, and details the competition in certain markets.
Namuel Diaz Ugueto, president.

NATIONAL COUNCIL FOR THE PROMOTION OF INVESTMENT (Conapri)
Avenida Francisco de Miranda, Centro Empresarial Parque del Este,

12th floor, La Carlota. Tel: (582) 237-5995.

Offers one-sided advice and information to investors on the benefits of the country. Adolfo Taylhardat, president.

Lawyers:

Legal advice in Venezuela is not hard to come by, but it is best to stick to the larger law firms to ensure quick and accurate information. Although we are not making recommendations, the following are established legal firms specializing in foreign investment and intellectual property regulations:

Benson, Pérez Matos, Antakly & Watts

Edificio Centro Altamira, 8th floor, Avenida San Juan Bosco, Altamira Tel: (582) 32-3801.

Anzola Boveda Raffalli & Rodriguez

Torre Britanica, 10th floor, Avenida Jose Felix Sosa, Altamira Sur Tel: (582) 261-8580.

Bentata Hoet & Asociados

Torre Las Mercedes, 2nd. floor, Avenida La Estancia, Chuao Tel: (582) 92-0720.

Baker & McKenzie.

Edificio Adlemo, 6th floor, Avenida Venezuela, El Rosal. Tel: (582) 32-4941.

Financial Advisers:

CNI Asesores Financieros

Torre La Previsora, 14th floor, Avenida Abraham Lincoln, Sabana Grande. Tel: (582) 973-2470.

Frank Amador, executive director.

Translators:

● Most five-star hotels have translation services.

● Also, the Association of Venezuelan Translators has established rates and several dozen members. Call President Carmen Teresa de la Ville, who also offers simultaneous interpreting (979-8415).

● One fast and accurate company is LinguaCorp, run by managing partner Francisco Pance (Calle Las Flores, Residencias Cavalier, 7-3 Sabana Grande. Tel: 762-0586). The company also works with documents sent by fax or modem from abroad and can handle legal documents.

Reference/Source Material:

VenAmCham Year Book
The best on the market, it lists almost 1,000 members. May be purchased in person or by mail order, for $75 (plus $5 postage) at the VenAmCham offices: Torre Credival, 10th floor, 2nd Avenida de Campo Alegre, Caracas.

Directorio Empresarial de Venezuela (Business Directory)
A list of the major business associations in Venezuela, available at: Centro Parque Carabobo, Level 13, Oficina 1313, Avenida Mexico (Tel: 574-9865), price $3.

Export Directories
The Foreign Trade Institute publishes a free export directory, available at Centro Comercial Los Cedros, Mezzanine 3 and ground floor, Avenida Libertador, (Tel: 531-0009), as does the Venezuelan Association of Exporters, available at Centro Comercial Concresa, 2nd floor, Oficina 435, Redoma de Prados del Este, (Tel: 979-7242), price $17.64.

In case of illness:

Many of the doctors speak English at these private clinics:

Clínica Institute Medico La Floresta
Calle Santa Ana y Avenida Principal
Tel: 209-6222.

Clínica El Avila
Avda. San Juan Bosco y Transversal 6
Tel: 208-1111.
For general treatment, ask for Dr. Ronald Stern, 9th floor (208-1984) who works with gastroenterologist Dr. Rosa Hernández. Both speak English and German.

A READING LIST

Books About Latin America as a Whole

Modern Latin America, by Thomas E. Skidmore and Peter H. Smith. Compact, readable overview of the region by two respected academicians. (New York: Oxford Univ. Pr.)

Open Veins of Latin America: Five Centuries of the Pillage of a Continent, by Eduardo Galeano. Heavy going, but gives the reader an idea of the animosity that many Latin American intellectuals feel toward the United States and their interpretation of history. (New York: Norton).

A Cast of Spaniards, by Mark Jacobs. A delightful collection of short stories by an American fiction writer who captures the mood and voice of the many Latin American countries in which he has lived. May be difficult to obtain except by ordering directly from the publisher: Talisman House, PO Box 1117, Hoboken, N. J. 07030.

About Argentina

Argentina: A City and A Nation, by James R. Scobie. (New York: Oxford University Press).

Argentina 1516 to 1982: From Spanish Colonization to the Falklands War, by David Rock. (Berkeley: University of California Press). *Argentina: Illusions and Realities,* by Gary Wynia. (New York: Holmes & Meier).

On Heroes and Tombs, a novel by Ernesto Sábato, one of Argentina's most revered writers. (New York: Ballantine).

About Brazil

Rebellion in the Backlands, by Euclides da Cunha. Classic work on the Brazilian government's brutal campaigns a century ago against religious mystic Antonio Conselheiro and his followers. The book jacket of one edition says it "has been called the Bible of Brazilian nationality." (Chicago: University of Chicago Press).

The Economic Growth of Brazil: A Survey from Colonial to Modern Times, by Celso Furtado. (Westport, Ct.: Greenwood Publishing Group).

Child of the Dark: The Diary of Carolina Maria de Jesus. This diary of a São Paulo slum woman is one of the few portraits of poverty in Latin America from the perspective of the poor themselves. (New York: NAL-Dutton).

Macunaíma, a novel by Mário de Andrade (Pittsburgh: University of Pittsburgh Press).

Dom Casmurro, a novel by Joaquim Maria Machado do Assis. (New York: Farrar, Strauss & Giroux).

Epitaph of a Small Winner, a novel by Joaquim Maria Machado do Assis (New York: Farrar, Strauss & Giroux).

The Hour of the Star, a novel by Clarice Lispector. (New York: New Directions).

Gabriela Clove and Cinnamon, a novel by Jorge Amado. (New York: Knopf).

About Central America

Inside Central America: Its People, Politics, and History, by Clifford Krauss. This work by a respected journalist puts the crises that swept Central America from the late Seventies through the beginning of the Nineties into historical perspective. (New York: Summit).

War and Peace in Central America: Reality and Illusion, by Frank McNeil. The region's decade of crises from the perspective of a U.S. diplomat caught up in them. (New York: Scribners).

Nicaragua: Revolution in the Family, by Shirley Christian. (New York: Random House).

Commandos: The CIA and Nicaragua's Contra Rebels, by Sam Dillon. (New York: Holt).

Blood of Brothers, by Stephen Kinzer. (New York: Putnam).

The Massacre at El Mozote, by Mark Danner. (New York: Vintage).

The Path Between the Seas: The Creation of the Panama Canal 1870-1914, by David McCullough. (New York: Simon and Schuster).

Panama Odyssey, by William J. Jorden. Intimidatingly long, but the definitive version of how the Carter Administration and the Panamanian government negotiated the transfer of control of the canal to Panama. (Austin: University of Texas Press).

About Chile

Modern Chile 1970-1989, by Mark Falcoff. (New Brunswick, N. J.: Transaction Publishers.)

A Nation of Enemies: Chile Under Pinochet, by Pamela Constable and Arturo Valenzuela. (New York: Norton).

Chile: The Political Economy of Development and Democracy in the 1990s, by David E. Hojman. (Pittsburgh: University of Pittsburgh Press).

Chile Through Embassy Windows, 1939-1953, by Claude G. Bowers. (Westport, Ct.: Greenwood Publishing Group).

Pinochet: The Politics of Power, by Genaro Arriagada. (Boulder, Colo.: Westview).

The House of the Spirits, a novel by Isabel Allende, a Chilean expatriate who is her country's best-known living author. (New York: Knopf).

About Colombia

One Hundred Years of Solitude, one of many acclaimed novels by Colombia's Novel Laureate, Gabriel García Márquez (New York: Simon & Schuster).

About Ecuador

Panama Hat Trail: A Journey to South America, by Tom Miller. (New York: Vintage/Random House).

About Mexico

Conversations with Moctezuma: The Soul of Modern Mexico, by Dick J. Reavis. (New York: Morrow).

The Labyrinth of Solitude, by Octavio Paz. A classic study of the Mexican psyche written poetically by Mexico's Nobel Laureate in literature. (New York: Grove).

The Wind that Swept Mexico: A History of the Mexican Revolution of 1910-1942, by Anita Brenner and George R. Leighton. An eminently readable, short account of the revolution and creation of the ruling PRI party that put in place the political system of today. (Austin: University of Texas Press).

Limits to Friendship: The United States and Mexico, by Jorge G. Castañeda and Robert A. Pastor. A former National Security Council staff member (under President Carter) and a Mexican political scientist discuss sources of U.S.-Mexican misunderstandings. (New York: Knopf).

Distant Neighbors: A Portrait of the Mexicans, by Alan Riding. Detailed, flavorful descriptions of how Mexico's contemporary political system works. (New York: Knopf).

Consider This, Señora, a critically acclaimed recent novel by Harriet Doerr, an American who lived many years in Mexico. (New York: Harcourt Brace).

About Paraguay

I, the Supreme, a novel by Augusto Roa Bastos, Paraguay's pre-eminent novelist, inspired by a 19th Century Paraguayan strongman. (New York: Vintage/Random House).

About Peru

The Modern History of Peru, by Fredrick B. Pike. Doesn't cover last couple of decades, but is good on earlier periods of Peruvian history. (New York: Praeger).

The Real Life of Alejandro Mayta, one of many acclaimed novels by Peru's most famous writer, Mário Vargas Llosa. (New York: Vintage/Random House).

About Venezuela

Venezuela: Tarnished Democracy, by Daniel C. Hellinger. (Boulder, Colorado: Westview).

INDEX

About the Authors

Judith Evans, who wrote about Argentina, is a financial writer and business consultant regarded as one of the leading foreign experts on the Argentine economy. She lives in New York and commutes almost monthly to Buenos Aires.

Bill Hinchberger, who wrote about Brazil, is a financial writer living in São Paulo. His work has appeared in *BusinessWeek, Institutional Investor, The Financial Times ARTnews, The Miami Herald,* and elsewhere.

Winston Moore, who wrote about Bolivia, is an Anglo-Bolivian business and financial writer living in La Paz. He holds a doctorate in government from Essex University in England.

Scott Norvell, who wrote about Central America, is an Atlanta-based writer and business consultant. He has lived in Guatemala and Nicaragua and still travels regularly to Central America.

Holly Johnson, who wrote about Chile, is a free lance journalist who has lived in Chile since 1986. She specializes in business and financial topics.

Ruth Sánchez and **Steven Gutkin**, who wrote about Colombia, were based in Bogotá for many years. Sánchez has been a correspondent for the Latin American economic magazine *América Economía.* Gutkin reported for *The Washington Post, Newsweek,* and The Associated Press.

Carlos Cisternas, who wrote about Ecuador, is a Chilean journalist who has lived in Quito for eight years. He specializes in political and economic coverage.

Lucy Conger, who wrote about Mexico, spent many years in Mexico covering the country's political and economic triumphs and crises, including the financial turmoil beginning at the end of 1994. She recently moved to São Paulo, Brazil, where she writes about the South American economies for the Reuters news service.

Esteban Caballero Carrizosa, who wrote about Paraguay, is a writer, consultant, and interpreter in Asunción.

Peter Hudson, who wrote about Peru and lives in Lima, puts his journalistic soul into the monthly column he writes on Peruvian soccer for an English publication, but he makes his living writing about politics and the economy, particularly Peru's developing capital markets.

Danilo Arbilla, who wrote about Uruguay, divides his time between his city home in Montevideo and his beach place in Punta del Este. One of Uruguay's leading journalists, he is editor of the weekly news and financial magazine *Búsqueda.*

Jane Knight, who wrote about Venezuela, is an economics journalist living in Caracas. She specializes in petroleum-related news and issues.